The Comintern in Spain before the Civil War

The Comintern in Spain before the Civil War

Red Tide Rising

Gustavo Martín Asensio

BLOOMSBURY ACADEMIC
LONDON • NEW YORK • OXFORD • NEW DELHI • SYDNEY

BLOOMSBURY ACADEMIC

Bloomsbury Publishing Plc, 50 Bedford Square, London, WC1B 3DP, UK
Bloomsbury Publishing Inc, 1359 Broadway, New York, NY 10018, USA
Bloomsbury Publishing Ireland, 29 Earlsfort Terrace, Dublin 2, D02 AY28, Ireland

BLOOMSBURY, BLOOMSBURY ACADEMIC and the Diana logo are
trademarks of Bloomsbury Publishing Plc

First published in Great Britain 2024
Paperback edition published 2026

Copyright © Gustavo Martín Asensio, 2024

Gustavo Martín Asensio has asserted his right under the Copyright,
Designs and Patents Act, 1988, to be identified as Author of this work.

Cover image: Posters for Spanish Elections (© Bettmann / Getty Images)

All rights reserved. No part of this publication may be: i) reproduced or transmitted in any form, electronic or mechanical, including photocopying, recording or by means of any information storage or retrieval system without prior permission in writing from the publishers; or ii) used or reproduced in any way for the training, development or operation of artificial intelligence (AI) technologies, including generative AI technologies. The rights holders expressly reserve this publication from the text and data mining exception as per Article 4(3) of the Digital Single Market Directive (EU) 2019/790.

Bloomsbury Publishing Plc does not have any control over, or responsibility for, any third-party websites referred to or in this book. All internet addresses given in this book were correct at the time of going to press. The author and publisher regret any inconvenience caused if addresses have changed or sites have ceased to exist, but can accept no responsibility for any such changes.

A catalogue record for this book is available from the British Library.

A catalog record for this book is available from the Library of Congress.

ISBN: HB: 978-1-3504-4335-8
       PB: 978-1-3504-4336-5
       ePDF: 978-1-3504-4337-2
       eBook: 978-1-3504-4338-9

Typeset by Integra Software Services Pvt. Ltd.

For product safety related questions contact productsafety@bloomsbury.com.

To find out more about our authors and books visit www.bloomsbury.com
and sign up for our newsletters.

*For my wife, Magdalena Katarzyna Bednarska,
and my sons, David, Gabriel, Samuel, and Josué Martín Bednarski. Ad Fontem!*

Contents

Preface	viii
Foreword	x
Introduction	1
1 Mobilizing All Our Forces: Introducing Comintern Operations in Spain 1923–36	15
2 Save the Children!: The Comintern Narrative of Victimization in Spain as the Cornerstone of the Popular Front Platform	39
3 A Vast and Concrete Ideological Penetration: The Comintern's Publishing Conglomerate in Spain 1931–6	63
4 Star Pupils: A Transnational, Comparative Approach to Comintern "Army Work" in France and Spain 1932–6	87
5 Schools of Communism: Revolutionary Opposition Groups in the Socialist Union UGT, 1932–6	119
6 They Paid for Our Olympiad: The July 1936 Popular Olympiad in Barcelona as a Case Study in Comintern Mass Organizational Operations	133
Conclusion	153
Epilogue	159
Notes	166
Index	231

Preface

This book is the unintended consequence of digging into my family history. In mid-2018 I submitted a formal request to the Spanish *Centro Documental de la Memoria Histórica* for the personal file of my great-uncle on my mother's side, CNT leader Eduardo Sanjuan Castro. I had only a vague personal recollection of him, as he died when I was still a child, but the oral traditions that circulated in my family about his career during the Spanish Civil War were utterly fascinating to me. The first batch of documents that arrived on my desk some weeks later did not disappoint. As is typical of government archives, multiple additional requests were necessary to obtain all the records kept under various branches and locations. Meanwhile, I began to dive into the period press and discovered a surprising number of references to his work as an activist and leader of the CNT-affiliated tobacco workers union. The documents revealed that, after the outbreak of war, Eduardo had used his connections to secure a job as agent in the dreaded Servicio de Información Militar (SIM) based on Calle Sorní 7 in Valencia. Eduardo's boss in the SIM was his close friend and fellow freemason Enrique Francés Giner. While putting all the documentary pieces together, I discovered that, for much of 1937, Francés Giner took frequent walks from his office on Sorní 7 to the Metropol Hotel, across from the Valencia bull ring, to report to a mysterious figure named "Alfredo" at the Soviet embassy, based at the hotel since late 1936. This was none other than Comintern secretary Palmiro Togliatti, who had had varying degrees of responsibility over Comintern operations in Spain long before the start of the war. I then began looking into Togliatti's and other Comintern leaders' pre-war communications with Comintern and party operatives in Spain, which grew significantly from 1931 to the early summer of 1936. The volume of reports, directives, letters, and other documents soon became unmanageable as a side interest and demanded a single and sustained focus. From the outset of this new research and writing project I was immensely blessed by the patient and encouraging feedback of Professor Stanley G. Payne. His generosity, kindness, and always challenging input have been truly priceless. I am also grateful for the feedback and encouragement of Professors Roberto Villa of Universidad Rey Juan Carlos and André Gounot of the Université de Strasbourg who read and commented on at least some of the work. Any and all errors in the book are fully my own. I also want to express my thanks to my *Doktorvater* Professor Stanley E. Porter who modeled for me the relentless pursuit of primary sources as the lifeblood of the humanities. Upon my arrival in London to begin my doctoral work, his first step with our entire research cluster was to take us to the manuscript reading room, at the British Library's old location on Russell Square, to read and handle ancient Greek papyri. His example and instruction set in motion a lifelong passion for research which continues to this day. Finally, none of this would have been possible without the patience and support of my wife Magdalena Bednarska, who put up with far too many absences because she believed this work matters. Kocham cię.

Foreword

*Stanley G. Payne, Emeritus Professor,
University of Wisconsin-Madison, USA*

The Bolshevik coup d'etat of 1917 precipitated the longest, most destructive civil war in modern European history (1917–22). Communist victory was an epochal event, conditioning much of the three-quarters of a century that followed. The Soviet Union that it formed in 1922 featured a constitution designed as a blueprint for communist world government. Though hopes for an immediate worldwide revolution were dashed and its abortive invasion of Eastern Europe repulsed, the Soviet regime was unique in modern world history—a government dedicated to the subversion and revolutionary overthrow of all other existing political systems.

Soviet leadership under Lenin and Stalin introduced a two-track international policy that pursued outwardly normal diplomatic relations abroad, but these were flanked by a simultaneous, largely separate program of parallel revolutionary agitation carried on by affiliated communist parties throughout the world. Diplomatic relations were maintained through normal embassies in countries willing to accept peaceful ties with a regime otherwise dedicated to international subversion.

Revolutionary activities were conducted by a new international network of communist parties known as the Third or Communist International (following its two nineteenth-century socialist predecessors), commonly called simply the Comintern. All its revolutionary initiatives in Europe had failed by 1923, and the focus momentarily shifted to East Asia, where it met with equal frustration. In 1924 the Comintern announced the opening of a "Second Period" that temporarily moderated international activity while the Soviet Union concentrated on building "Socialism in One Country," a program to construct a fully communist system and, hopefully, transform the country into a military superpower. The latter process had gotten underway by 1928, at which point the Comintern announced the opening of a new "Third Period." This formulation produced one of the only two major forecasts that the Soviets actually got right, for it declared that the era of postwar stabilization would soon come to an end, to be followed by an imminent worldwide crisis of capitalism. The Comintern proposed to exploit this through a new revolutionary offensive, climaxed by armed insurrections and/or renewed civil war. Compromise tactics must be abandoned, as communists sought leadership of revolutionary forces, forming only "united fronts from below" under communist domination.

A Spanish Communist Party had been organized, partly by Soviet initiative, in 1920, but during its first decade Comintern interest in Spain was focused partly on the country's utility as revolutionary gateway to Latin America. Historians have rarely taken notice of the party's abortive attempt to spark revolutionary insurrection during the regime crisis of August 1923, since the initiative fell flat. The takeover of Spanish government by a new left-liberal Republican coalition in 1931, however, sparked the Comintern's interest. Though the inauguration of the Second Spanish Republic is usually seen as establishing the only new liberal democracy in a Europe rapidly moving toward authoritarianism, the leaders of the Comintern more perceptively viewed this as initiating a new revolutionary process. Two years later, after Hitler's seizure of power in Germany, Spain potentially offered the only such opportunity in Europe. It became a major focus of Soviet interest for the first time, leading in 1932 to the appointment of new party leaders thoroughly subservient to Moscow. Though historians' opinion often holds that Spanish Communism became influential only after the start of the Civil War in 1936, in fact it grew slowly but steadily from 1931. By that time the Comintern had years of experience in the arts of infiltration, "front" operations, propaganda manipulation, and subversion, all of which it employed in Spain to increasingly good effect. A particular target was the infiltration and manipulation of the much larger and well-established Spanish Socialist Party, which formed part of the original Republican governing coalition. The socialists veered increasingly toward revolution, partially under communist influence, from 1933 on. This is the historical situation that attracted the interest of Gustavo Martín Asensio, who has worked for a quarter century in the global high tech and telecommunications industry. Though presently business consultant for a Scandinavian telecommunications service provider, he has an extensive scholarly background. In 1999 he completed a Ph.D. in Hellenistic Greek and Linguistics at the University of Surrey (United Kingdom) and has published a book and several scholarly articles on the Greek language and New Testament studies. His research on the contemporary history of Spain was initiated by inquiry into the career of his great-uncle, Eduardo Sanjuan Castro, a notable figure in the anarchosyndicalist Confederación Nacional de Trabajo (CNT—National Confederation of Labour) during the era of the Spanish Civil War. As he explains in the introductory chapter of this book, he was surprised to find Sanjuan's immediate superior, an official in the Republican SIM (Military Intelligence Service), reporting regularly to the shadowy figure of Palmiro Togliatti, chief Comintern adviser in Spain (and later long-term head of the Italian Communist Party). This perplexed him and led to further research on the increasingly influential role played by the Comintern during the Republic, well before Communism achieved hegemonic status during the war. As Martín Asensio explains, most preceding historians have assumed that this was a comparatively unimportant topic in the history of the prewar Republic (1931–6), pointing to the party's modest membership. Such an assumption ignored the amount of attention that the Comintern had been devoting to the only West European country in which an active revolutionary process was already under way. By that point the Comintern had become well-trained in infiltration, propaganda, and subversion. With Soviet finance, agents, experience, and Comintern guidance at its disposal, Spanish Communism played an increasingly active and influential role.

Preceding historians had been impeded by the unavailability of Soviet primary sources, but that gap has been filled through progressive opening of Russian archives during the past quarter century and more. This opportunity is brilliantly exploited by Martín Asensio, primarily through extensive electronic research, combined with the use of other materials. His highly original study achieves a noteworthy historiographical breakthrough, revealing for the first time the full range and influence of Comintern activity, showing the communist contribution to the radicalization of the broader Marxist left and to the eventual breakdown of Republican institutions. That in turn helped to precipitate a deadly civil war that became a major problem for European international relations.

In this book Martín Asensio brings into focus the major areas of Comintern activity: massive publication and distribution of propaganda (sometimes through disguised media); concerted infiltration of the socialist party; infiltration and radicalization of the large socialist trade union system (a key to sharpening social and political conflict); infiltration and subversion of the armed forces (together with the initiation of an armed communist militia); domination and expansion of communist influence over the major sector of organized leftist athletics (in turn a feeder for the communist militia); the important communist role in facilitating the broader Popular Front alliance of 1936; and exactly how the shift to greater use of elections was related to the continuing revolutionary goals of the movement. Possibly most important of all was the initiation and expansion of the "victimization" propaganda campaign in 1934–5. This transformed the thousands of violent revolutionaries involved in the socialist and communist insurrection of 1934 from perpetrators into "victims"—one of the great propaganda feats of the twentieth century. It was a principal key to the leftist victory in the corrupt and fraudulent Popular Front electoral process of 1936 and the breakdown of the Republic itself a few months later.

As is customary in the academic world, historiography in Spain has been dominated by a predominant politically correct viewpoint. Only a few courageous university historians and independent scholars dare to challenge it, for since 2022 this has been reenforced by the only official censorship legislation in effect on the national level in any of the Western world's nominal democracies. Ever since 1808, Spain has been a leader in radical political innovation and now censorship of historical expression has the force of national legislation behind it. Thus in Spain "cancel culture" is no mere academic fad: Tocqueville's "soft despotism" is more advanced than in any other Western country.

Gustavo Martín is not, however, advancing a political polemic, but a sober, massively documented study based almost entirely on primary Soviet sources. His principal data are drawn directly from the reports of Comintern agents and communist leaders themselves. The result is a major contribution to the history of the Comintern, Spanish Communism, and the progressive breakdown of the Second Spanish Republic. It is a focused research monograph that also invalidates a significant part of the preceding historiography. In 1938, while the Civil War raged, Spain's leading philosopher, the internationally famous José Ortega y Gasset, wrote tellingly that the most important thing to know about the conflict was simply the nature of its origins—the background from which the war had sprung. Therein exactly lies the significance of this book.

The war that began in 1936 brought Spanish Communism to world prominence, though for the party and its Soviet sponsor the Spanish experience proved paradoxical. Throughout the "Third Period" of Comintern activity from 1928 to 1935, the movement adhered to its announced strategy of radicalization à l'outrance, seeking culmination in insurrection, civil war, and the triumph of Communism. Aside from certain achievements in Spain, however, that strategy had failed everywhere else. By contrast, Benito Mussolini had grasped nearly fifteen years earlier that the "communist strategy" was doomed to failure in an institutionally coherent Western country such as Italy. Thus he rejected a "communist strategy" of insurrection in favor of a "fascist strategy" that sought alliance with broader electoral forces later to make possible a nominally legal transition to a one-party dictatorship, as finally occurred at the beginning of 1925. Adolf Hitler, by contrast, had followed the "communist strategy" in Munich in 1923, very nearly losing his life, since the comrade with whom he marched arm-in-arm during the insurrection was quickly shot dead. Hitler may have shown greater personal bravery than either Lenin or Stalin, but failed completely. He learned his lesson, thereafter switching to Mussolini's "fascist tactic," which eventually made him dictator in 1933. Stalin was much slower to learn, but eventually, after the destruction of the largest communist movement in Europe, also eventually switched to the "fascist strategy," announcing a new Popular Front tactic of electoral coalition in 1935.

Simplistic and blinkered Western historiography for many years insisted that this demonstrated Soviet abandonment of revolutionary tactics, but Martín Asensio demonstrates this was not the case. All that was ever necessary was to read in detail the officially published Comintern statements, but so simple an effort was too much for many Western historians (though, as Martín Asensio points out, the noted British diplomatic historian Jonathan Haslam has finally come round to it in his declining years). Comintern spokesmen made clear from the beginning that the Popular Front represented no more than a temporary shift in one major aspect of tactics, part of a three-step strategy that would begin with elections to form Popular Front all-leftist governments in various countries, to be followed by a transition to an all-worker revolutionary government (as in Russia in 1917), climaxed by a third-phase transition to a purely communist "democratic worker dictatorship." There was no deviation whatsoever from this plan for four years. Conditions in Spain in the spring of 1936, as Martín Asensio shows, filled Comintern leaders with jubilation. The only Popular Front election anywhere had produced an all-leftist government that, although it included no socialist or communist ministers, adopted increasingly radical measures. Constitutional order was subject to frequent, rarely restrained breakdown, with revolutionary seizures of and much destruction of property; arbitrary arrests of many hundreds of rightists; the burning of scores of churches; prohibition of religious services in some provinces; the closing of Catholic schools; the beginning of the packing of the judicial system and the incorporation of hundreds of revolutionary militants into the police forces (rather like Nazi Hilfspolizei in Germany in 1933). Hundreds of politically motivated killings were climaxed by the kidnapping and murder of the leading spokesman of the parliamentary opposition by a mixed squad of Republican police and revolutionary militants. As Martín Asensio demonstrates, to Comintern leaders this was for the first time "revolution on the march" after years of frustration. For five years, the Comintern had promoted maximal radicalization, but by the spring of 1936, when some Spanish party leaders talked of a direct revolutionary takeover, for the first time Comintern chiefs pulled back. They declared that Spanish leaders were trying to go too far too fast, and insisted on adhering (at least generally) to the grand plan of 1935. In Spain all anti-leftist forces had been rendered impotent, and pro-revolutionaries controlled nearly all institutions. Thus a nominally legal transition to revolutionary control could soon be carried out without much institutional rupture. The consequence, however, was that it sometimes became difficult to keep all communist militants in line. For five years the Comintern had encouraged ultimate revolutionary civil war, but by June 1936 it sought to avert any overt blow-up, knowing that in an outright civil war the rightist opposition might have a better chance. As matters stood, if absolute breakdown could be avoided, the revolutionary left might win complete power through nominally legal means. In the final days before the military insurrection, the Comintern advice was simply to use the latest crisis as a wedge to complete total leftist takeover of all institutions, nominally employing as much as possible whatever was left of Republican legality.

When half the army, assisted by civilian volunteers, began an insurrection on July 17, 1936, some revolutionary leaders wanted to dissolve what was left of the armed forces, to be replaced by a mass revolutionary militia that could guarantee an immediate all-out collectivist revolution. The Comintern quickly tried to veto that, insisting that the revolutionary process sustain the Popular Front instead, with its cover of a nominally democratic coalition Republic, and restructure a regular army to suppress the rebellion. Communist party membership had been expanding rapidly since 1935, and the wartime crisis brought it fully to the fore as it became a genuine mass organization for the first time. As Martín Asensio explains, the Comintern had shown the way to overcoming the debacle of the failed socialist revolution of 1934, and it was the first to set the guidelines by which to wage the Civil War, sheltering under the propaganda myth of Republican democracy while organizing a fully structured regular army to win the conflict.

The main obstacle faced by Spanish Communism was that by this point the revolutionary process initiated in 1931 had gone much too far for leftist moderates and the Comintern to be able to hold it back. All the revolutionary left—majority socialists, anarchosyndicalists, the very small anti-Stalinist communist party POUM (Worker Party of Marxist Unification) and even a small sector of the more moderate left—insisted on immediate socioeconomic revolution. The minority Republican government gave in to them, largely replacing the armed forces with revolutionary militia who prioritized large-scale collectivization and wreaking violence on presumed civilian enemies. This made it possible for the rebels, soon given modest military assistance by Italy and Germany, to gain millions of supporters and grow much stronger.

The situation of Spanish Communism grew more paradoxical yet. Through the Comintern, Soviet policy insisted that all effort be concentrated on the military struggle, else the revolution was doomed. This required that the Spanish Revolution—the only mass violent collectivist revolution in West European history—be channeled and controlled, thoroughly subordinated to the military struggle. The communist line—supported by the moderate left—was obviously correct, but was generally rejected by the extreme revolutionary left, whose militants were much more numerous. This produced the final paradox that the greatly expanded Spanish Communist Party, proud of its association with the only successful revolution of the century in Russia, were now accused of promoting "counter-revolution" instead. Within Republican Spain, communist spokesmen found themselves condemned to pass the entire struggle repeatedly arguing that they were not at all counterrevolutionaries, but rather representatives of the only known successful revolution, and that only their program could achieve victory. Collectivist revolution had been imposed throughout most of the Republican zone, and communist policy did not advocate renouncing most of that but simply moderating its operations to concentrate strength for winning the war. Soon they were drawing attention to Lenin's NEP (New Economic Program) of 1921, which had restored a temporary limited capitalism and market economy to the Soviet Union to enable its economy to recover. The economy's "commanding heights," however, remained in the control of state socialism. This, they said, was similar to what they were trying to encourage in Republican Spain.

Just as the Comintern had promoted the "myth of victimization" to enable the left to recover from its self-inflicted prewar disaster, it stressed the crucial importance of maintaining the myth of the "democratic Republic," described as "just like France or the United States." Comintern policy was always carefully related to geopolitics, and from the beginning Soviet leadership saw the importance of trying to gain support from Western democracies, especially France and Great Britain. The problem was that many leaders in the latter countries were too nearby and too well informed to be overly impressed by the illusion of Republican democracy, though in later decades this ploy proved surprisingly successful with historians less alert than the contemporary Western leaders. The extensive resources of the Comintern propaganda machine were never able fully to offset this.

Spanish revolutionaries entered the struggle with most immediate power factors on their side—most of the territory with the majority of the population, most of the large cities and industrial production, most of the country's financial strength, half of the regular army, and most of the navy and air force. Their greatest weakness was internal disunity and the revolution itself, which sapped their strength and impeded concentration of resources. Though the left generally resisted outright communist control, they inevitably looked to the Soviet Union for military support. For various reasons, this was a serious dilemma for Stalin, but, two months into the conflict, the Spanish left showed that it was making some effort to follow Comintern advice by forming a fully organized multi-party coalition government under the most prominent revolutionary leader, the socialist Largo Caballero. Stalin then agreed in September 1936 to send Soviet arms and Soviet combat personnel to Spain. This helped to stabilize the fronts by the end of the year, ensuring that the conflict would last longer and become more deadly.

In 1937 communist power reached its peak in Spain. The newly formed Spanish Republican People's Army was modeled on the Soviet Red Army, with its red star insignia, clenched-fist military salute and system of political commissars. Communist propaganda often predominated, though never exclusively so. Communist attention above all concentrated on the Republican military, in which for some time a partial communist hegemony prevailed, though this always encountered resistance. The most ardent rival of Stalinism, the quasi-Trotskyist POUM, was completely suppressed. In general, Soviet policy followed its standard two-track course. Stalin hoped to provide enough assistance for the Spanish revolution to win, but on Comintern, not Spanish revolutionary, terms. For this to happen, it was necessary politically to maintain what Burnett Bolloten has termed the "grand camouflage" of disguising the violent revolution (and most of the Western left, then and now, has assisted in the enterprise). The predominant concern, however, was always Soviet geostrategic interests, and that required constant calculation. Full-scale Japanese invasion of China in 1937 opened the danger of conflict on the Soviet eastern border, with the nightmare of a Soviet war on two fronts. From that time large-scale Soviet military aid to the Chinese government (itself strongly anti-communist) increasingly superseded support for the Spanish revolution, even though Comintern policy continued to insist (again largely for Soviet geostrategic purposes) on all-out resistance to the Nationalist counterrevolutionaries of Franco.

During the Spanish conflict, leftist forces tended more and more to divide between pro- and anti-communists, limiting the degree of hegemony which the communists could achieve. By 1939 the struggle had become militarily hopeless yet the Comintern was instructed to demand resistance to the bitter end. In

March 1939 this became too much for the rest of the Spanish left, which erupted in an anti-communist military revolt in Madrid. That precipitated the flight of the communist leaders and the end of the Civil War that the Comintern, however contradictorily, had done so much to provoke.

The Spanish Civil War of 1936–9 was Western Europe's largest modern civil war and was also the most dramatic and closely watched development in Europe during the 1930s prior to the military aggressions of Germany. Its complications have often defied historians, and it produced no greater complexity than the role of Communism. Gustavo Martín has given us a strikingly original and well-documented monograph that for the first time explains in detail how this began to develop during the five years of the prewar Republic.

Introduction

The debate over the nature and degree of sincerity of Soviet collective security policy in the 1933–9 period went on for decades. Two volumes published in 1984 are representative of the major sides in this debate. Jonathan Haslam's *The Soviet Union and the Struggle for Collective Security in Europe: 1933–1939*[1] is representative of the historiography that saw the Soviet collective security policy in the period as a genuine effort to secure peace in the face of the fascist threat. Thus, genuinely concerned over the Nazi regime's threat to world peace, Stalin would have forced a radical turn from prior Soviet pursuit of communist revolution in Western capitalist countries. Jiri Hochman's volume, *The Soviet Union and the Failure of Collective Security, 1934–1938*,[2] however, is representative of the literature that interprets much of the Soviet foreign policy outreach in the period as a ploy and a means of shifting confrontation to the capitalist nations, while the Soviet Union continued to pursue an alliance with Hitler. Hochman further argued that this "peace-making" outreach in the West also enabled Stalin to carry out the Great Terror at home and continued communist subversion abroad. Marilynn Giroux was right to express frustration by the debate as summarized in Haslam's and Hochman's volumes, as a historian denied access to the archival materials needed to settle the dispute.[3]

We see a fine instantiation of the debate ten years later in the Gabriel Gorodetsky-edited volume *Soviet Foreign Policy 1917–1991. A Retrospective.*[4] Here Haslam refines his position to argue that Litvinov's diplomatic outreach to the West in our period represented an authentic Soviet option for peace which Stalin may have shared, had Molotov not had the upper hand.[5] Haslam downplays Stalin's Bolshevism in this period, a key piece in his argument which we shall address below. In his contribution to this volume, Teddy Uldricks suggests that the real foreign policy of the USSR is not to be found either in Litvinov's peace orations in Geneva or in the persistent secret pursuit of a deal with Hitler. Uldricks defends instead a third interpretation which is fully consistent with the Leninist worldview that Stalin always held. Since the days of the Bolshevik revolution, the constant preoccupation of Soviet leadership had been that of an all-capitalist coalition that would encircle the USSR and bring to an end the Soviet project. Lenin thus argued that in the absence of worldwide revolution, the only valid strategy for defending the integrity of the USSR was to pursue alliances in such a way as to keep the capitalist nations divided among themselves. It is this Soviet foreign policy concern and no other, argues Uldricks, that provides a coherent explanation of Soviet dualism in the period.[6] As Silvio Pons put it in 1995, benefiting already from limited access to the Soviet archives, the capitalist world's intervention in the Russian Civil War became the archetype of an ever-present all-capitalist, all-imperialist alliance against communism that drove Soviet foreign policy.[7]

James Harris and Stephen Kotkin have, I would argue, all but settled the issue by means of their exhaustive research and exegesis of soviet archival sources, especially in Stalin's personal archive.[8] Harris, exploring Stalin's personal correspondence and diplomatic archives, concludes that, following both his Bolshevik ideology and consistent intelligence reports, Stalin was focused on neutralizing a feared capitalist alliance against the Soviet Union whose leaders were not primarily Germany and Japan, but Britain and France.[9] Harris shows that the source of these intelligence reports was often military intelligence (the OGPU), and that Stalin was often discussing these materials with Molotov and other committed Bolsheviks, while consistently restraining and bypassing Litvinov and others in the Foreign Commissariat in this period. Kotkin rubs our noses up against a fundamental fact confirmed time and time again by the documentation. In their private conversations, Stalin, as well as Dimitrov, Molotov, and all the top Soviet leadership did not diminish or relax their communist, Marxist-Leninist worldview, nor the vocabulary that expresses it. While the doors to the archives remained closed, one could have imagined, suggests Kotkin, Stalin and the Soviet leadership meeting in private and commenting, with a sigh of relief: "alright, finally alone. Enough with all the nonsense about the bourgeoisie and proletarian revolution. Let us get on with the real agenda." Stenographic records and other documentation, however, reveal there was, in fact, no difference in worldview, vocabulary, and outlook between the public and private conversations of Stalin and the Soviet leadership in our period. These were devoted communists and followers of Lenin through and through. This insight is not a trivial one, as Haslam argued in his early writings on the subject that Stalin, together with Litvinov, was "never a true ideologue in the manner of Lenin" and remained open to a non-Bolshevik policy until Molotov won him over to his side.[10] This, as we will show, amounts to allowing the trees of flexible Leninist agit-prop to block from view the forest of an unchangeable Bolshevik strategy.

Further, and more importantly, Kotkin's work has removed what was perhaps one of the leading remaining sources of support for the notion that, in 1924, Stalin had moved away from the Leninist doctrine of active support for world revolution. Relying on personal letters, speeches, and other archival material, Kotkin shows that the traditional interpretation of Stalin's 1924 article "Socialism in one Country" as a break with Lenin's policy of worldwide revolution is the product of heavy filtering through Trotsky's later "permanent revolution" polemic. Rather than an abandonment of support for world revolution, the tract was a defense of Soviet success since October 1917 and a justification of building socialism in Russia *first*, while the right conditions and opportunities arose elsewhere. Thus, for Stalin the victory of socialism in the Soviet Union had an international character, and final communist victory would involve proletarian revolution in other countries as well. The key section of Stalin's article, argues Kotkin, was that in which the dictator details the conditions that were needed for the success of the Bolshevik revolution, especially that of imperialist war among capitalist nations. The Great War was a conflict that fully occupied imperialist countries and consumed their resources, thus enabling Bolshevik revolution to proceed in Russia. As Uldricks had argued before, though without Kotkin's exhaustive command of the archives, Stalin's greatest fear was the encirclement of the Soviet Union by an all-imperialist coalition. Consequently, Soviet foreign policy, according to Stalin, had to pursue alliances that would divide the Western capitalist nations, "as wars between our enemies are our greatest ally."[11] The Franco-Soviet pact of 1935 should be seen in this light, as should the "anti-fascist" and later popular front tactics driven by the Comintern globally in the period of 1933 to 1936. Stalin believed firmly with Lenin that imperialist war, and not only class struggle would trigger revolution in capitalist nations. Stalin's final words in his famous tract are transparently clear:

> Therefore, not only those are wrong who forget the international character of the October Revolution and declare the victory of socialism in one country to be a purely national, and only a national, phenomenon, but also those who … are inclined to regard this revolution as something passive, merely destined to accept help from without. Actually, not only does the October Revolution need support from the revolution in other countries, but the revolution in those countries needs the support of the October Revolution, in order to accelerate and advance the cause of overthrowing world imperialism.[12]

In what is, arguably, his magnum opus published in 2021, Haslam seems to have come full circle. In *The Spectre of War*, Haslam intends to correct a long-standing downplaying of the threat posed by Soviet communism to Western democracies in the interwar period. Haslam asserts that soviet diplomatic talk of collective security was believed, first and foremost by "liberals and socialists," a naiveté which rendered them irrelevant to Western leaders who understood Moscow's true intentions. Far from abandoning Lenin's world-revolutionary strategy, Stalin remained committed to it, though pursuing a duplicitous set of tactics that always included Comintern-led infiltration and subversion of the same Western nations Soviet diplomacy was engaging with. Haslam thus seeks, in line with Kotkin, to reconnect the historiography of the Cold war with an account of the interwar period that keeps the real threat of Soviet communism at center stage.[13]

This interpretation best explains the duplicity of Soviet activity in Europe in the period: anti-fascist and popular front tactics in France and Spain while pursuing secret deals with Nazi Germany; campaigns for peace and against war while supporting, as we shall see in detail, socialist-led armed insurrections in Austria and Spain and building up the Soviet army and its arsenals; defense of parliamentary democracy while training and deploying Comintern operatives in the infiltration of trade unions, cultural and sports organizations, and armed forces of European nations; publishing edited VII Comintern Congress documents supporting anti-fascist collaboration with petit bourgeoisie and social democrats while distributing secret military tasks to its European sections, including those with "bourgeois democratic" governments, after the VII Congress. The governments of Britain and France understood and were carefully tracking these activities through the resources of their intelligence services, a fact that always influenced diplomatic relations with Russia.[14] Indeed, even the early Haslam was forced to concede that "[h]owever much Mother Russia attempted to conceal the fact, her revolutionary petticoat kept dropping below the hemline of her ill-fashioned dress."[15] As Kotkin has shown, Neville Chamberlain's choices as he traveled to Munich in September 1938 were more limited than is often granted. Without wishing necessarily to rehabilitate Chamberlain, Kotkin refers to the British prime minister's letters to his sister Ida in those days. In this correspondence, Chamberlain contemplated the consequences of an alternative pact with the Soviet Union, a path recommended to him by many in Britain: "[h]ow then, shall we extract the communists from Central Europe?"[16] The Western allies would be forced to face this very scenario in 1945.

Thus, contrary to popular opinion, the VII Congress of the Comintern did not bring about a fundamental change in Bolshevik doctrine nor a turn away from the pursuit of world revolution. The fact that there could be no radical break with the past was evident in Dimitrov's early dialogue with Stalin in the run-up to the Congress.[17] The real break brought about by the VII Congress was a break with rigidity and cut-and-paste Bolshevism in favor of Leninist flexibility in tactics with complete adaptation of these to local situations. The strategy, however, remained the same. This was made evident, for example, in the conditions established at the congress for unity with the socialists. These included "complete break of the social democrats with the bourgeoisie, and recognition of the need to remove the bourgeoisie from power revolutionarily and establish the dictatorship of the proletariat in the form of soviets."[18] These conditions were not taken lightly. In fact, the youth branch of the French party was, simultaneously with the congress, signing a unity of action agreement with their socialist counterparts affirming the essence of the Bolshevik revolutionary agenda.[19] These conditions were also mentioned explicitly in the letter that the group of Spanish socialists, communists, and anarchists took home from their Moscow exile in March 1936, with the approval of the Comintern leadership.[20] Speaking to the Executive Committee of the Communist International (ECCI) in January 1936 about the great impact of the VII Congress in Spain, Victorio Codovilla celebrated the left wing of the socialist party had "justly interpreted that the Comintern has not capitulated, it has not changed its line, the Comintern has adapted its tactic to the current situation in order to gather the forces against fascism."[21] McDermott and Agnew were, therefore, correct to affirm the VII Congress brought changes in tactics but certainly not in strategy. Indeed, "there was nothing in [Comintern General Secretary] Dimitrov's speech which openly challenged the universal applicability of the Bolshevik model of revolution."[22]

The literature on the specific application of Soviet foreign policy to Spain in the period of the Second Republic and before the outbreak of civil war (April 14, 1931–July 17, 1936) seems in dire need of updating. Herbert Southworth, a former employee of Juan Negrín during and after the Spanish Civil War, dedicated decades to a systematic *exposé* of manufactured francoist documents purporting to demonstrate Soviet communist plans for insurrection in Spain in the summer of 1936. We will discuss Southworth's work in detail in Chapter 1, but his, at best, partial understanding of the larger context is worth addressing here briefly. In his passing discussion of Soviet foreign policy in 1933–9, Southworth sided squarely with the Soviet collective security school of thought we have discussed above, and cited Cattell as his authority, together with an exiled socialist leader of the postwar period, Ramos Oliveira. Southworth cited Cattell to argue that the American historian rebutted "the whole concept of a communist plot in the overall European picture of the time." As we have seen above, however, Cattell, writing before the opening of the Soviet archives, admitted at the outset of his work that the Soviet Union refused to abandon "even for the moment" their goal of subversion and world domination. Paul Preston also fails to engage in any detail with the debate on Soviet foreign policy in the period as summarized above and argues that in 1936 spreading revolution "could hardly have been further removed" from Soviet policy, since Stalin was concerned above all with "collective security, cooperation with Britain and France against the German threat."[23] Writing in Preston's 1984 edited volume, Smyth affirms that "Soviet leaders sought only a peaceful international existence which would permit them to complete their gigantic domestic experiment."[24] Ángel Viñas, thoroughly committed to the sincerity of Soviet collective security in the period, attaches significant value to the recently published Ivan Maisky diaries[25] as a reliable source of Soviet intentions in the period. Yet, Viñas ignores the constant conflicts both Maisky and Litvinov had with Moscow, and the fact that Stalin, true to his steadfast Leninist ideology, allowed Maisky and Litvinov to continue their anti-fascist outreaches while keeping a separate track open toward Germany that his two diplomats knew nothing about.[26] Additionally, and to the dismay of both Maisky and Litvinov, Stalin kept all the subversive activities of the Comintern running at full speed in 1935 and early 1936, of which Spain is a case in point. Viñas and Preston refuse to accept that, Litvinov notwithstanding, all foreign policy was for Joseph Stalin, in Kotkin's words, a "two-faced intercourse with enemies." Consequently, Southworth, Preston, and others have argued that Soviet subversion in Spain occurred only as a result of the July 1936 military uprising, relegating opposing views to the dustbin of francoist conspiracy theory. This thesis has become a key tenet of much of the historiography of the Spanish Second Republic in the past forty years, often merely stated without any serious attempt at justification or deep engagement with primary sources.[27]

Contrary to Southworth, Preston, and Viñas, Stanley Payne has argued that Soviet involvement in Spain in the Second Republic period was significant and consistently subversive from 1931 to 1939.[28] Payne suggests that the VII Comintern Congress, far from abandoning the Leninist dogma of world revolution, refined and re-launched a duplicitous two-track strategy that has been, by design, widely misunderstood. On one track, a united front pursuing insurrection and revolution in Spain remained the fundamental communist tactic. In parallel, a second track involved the Concentración Popular and Popular Front coalitions against fascism including not only socialists but also "petit bourgeoisie" republican parties and explained in attractive democratic terms. The twin track approach was, argued Payne, fully consistent with the Soviet policy of keeping normal diplomatic and commercial ties with Western democracies, while simultaneously sponsoring and supporting insurrectional activities through its Comintern resources in those countries. What was missing from Payne's work was thorough documentation in the Comintern and other archives that would substantiate a significant level of subversive and insurrectional Soviet activity in Spain from 1931 through June 1936. Antonio Elorza and Marta Bizcarrondo's volume *Queridos Camaradas* could have provided such documentation. Their work, however, while groundbreaking in a number of ways, was plagued by a several limitations, most of them, perhaps, self-imposed. To begin with, the apology made in the introduction to the communist party of Spain for presenting material that would shed a negative light on its past was puzzling.[29] Secondly, the volume does not cover most of the available archival material detailing the illegal[30] and subversive activity of the Comintern in Spain in the period, to wit, the detailed planning, training and operations of "work" in the army and navy, the training and support for armed insurrection both before and after the VII Comintern Congress, the careful management, beyond simply finance, of the campaign post-October 1934 which merged into the Popular Front campaign, the direct and leading role of the Comintern, starting in January 1935 in the promotion of and recruitment for the Popular Front platform which reached socialists and republicans from the start, the Comintern design and planning of the July 1936 Popular Olympiad in Barcelona, etc. Elorza and Bizcarrondo's decision to present the archival material maintaining the "spider web" structure of the communications between the Comintern and the Spanish section and vice versa, kept the authors from presenting consistently and clearly the twin-track tactics of Soviet policy throughout the period. The authors wished to argue, for example, that the German militarization of the Rheinland on March 7, 1936, "destroys Soviet peace policy and the principle of collective security."[31] Soviet and Comintern policy for Spain from then on, argued the authors, becomes far more defensive than offensive or revolutionary. Yet, Elorza and Bizcarrondo go on to admit, without any detailed commentary, the duplicitous Soviet policy evident in the signature of a new commercial agreement with Germany on April 29, 1936.[32] Further, the authors refer in passing to the renewed emphasis, in a May 1936 Comintern resolution, on the role of armed militias and infiltration of the army, as well as the instructions to erase "enemies of the Republic" from the political map and thus ensure a victory of revolutionary forces over the counterrevolutionary ones. These inconsistencies are not resolved in a coherent interpretation of the documents in Elorza and Bizcarrondo's volume.

The archival documentation we shall discuss in detail in this book demands a thorough reassessment of the level and nature of Soviet involvement in Spain *before* the outbreak of civil war. In Spain, the Russian Revolution had a powerful impact that shook the socialist party and the anarchist union Confederación Nacional del Trabajo (CNT) to their core in the years 1917–21. The mimetic and short-lived socialist and anarchist revolutionary insurrection of August 1917 was, contrary to traditional interpretations, a violent uprising that exceeded any single episode of armed violence since the Carlist wars.[33] As would be the case in a socialist-led insurrection in October 1934, the romantic label "revolutionary strike" became a smokescreen conveniently placed in front of violent processes which resulted in significant death and destruction. In January 1919 the leadership of the Spanish Socialist Party PSOE expressed for the first time in a party congress its commitment to the Bolshevik revolution, whose principles were affirmed to be "exactly the same"[34] as those that should drive socialist party action in Spain. Before the end of the year, however, the party would vote to remain, for the time being, within the socialist II International, a decision that provoked the schism of its youth organization, who voted unconditionally in favor of joining the III International. Over the next 16 months, the socialist party would suffer the exit of its youth to form the Spanish Communist Party (PCE) and of an additional group of dissidents one year later, who would form the Workers' Communist Party. Both groups would eventually merge under the existing PCE label, the Spanish section of the Comintern.

The initial fervor for the Bolshevik revolution would die down in Spain after 1921, a lull that would last a decade. As Roberto Villa has shown, the same coalition that prepared and carried out the August 1917 insurrection would re-emerge in late 1930 in the Pacto de San Sebastian and its revolutionary committee. As in 1917, Catalan separatists, socialists, left wing and moderate republicans, and a fraction of the military banded together to promote, not parliamentary democracy, but regime change via a coup, which was launched but failed in December 1930. The edict published in Jaca on December 12, 1930, left little doubt about the nature of the regime it intended to establish. Signed by Fermín Galán, leading member of the revolutionary committee, the edit warned: "[a]nyone opposing, by word or in written form … the new-born republic will be shot without trial."[35] After a municipal election was won in the provincial capitals by republican candidates, though the overall nationwide vote was won by monarchists, the Spanish II Republic was proclaimed. The communists understood from the start that elections were useful even if one did not believe in the democratic process. Speaking in January 1935 about the

April 1931 municipal elections, Comintern agent in Spain Victorio Codovilla warned the ECCI that, just as the left had used local elections to establish the republic in 1931, the "reaction" could try to use the 1935 municipal poll to close the revolutionary period.[36] A day after the 1931 vote, the socialist organ *El Socialista* put forth an interpretation of the new regime, in line with the vision of the revolutionary committee of 1930: "[i]t is for us now to enjoy the pleasure of observing the triumphant revolution ... to the conservative sectors we warn, if anyone insists on disappointing ... they will be responsible for unleashing the violent revolution."[37] With the advent of the "Spanish revolution" on April 14, 1931, the Comintern, present in Spain with financing, training, and support since the early 1920s, began to focus on Spain to a far greater degree. Moscow's efforts in Spain, as we shall see, zeroed in not primarily on growing PCE membership but on the standard Bolshevik playbook of "work" in the autonomous, socialist, and anarchist unions, the setting up and expansion of "mass organizations," the creation of a large network of publishing houses, and, especially, "work" in the armed forces. In parallel with its operations in Spain, the Comintern began to bring the most talented and qualified communist leaders to the International Lenin School in Moscow, with student numbers increasing year by year until March 1936 in which fifty-three Spaniards were attending the school. The training provided in Moscow covered theoretical matters, as well as the fundamentals of legal and illegal work, including armed insurrectional training and systematic infiltration of the armed forces. Communist cell work in the Spanish army was so successful that in early 1936 the leadership organized a congress in Madrid, with cells representing every single barracks in the city. In the navy, communist cells on board the largest vessels included most corporals and hundreds of NCOs, according to a report held at the PCE archive.

The Comintern's mass organizational work in Spain, a success story among Western European sections, allowed it to punch well above the weight of official PCE membership in Spain in our period. Indeed, in early 1935, the communist-controlled sports organization FCDO alone boasted 50,000 members, exceeding by itself the number of PCE members at that time. According to internal Comintern reports, Friends of the Soviet Union in Spain had 20,100 members in July 1933, many of which were cultural influencers with large networks of followers through press, publications, and events. According to another report from 1933, the various Comintern-managed anti-war committees in Spanish provinces boasted 76,000 members, with 31,000 in Asturias alone. Spain's branch of International Red Aid, Socorro Rojo Internacional (SRI) was launched in the country in late 1931 and within two years had offices in most provincial capitals.

Its leadership and generous funding of the agitational campaign that followed the October 1934 insurrection made the SRI indispensable to the leadership of the socialist party, as we shall detail in this book.

The beginning of the Bolshevization of much of the socialist party in this period can be traced back to Largo Caballero's address to the socialist party's summer school in August 1933. In this speech, Caballero expressed his merely instrumental view of parliamentary democracy and his positive assessment of the revolutionary maturity of the Spanish proletariat, which he compared with its Russian counterpart in October 1917.[38] The Bolshevization process gained significant momentum in 1934, as, after losing the elections to a conservative-republican coalition, the socialist leadership prepared an armed insurrection, gathered weapons, and trained its members, often using Comintern-printed manuals. Having joined the fight in the last-minute following Comintern approval, the Spanish communists delivered their master stroke, claiming overall leadership and crafting a masterful narrative of fascist repression and proletarian victimhood that would become the cornerstone of the Popular Front. Comintern agent "Medina" (Victorio Codovilla) was in contact with Caballero and other socialist leaders before the insurrection and was assured of thorough preparation and final success, as we shall see. Frequent communication from both Medina and Ercoli (Palmiro Togliatti) and other Comintern officials in Moscow, Madrid and Paris continued throughout 1935, as communist infiltration of the socialist union UGT and youth was reaching its desired outcome. Before traveling to a meeting of the socialist II International in 1935, Julio Álvarez del Vayo consulted with Ercoli on what his course of action should be at the congress. Ercoli responded by instructing that del Vayo should stir up dissention between left and right fractions and inform those in favor of the Popular Front to contact the Comintern directly. The doctrinal and tactical convergence of the Spanish socialists with the Comintern in 1933–6 is an essential enabler of the processes we will discuss in detail in this book. North of the Pyrenees French socialist leader Léon Blum remained at best guarded in his relationship to the PCF, seeing the communist party as "une sorte d'armée de métier de l'insurrection" and a "parti nationaliste étranger."[39] Even as his party was signing the unity of action pact with the communists, he was convinced of the fact that the new attitude of the communists had its origin in Moscow.[40] South of the border, however, Caballero, Del Vayo, de Francisco, Nelken, and many other socialist leaders and influencers moved from open admiration to full alignment with Soviet communism as expressed by Caballero: "we are different only in name."[41] The various Comintern representatives understood these socialist leaders and the mases who followed them offered Moscow fertile and well-ploughed ground, and the consensus was expressed by Codovilla in January 1935 when he told the ECCI that these top socialists "are on their way to us." All the mentioned legal, semi-legal, and illegal Comintern operations in Spain were instrumental in the achievement of its top objectives by early 1936: the merger of socialist and communist unions, as well as youth organizations totaling 150,000 military-age members under communist control. With the Popular Front government in power as of February 1936, the Comintern's policy for Spain remained unchanged, in line with its understanding of the high level of revolutionary maturity in the country. As we shall detail in the epilogue, the "bourgeois-democratic" and proletarian phases of the revolution were overlapping in Spain in the spring of 1936, and the Comintern's Spanish section, in a fine display of Bolshevik flexibility, embraced the opportunities this presented. The "October path" remained firmly occupied by socialists and communists through to the summer of 1936.

Most of the archival documents we discuss in the book are held by the Russian State Archive of Socio-Political History (RGASPI) and were obtained in a few cases directly and, for the most part, from four separate online repositories. The Covid pandemic, followed by Vladimir Putin's *Vernichtungskrieg* in Ukraine, has made these repositories the sole means of accessing the relevant material for the foreseeable future. The first of these, the Electronic Library of the Russian Historical Society,[42] is a thematically arranged collection of Comintern-related documentation reproduced in separate volumes and including some material from *Pravda* and other sources. This is a very valuable collection because it includes RGASPI files not available in other online sources, especially several detailing the subversive and illegal activities of the Spanish and other sections. The second source is the Soviet Era Documents Collection of the Federal Archival Agency of the Russian Federation, which contains much of Fond 495 of the Comintern material held by RGASPI, that is, the secretariats, commissions, and local sections of the Comintern.[43] The digitization and classification work for this repository was carried out with the cooperation of the International Committee for the Computerization of the Comintern (INCOMKA), including also, for example, the Library of Congress. Access to the materials in Fond 495, however, has been made much easier by the InfoRost platform in terms of usability and user interface.[44] Lastly, we have consulted the substantial documentation hosted by the Portail Archives Numériques et Données de la Recherche (PANDOR).[45] This online repository contains over half a million pages of archival material related to the French section of the Comintern, but includes many documents from the Spanish section or related to Spain, given the membership of both sections in the Comintern's Roman Land Secretariat. This material also includes documents of or related to the Spanish section that are not available in the other online sources, for example, the letters from the headquarters of the French Communist Youth to its sections on the Barcelona "Popular Olympiad," which we discuss in Chapter 6. In addition to the RGASPI files mentioned, we have obtained copies of all the decrypts of Comintern communication from and to Spain in our period, as well as the personal files of relevant individuals, all held by The National Archives.[46] This material becomes particularly useful in conjunction with the RGASPI documentation and yields important insights that would be unattainable by research in either of the archival sources alone. For example, the communications between the Spanish section and Moscow in February 1936 illustrate and complete the various 1935 to January 1936 RGASPI-held reports on Comintern promotion of the Popular Front, with last minute instructions to urge electors to vote "en bloc" for Popular Front candidates. The 1933 and 1934 reports on Spain produced by Willi Münzenberg in Paris are also complemented by the March 1936 decrypts confirming Münzenberg was in Madrid personally to drive publication efforts and negotiate with socialist leaders. Lastly, the Historical Archives of the Spanish Communist Party, the British Labour Party Archives, and the International Institute of Social History in Amsterdam have also yielded several interesting documents that shed additional light on our investigation. Among these, the 1939 report on communist cells in the Spanish navy from 1932 through 1936, or Fernando Claudin's typewritten account of his return from Moscow to fulfil his communist duties as a conscript in an artillery regiment are just two examples of several.

In the days before PowerPoint and Google slides, teachers, business leaders, and other communicators often relied on overhead projectors and cellulose acetate transparencies. Superimposed and projected on a physical screen, these transparencies would display layers of information to be explained step by step: political structure above official organizational charts, physical geography above political geography, etc. In the present work, Spanish, French, and occasionally British period press sources are regularly deployed as an additional primary source layer that grounds the archival data in events as reported in widely read period newspapers. Thus, we can see how instructions delivered by Elena Stasova of Red Aid in Moscow regarding the political utilization of Asturian orphans were implemented, under the leadership of Pasionaria, days later, as reported on by a regional daily. Further, we verify that the letter sent by the Comitè Català pro Esport Popular to President Azaña in early 1936, requesting funding previously granted to the Spanish Olympic Committee, was delivered immediately after the Comintern's sports organization issued an instruction to carry out precisely such an action. British press coverage of the "parliamentary delegation" to Madrid and Asturias in November 1934 is similarly complemented by internal communications from the Labour Party archives on the unauthorized activities of Ellen Wilkinson in Spain. Coverage in the French press of the return of French "athletes" to Marseille in August 1936 illustrates and confirms material from the French communist youth leadership to its regional leaders months earlier. Though the present volume is primarily the fruit of research in previously neglected archival material, I believe the additional effort to bring period press to bear on the events and persons referred to in these documents confirms, once more, Burnett Bolloten's thesis: "[i]t is impossible to understand the passions, the emotions, and the real issues that touched the lives of … participants without consulting the press."[47]

Lastly, a note on the structure of the book. The chapters do not follow a strict chronological order from one to another. Rather, they reflect the hub and spoke structure of Comintern organizations in the countries in which they operated. Elorza and Bizcarrondo, as we have already mentioned, referred to the "spiderweb" shape of Comintern archival material, a shape they sought to retain in their book, together with a more chronological approach. In the present volume, Chapter 1 introduces the key areas of Comintern operations in Spain, especially during the years of the II Republic and until the outbreak of war. These topics are then developed in the following chapters: the design and deployment of the Popular Front tactic after October 1934, the network of Comintern publishing houses and supporting organizations and personnel, army work in France and Spain, infiltration of the socialist trade union UGT, and the Barcelona Popular Olympics as a case study of Comintern mass organizational work in Spain in July 1936. The discussions of the various Comintern organizations in each of these chapters follow their own separate chronologies within our period. The hub uniting these spokes, intentionally kept hidden by Comintern design, is the "M" for Moscow written by "Klavego" (Ettore Quaglierini) in his organizational chart of Comintern publishing in Spain, as we will discuss in Chapter 3. The Comintern's representatives in Spain, their managers in Paris, Berlin or the Soviet Union, and the Europe-wide networks of financing, training, and best practice will become familiar to us as we read through the material and will reveal the true nature and aims of the myriad of local organizations they set up in Spain throughout our period. The picture that emerges is that of a skillfully crafted, far-reaching network, its power and efficacy greatly exceeding that of the sum of its individual parts.

1

Mobilizing All Our Forces

Introducing Comintern Operations in Spain 1923–36

Introduction

Of the most debated topics in Comintern historiography few generate more ink than the question of the degree of subservience of local sections to Moscow, especially in the Third Period and in that of the Popular Front.[1] In the case of the Spanish section, a significant consensus exists that it was, in fact, a paradigm of progressive Stalinization under tight supervision from the center. The consensus extends also to the fact that Spain was the country, together with France, in which the theses of the VII Congress were most thoroughly applied.[2] Elorza and Bizcarrondo[3] began to detail, on the basis of then newly available Soviet archival material, the extent and varying degrees of success of the Comintern's activity in Spain from the 1920s to the end of the war. Their treatment of the period of 1931 to 1936, however partial (see introduction), attests to the sociopolitical weight achieved in Spain by the Comintern's fully funded network of front organizations, fellow travelers, films, publishing, and a PCE closely managed by more Comintern representatives than is usually acknowledged. Other historians have argued that the influence of the Comintern and its Spanish section in Spain until the Spanish Civil War was proportional only to the PCE membership, and therefore, it "played merely a peripheral role,"[4] "lacked any real influence,"[5] or was "casi insignificante."[6] Following from this assumption, any hypothesis of

---

The title is taken from Ercoli's (Comintern Secretary Palmiro Togliatti) triumphant speech to the ECCI on April 1, 1936. He warned the Comintern sections not to suggest the broad masses could not be mobilized, and added, "No comrades. We have achieved the united front in France and Spain. A popular front for peace can only be created by mobilizing all our forces." (die Mobilisierung aller unserer Kräfte). The German text of Ercoli's speech is available at RGASPI F. 495 Op. 2 D. 241, for example through the InfoRost platform https://komintern.dlibrary.org/ru/nodes/91-fond-495?view=lis

substantial, especially subversive Comintern influence in Spain prior to the outbreak of civil war is dismissed as the product of 1936 right-wing communist plot mythology. The influence of Herbert Southworth in this school of thought is substantial.[7] Southworth submitted his final manuscript of *Conspiracy* the same year Elorza and Bizcarrondo published their volume, which excuses Southworth for not having taken their findings into account. Southworth would have benefited from a survey of the material in the Soviet archives, however, as he spent 128 pages summarizing his decades-long work of discrediting four poorly crafted francoist "documents." The "documents" claimed to prove a communist plot to bring about armed insurrection had existed Spain in the spring of 1936. These documents, Southworth explained, served a fundamentally apologetic purpose for the military insurrection of July 17, 1936. The text on these four sheets of paper claimed that a communist plot was in place in the spring of 1936 to infiltrate and neutralize the Spanish army, bring about a left-wing armed insurrection against the Popular Front government, and establish soviets in Spain. The documents also claimed a meeting had been held in Valencia involving Comintern emissaries, French Communist Party leaders, and Spanish communists to prepare armed insurrection. The July 17 military uprising had become necessary, thus went the logic of those who penned the pamphlet, to preempt the communist plot. Having painstakingly demolished any claim to the authenticity of the documents, Southworth argued the discussion of what led to the Spanish Civil War could proceed to the, in his view, correct parameters of global class warfare.

In this chapter, we will begin to discuss relevant Comintern archival material in order to present a first survey of what the Third International saw as its semi-legal and illegal operations in Spain, with a focus on the 1931 to early 1936 period. The picture that emerges is that of the fundamentally subversive, revolutionary, and insurrectional objectives of the Comintern in Spain which remained unchanged after the implementation of the theses of the VII Comintern Congress. In the course of our discussion, we will remind our readers of a hermeneutical principle that must be kept in mind when attempting to understand and interpret Comintern texts. Those who emphasize the progressive Stalinization of the Comintern do not always take into account one fundamental Leninist tenet, fully digested by the Soviet and Comintern leadership and which often inspired its policies. That principle is simply this: while Soviet communism is inflexible as to its fundamental principles and revolutionary aim, it is completely pragmatic and adaptive as to slogans and tactics on the basis of local needs and specific situations in time. Thus, the

Central European Lands Secretariat of the ECCI, in a January 1930 letter to the German party writes: "[i]t is important, as Lenin loved to express, to listen to the core slogans of the masses and then make them the driving force of the revolution."[8] The leaders of the Spanish party were always urged not to ignore this principle, and this led to regular reprimands from *La Casa*. Thus Stepanov, in a speech at the political secretariat of the ECCI on the situation in Spain in February 1933 writes: "[t]he main task of the Spanish party is to find out where the masses are going, in which direction they are going"[9] to deploy tactics on that basis. I believe the communications between the Comintern and its Spanish party from 1923 through early 1936 as discussed in this chapter will make this abundantly clear. The material we have studied demonstrates that the adaptability of slogans and tactics never changed the central aim of the Comintern in Spain: to turn what they saw as an ongoing bourgeois-democratic revolution into a communist-controlled proletarian revolution through the armed seizure of power. The standard Comintern playbook to achieve this is in Spain, as it was elsewhere, is reflected in the sections of this chapter and will be developed throughout the book: work in the non-communist unions and among cultural influencers; pursuit of revolutionary agitation with maximum sensitivity to local conditions, training for armed insurrection and work within the armed forces, and deployment of anti-fascist and popular fronts to achieve the merger of the unions and youth sections under communist control.

Moscow Gold for Moscow's Work: Snapshots of Early Comintern Operations in Spain

A thorough financial and political dependence of the Spanish section on the Comintern is evident in the earliest correspondence between the Spanish section and *La Casa*. Financial dependence establishes political dependence, and the level of accountability imposed by the Comintern already in the 1920s becomes standardized throughout the period of our study. On August 17, 1923, just before the establishment of the dictatorship of Primo de Rivera, Osip Pyatnitsky writes to the Executive Committee of the Spanish party, in response to their request for 5,000 Pts.[10] Pyatnitsky, an early manager in the OMS,[11] the secretive branch of the Comintern responsible for subversive operations and covert financing of the sections, demands to be given a full accounting of expenses to date. Our representative who attended your congress, writes Pyatnitsky, has asked for 5,000 Pts. to be allocated for travel to industrial centers for propaganda and agitation. Before considering this, he continues, we ask you to inform us what you have received thus far in 1923, how you spent these funds, and what your expected needs are until the end of 1923. Pyatnitsky also asks for specific details on funds that were sent for a publication or publishing enterprise:[12] how was the publication organized and what was published thus far? "Our representative" is a reference to Jules Humbert Droz, the leading Comintern emissary to Spain in those years, whose strained relationship with the Spanish party leadership was discussed in detail by José Bullejos. Bullejos also described the efforts the party was engaged in in 1923 to win over the anarchist masses and to unify the party, still plagued by factional dissention, and the burden of what he saw as Humbert Droz's authoritarian ways.[13]

Financing for the Spanish section is further detailed in the December 1924 minutes of the meeting of the Politburo of the Central Committee of the CPR(b),[14] dealing with the approval of the ECCI budget and that of individual sections. With Molotov and Pyatkitsky present, the meeting approved the 1925 ECCI budget of 4.1 million rubles presented by the appropriations committee. Of this amount, 10,000 gold rubles was allocated to the Spanish party, double the amount for Ireland and ten times the amount of Portugal, but far less than the French section, which received 600,000 gold rubles. From time to time, unplanned activities or emergencies arose which required additional funding. In a telegram[15] sent on the 19th of November 1927 Kruglov ("Noel"), located in Berlin, asks OMS Manager Abramov for urgent explanations to a request for 25,000 French Francs made by the Spanish section: is this for travel? asks Kruglov. Alexander Abramov Mirov (see note 11) was at this time the OMS resident in Berlin, with OMS responsibility for Western Europe, especially over the correct management of Comintern funds. According to the administrative notes handwritten on the document, both Abramov and Pyatnisky read this telegram.

Once the Second Republic was established in Spain on April 14, 1931, the Comintern began to focus on its Spanish section and allocated to it more personnel and funding. The Comintern understood the regime change in Madrid as the inauguration of a bourgeois-democratic revolutionary period that would lead necessarily to proletarian-socialist revolution, a perspective shared by many in the socialist camp.[16] Consistently with that vision, the center intensified its investment and operations in the country. Starting in October 1931, we see several detailed Comintern communications to the Spanish party with itemized expense reports and associated instructions. An October 5, 1931, communication,[17] for example, details the budget for the setting up of a live-in base, including a 525 pesetas security deposit for three months paid on July 15 which is to be refunded, rent from July 15 to August 31 at 272,50 pts., electricity bill at 1,35, ashtrays, half a dozen candles and paper for 5,25, bed linen at 100 pts., furniture cost plus transportation at 1,030 pts., and even various kitchen items bought by Maria. This is likely a reference to Tina Modotti, aka "Maria,"[18] one of the Comintern emissaries in Spain at this time, romantically involved with the Comintern's leading man in Spain at the time, Victorio Codovilla. Maria was working for Elena Stasova, the head of MOPR (International Red Aid in its Russian acronym, SRI in Spanish) but was officially in Spain first as a journalist and later as a representative of the Soviet Ministry of Natural Resources.

For the March through November 1931 period, two additional documents[19] detail salaries and operational expenses. For example, on July 28, 300 pts. were spent by Navarro for a rally with the unemployed. This is a reference to Barcelona-based PCE leader Francisco del Barrio Navarro, who did indeed work in agit-prop among the unemployed before traveling to the Soviet Union. We also find a reference to the well above average[20] 350 pts. monthly salary of (Jesús) Larrañaga (Laran'yagui in the text), and 400 pts. for Roldán's salary, probably in reference to Manuel Roldán Jimenez.[21] Roldán was a former CNT gunman who joined the PCE and was one of the leaders of the Union Local de Sindicatos, with a majority of its members from the PCE, but also including anarchist and socialist members. Roldán was later expelled from the PCE and joined PSOE in 1936. A further 600 pts. were allocated to Roldán for the administration of "Unión Sindical," in reference to Unión Local de Sindicatos.

Particularly interesting is the reference to 500 pts. allocated to [Lucio] "Santiago" for "work" among the railway workers. This is an example of what the Comintern understood, and constantly stressed to its sections by work among or within the trade unions. This work did not have as its aim mere collaboration but, rather, agitation and infiltration of non-communist unions to undermine their leadership and control their decision-making, a topic we will elaborate fully later in this book. The Sindicato Nacional Ferroviario was one of the jewels on the crown of the socialist UGT Its leadership understood how crucial it was for them to invest in the protection of the union against the intrusion of communists, efforts which led to the identification and expulsion of Lucio Santiago and other communist infiltrators in 1931, probably shortly after he incurred in the abovementioned 500 pts. expense.[22] Often, work among the unions yielded far more positive results. In their confidential reports to La Casa, PCE leaders and Comintern representatives detailed the successful infiltration of non-communist unions, especially those associated with UGT

These unions were strong in critical sectors of the Spanish economy, and communist influence, if not outright control, of strike committees and other decision bodies was essential to the Comintern's revolutionary aims.[23] For example, in a September 5, 1934, report on the situation in Spain, the leadership reports successful penetration of the top leadership of multiple trade unions, most associated with UGT, including the top unions of metalworkers and transport.[24] The party believed these efforts to have been a success, and by late 1934 claimed 200,000 unionists under its influence.[25] Significant control of the leadership of socialist unions also enabled the communist infiltrators to avoid expulsion once they were found out, and an example of a union of metal workers in Trubia, Asturias is provided in the same document. Infiltration of socialist and anarchist unions also supported recruitment for the PCE. In an openly critical letter to the Spanish section dated January 23, 1933, Stepanov[26] writes that current recruitment in the unions is carried out by PCE personnel as members of the unions and not as agitators, with a focus on quantity, rather than quality. Even so, Stepanov continues, recruitment must be extended via MOPR (Red Aid in Spain, Socorro Rojo Internacional),[27] and other Comintern mass organizations such as Friends of the Soviet Union (Amigos de la Unión Soviética),[28] which boasted 20,100 members in 1935,[29] second only to France, theater, film, and sports groups, etc., all increasingly present in Spain in the early 1930s. As we shall see below, one of the most successful moves of the Comintern and its Spanish section in their efforts to control the unions was the recruitment of UGT for the Anti-Fascist Front. The Anti-Fascist Front membership and political platform was later used by the Comintern for the launch of the first version of the Spanish Popular Front concept in early 1935. After claiming to have secured the support of the socialists on to this early Popular Front platform, Cominternian extraordinaire Hugo Eberlein would report back to Moscow that the UGT saw no further obstacles to the full merger (see below on this). The eventual merger of the unions in 1935 was the conclusion of a long process of infiltration and control that, in the words of Victor Alba, "anyone who knows the methods of communist action could have foreseen."[30] Though PCE membership numbers mattered both in Madrid and in Moscow, these documents illustrate that the Comintern was, already in 1931, investing in a large network of cultural and political influence and infiltration that extended well beyond its official party membership. Thus Bullejos:

> The constant increase of the Communist Party's influenced was not only manifested in the growth of its members, but also in the conquest of large

numbers of sympathizers ... which we grouped in the so-called auxiliary organizations. Red Aid was the most important of these.[31]

Socorro Rojo did become one of the most popular organizations in Spain, certainly by early 1935 when its distribution of over a million francs to the participants in the October 1934 insurrection achieved their intended purpose of "deeply penetrating and conquering the socialist masses for the PCE."[32] Red Aid had become a "serpent's embrace" and the merger of the unions and youth organizations was soon to follow.

The spread of the Comintern's far-reaching network of influence required the set-up and financing of a legal as well as a semi and illegal apparatus in each country, and Spain was no different. In a letter dated July 22, 1933,[33] the Central Committee of the PCE was instructed to carry out a restructuring which involved a leader and a treasurer who would distribute funds to a paid illegal apparatus secretariat. Publishing was to have both a legal and an illegal section, and other illegal activities were to be mass agit-prop campaigns, and "work in the army" (see on this below). The activities of the PCE and front organizations in 1933 were going to require substantial funding, and the OMS sent Margarete Buber to deliver personally "a considerable sum of dollars" to the new leaders José Díaz and Vicente Uribe, while her husband Heinz Neumann was already operating in Spain as "Octavio."[34] The new organization and the joint focus on legal and illegal agit-prop activities evidence the fundamental revolutionary orientation the Comintern wished its Spanish section to maintain. This orientation matched and was based on their perception of the readiness of the Spanish proletariat to move on from the democratic bourgeois revolution.

"Revolution in Our Guts": Capturing the Passions of the Spanish Proletariat

Bullejos wrote about the period just before and after the arrival of the Second Republic, "The relationships between the Comintern delegates and us had never been cordial since we disagreed about the interpretation of national problems and the tactics to apply to these."[35] Much of the narrative that follows reads like a poorly veiled attempt at self-justification by Bullejos. From a Comintern perspective, the RGASPI documentation reveals the extent to which the Spanish leadership under Bullejos had failed to understand and apply the most fundamental elements of communist agit-prop and was bound by what Manuilsky would call, speaking in 1934, "a mechanical understanding of bolshevization." The generous flow of Moscow gold and brain power into Spain, which increased progressively since 1931, enabled the center to make the necessary changes that would turn Spain into a Comintern showcase in early 1936.

The PCE leadership and the Comintern did see eye-to-eye on a number of points throughout the period of our study. Among them was the fact that, with the advent of the Second Republic, Spain had entered a revolutionary path. In his May 19, 1931, address to the ECCI's Political Secretariat in Moscow,[36] Bullejos explained that Spain was now in a bourgeois-democratic revolutionary phase and would be led to a proletarian socialist revolution "in soviet form." Bullejos engaged in the expected self-criticism of past performance and mentioned openly that the party was divided in its understanding of the two revolutionary phases. That Spain was ripe for revolution, however, was hardly questioned by the Comintern leadership in the period of our study. In a passionate speech to the ECCI on April 17, 1932,[37] Dmitry Manuilsky reflected on the negative consequences of being too attached to formulas, and the urgent need, when preparing revolutionary slogans and actions, of considering carefully the current conditions in each country. Manuilsky was highly agitated, he continued, when he considered the inadequate slogans used at the recent French union conference. "The revolutionary way out of the [capitalist] crisis is in our guts," he affirmed, but, following the guidelines of the XI plenum, the details must be worked out on the basis of the concrete situation of each country. He added: "[w]e cannot say that a revolutionary crisis has gripped the capitalist world in every country ... but undoubtedly [in] China it has, [in] Spain it has" (No, nesomnenno, Kitay da, Ispaniya da). Nearly a year later, Stepanov addressed the Political Secretariat of the ECCI[38] on the situation in Spain and discussed the revolutionary mindset of the peasants and factory workers, and expressed his belief that a revolutionary seizure of power was close. What was needed was to understand where the masses are going and to draw them away from the reformist and anarchist parties.

The Comintern's revolutionary orientation in Spain did not change throughout the period of our study. Contrary to long-held opinion, the VII Congress of the Comintern and the new tactics based on the united front from above and popular front did not change the Comintern's assessment that Spain was already ripe for revolution. Nor did they change the ECCI's fundamental belief in proletarian revolution and the dictatorship of the proletariat as being the raison d'être of the Comintern and the CPR(b). It is surprising to read scholarly work[39] that takes some of the published Comintern documents from this period at face value, drawing conclusions on that basis. Such superficial readings fail to understand the nature of slogans and agit-prop and the unchanging underlying revolutionary objectives the Comintern required all its sections to pursue, though adjusted to the particular situation of each nation. The work of the ECCI's preparatory commission in discussing the agenda for the VII Congress makes this point abundantly clear. In a June 14, 1934, meeting[40] Manuilsky engaged in self-criticism in the name of the ECCI and asked how it was possible that the fascists, in reference to the German NSDAP, had managed to draw the discontent of the masses into their own political format, and not the communists. The answer he suggested was that the slogans held during the Third Period, though correct in most cases, were too abstract, too theoretical, and divorced from the concrete experience and demands of the proletariat. Additionally, the leaders had held a mechanical understanding of bolshevization, that is, an inability to consider specific phases and flexible tactics as effective means to that end. He then discussed the new tactic of the united front, and illustrated it with an example from Spain: "[l]et's say there is a crook in Spain, Largo Caballero, who will use the slogan of the dictatorship of the proletariat." Our colleagues in Spain, he continues, will say to him, you are a crook and a trickster, and we know that he is. But the large masses, the socialist and anarchist mases don't have full clarity on this. Therefore, Manuilsky concludes, from a standpoint of exposure, we will make the united front our wide appeal to the masses, the united front will be a tool for exposure (orudiem razoblacheniya). In Marxist lingo, this phrase refers to the instrument one uses to expose, to reveal the inconsistencies of bourgeois capitalism. The concern with this dialectical tactic, he adds mentioning France as an example, is that the Comintern may end up strengthening the socialists as a result. He concludes by suggesting relevant slogans, such as the fight against fascism and war. On a further preparatory discussion led by Pyatnitsky on August 29, 1934,[41] Pyatnitsky and his audience agree that Spain is among those countries in which the powder keg of revolution is about to ignite into insurrection, even if Spain does not play as big a role as other countries. Naturally, there were multiple follow-ups to this discussion from Kun, Pyatnitsky, and others, but space forces me to jump to the summary of one of the final drafts of the resolution on soviet power. Dated July 21, 1935, with most delegates already in Moscow, is the final draft of the resolution on the "Report of Comrade Dimitrov, For Soviet Power." This text is crystal clear: "[t]he goal of our struggle against fascism is not to restore bourgeois democracy, but to win Soviet power." The final draft of this key resolution further stated that one can be an anti-fascist and not pursue soviet power, and the Comintern will now pursue a united front with such anti-fascists. However, only a consistent (capitalized in the Russian text) anti-fascist is ready to fight for soviet power and pull out the root of fascism, which was believed to be bourgeois democracy. The leaders of the majority socialist faction, including the key Madrid socialist federation FSM, the UGT union, and the youth, shared this perspective, especially after their 1933 electoral loss.[42]

The victory of the Popular Front in February 1936 represented for the Comintern in revolutionary terms not a point of arrival but merely a further stage in the development of its revolutionary policy. Victorio Codovilla, writing in September 1936, had this to say about the Popular Front victory in February 1936 and its impact in the country in the following months: "[i]t became clear to everyone that [the Popular Front government] threatened the privileges of large landowners, military cliques, the church, etc. … everything that represents the Spain that should have been destroyed and was not destroyed on April 14th [1931]."[43] Once trade union and youth organizations had been brought under single communist control, all that remained was full absorption of the socialist party and as much of the CNT membership as possible to create a single, united proletarian party that would complete the revolution. Until then, maximum care had to be exercised in the correct employment of tactics and the avoidance of maximalist positions before all the requirements were in place. Fundamentally, in the words of Stalin often quoted by the ECCI, "the revolution does not happen by itself" and requires the wise and measured deployment of the full resources of international communism. For the Comintern, as we shall see, preparing for revolution involved necessarily armed insurrectional training and infiltration of the bourgeois armed forces.

The Iron Fist of Revolution: Preparing Armed Insurrection

As early as 1931, members of the Spanish section were attending armed insurrection and weapons training at joint Comintern and military intelligence schools in Moscow. In a February 13, 1933,[44] memorandum to the ECCI, the ECCI's referent of the organizational department addressed the status of military insurrectional training in the years 1931–3. His name was Karol Sverchevsky, who signs using his alias "Walter," a Pole with a long career in the Red Army, including the general staff. He would later be known in Spain as "General Walter" during the Spanish Civil War. Sverchevsky's report provides several lessons learned with a view to improving the quality of students, curriculum, and results.

The document mentions that three students from Spain attended these special courses from 1931 to 1933, and a note on the margin added by Sverchevsky in 1936 mentions an additional eleven Spanish students who attended from 1933 to 1935. The Spaniards attended the French-speaking version of the courses, along with French and Italian comrades. The breakdown of the curriculum was as follows: military technology: 30 percent; general tactics: 25 percent; political: 25 percent; military-political: 15 percent; desk (work?), technical: 5 percent.

Walter's understanding of what constitutes the core course is abundantly clear. "The main emphasis of the study is … theory and practice of armed uprising,[45] decomposition or degradation (razlozhenie)[46] of the bourgeois armed forces, street fighting, subversive affairs, and complete mastery of … manual and automatic weapons." Walter added that military instructors were drawn from the IV Directorate, a reference to the military intelligence unit of the Red Army in the interwar period and predecessor of the GRU. The head of the IV Directorate in our period was Yan (Ian) Karlovich Berzin who would later become chief military advisor to the Popular Front government during the Spanish Civil War. The special school was located at Pyatnitskaya Street with an additional site at the Bakovka railway station of the Belorussian line near Moscow. Walter was particularly worried about the subversive affairs course, which lacked, in his view, consistently committed instructors. To remedy this, Walter wrote that (all caps in the Russian text): "[i]t would be desirable to create your own subversive chemical lab with two staff." Walter is also concerned with the insufficient textbooks and adds that only Neuberg's text on armed insurrection and "Rovetsky"[47] on street fighting are available. The reference to Neuberg is easily understood. Walter is referring to the booklet published originally in German in 1928, and in French in 1931 by the Comintern-financed Bureau D'Editions under the title of *L'Insurrection Armée*. The Spanish section of the Comintern published the booklet in Spanish in 1932 through its publishing house, Editorial Roja.[48] The term "insurrección armada" was made progressively familiar in Spain through the book printing and distribution by the Comintern publishing houses, but far more so through the promotion of the book's armed insurrectionary principles and tactics in the publications of PSOE, Juventudes Socialistas, and UGT.[49] From 1931 to early 1936 the phrase appeared with increasing frequency in the Spanish periodical literature, as a survey of the period press reveals.[50]

In early 1934, an urgent letter[51] was sent to the Central Committee of the Spanish party instructing them to accelerate the sending of students to the International Lenin School (ILS), which included both armed insurrectional/

military and political training since 1928.[52] The Spanish party had been "extremely slow" in sending the students and only two had been sent up to the time of writing, and had done so without the required absolute secrecy. At that rate the full class of thirty would not be ready to start by the end of May. Additionally, the quality of the students was low and two were considered illiterate (Mas and Montero). The center stressed to the Spanish party the requirement to include women, Komsomol members (youth), members of the communist factions within UGT and CNT, and especially more students coming from the "oppressed nations" of Catalonia, "Vizcaya" (in reference to the Basque region of which Vizcaya is a province), and Galicia. Students are required to have experience in strikes and pitched battles, to come from large factories and strategic sectors like transport. In January 1935, the Political Commission of the ECCI writes the Spanish section[53] again in relation to ILS students and courses. The letter stresses some of the same points as to students from "oppressed nations," women, etc., but makes several references to the October armed insurrection: the setting up of two separate classes is justified "based on the situation in the country and the prospect of a new upsurge in revolutionary waves [emphasis mine]," and the requirement for new students is that they be tested in class battles, advanced fighters, especially from the October armed struggle. Lastly, the ECCI stressed that most of the students should not be political immigrants, that is, the large group of socialists and communists that was already in Moscow evading Spanish justice, so that they can return home immediately "for work within the country." It appears at least some of the "political immigrants" were enrolled. Among the socialists who had been involved in the October insurrection and were now hosted by the Comintern in the Soviet Union were Margarita Nelken, Enrique de Francisco, Laureano Briones, Graciano Antuña, and many others, who evidenced clear commitment to the Comintern during their stay and upon their return.[54] The curriculum of ILS would also be exported to Spain in 1936, as a letter from the Spanish Sector of the Roman Lander Secretariat informed the ECCI on April 1, 1936. A two-month school was to be set up in Madrid and Barcelona, as a "branch" (philial) of ILS but under the management of the PCE. The school should provide training for communist local leaders as well as the leadership of the socialist party and UGT, and the left-wing intellectuals. Responsibility for the school should be given to comrade M., probably a reference to "Moreno," that is, Stepanov, and a budget based on 1935 data is provided for the "Spanish Sector ILS" including uniforms and per diem for fifty-three people, totaling 226,000 French francs. In spite of the prospect of local branches of the ILS in Spain, socialist leader del Vayo seemed to have preferred sending eleven socialists to Moscow for training in February 1936.[55]

Naturally, the OMS had a key role to play in the subversive work of the Comintern's sections. The Abramov file at TNA (see note on OMS above) opens a window into OMS operations in Spain that would be otherwise closed, due to the classified status of this material in Moscow. The file reveals that the OMS was also running its own secret school for cipher wireless operators in Moscow, one of the key elements of the Comintern's subversive operations in Spain. Abramov ("Doctor") was actively engaged in recruiting Spanish students for this course in November 1935, urging Victorio Codovilla ("Medina") and Carlo Codevilla ("Raul"), the OMS representative in Spain, to personally select the students. The leading cryptographers associated with this OMS operation in Spain in our period were "Rosa" (Irina Benz) and "Pascal" (Lydia Dübi). The OMS personnel in Spain were involved in all the subversive operations beyond communications, and included the delivery of 200,000 francs just before the February 1936 election, delivery of fake passports and visas, liaising between the socialists and communists in Moscow in 1935 and Abramov and his organization in Spain, etc.

In addition to various forms of armed insurrectional training provided to socialist and communist students, the Comintern's Organizational Department stressed the absolutely essential "work in the armed forces" that its sections were to carry out. This message from the center was particularly stressed for all sections, including Spain, *after* the VII Comintern Congress. In a detailed secret memorandum representing the Organizational Department of the ECCI, "T. Lechen" addresses how the Comintern has and will assist the sections with work in the army. T. Lechen is none other than Tuure Lehen,[56] aka "Alfred," the master insurrectionist and guerrilla leader who had co-edited the leading textbooks on the subject for the Comintern. Lechen affirms the ongoing absolute centrality and urgency of insurrectional and degradational work in the army "in spite of the united front" (Nesmotrya na edinii front). The work of supporting the sections in their military work in the past (special schools, mass work in the army, etc.), suggested Lechen, needed to be updated and strengthened. In an additional secret memorandum on military work by the sections written in December 1935,[57] "Zeisser" referred to the VII Congress *unpublished* military tasks[58] which included infiltration of the armed forces and preparation for armed uprising by all sections. "Zeisser," Wilhem Zaisser,[59] is another German military expert, tested in multiple insurrections from China to Europe and Morocco. He was an instructor at both the military school at Bakovka station (see above) and the ILS. Zaisser wrote that the ECCI had to continue supporting the sections in these tasks and that the experiences of sections on armed insurrection and civil war had to be collected for the benefit of all. The message of the essential nature of "work in the army" was delivered to the Spanish section in no uncertain terms in the run-up to the socialist-led October 1934 armed insurrection. In a September 15, 1934,[60] letter from the ECCI to the Central Committee of the PCE; la Casa detailed directives for the preparation of the struggle for power. The letter contained a significant degree of wishful thinking, given the fact that PSOE, UGT, and FJS kept the PCE out of the gathering of weapons and other preparations until the last minute. However, the letter is illustrative of the Comintern's intense dedication to training and preparing all its sections for armed insurrection, including working within the armed forces to infiltrate and degrade them. The ECCI approved the participation in any armed insurrection and encouraged the PCE to try to lead it, "even when the movement begins under the leadership of another party." While the ECCI approves the joining of the socialist-led Alianzas Obreras, the ECCI wants the PCE to raise within them the key question of taking control of the army, and PCE must invite the socialists to create anti-fascist cells within it. Without "army work," no victory is possible, it concludes.

The PCE, including by 1935 several of its members who were also card-carrying UGT and socialist youth members, had a number of graduates of Moscow-based armed insurrectional training, and managed to develop a substantial network of army cells by early 1936. The best-known and probably most successful implementer of Comintern "army work" was Enrique Lister, a graduate of both the ILS and Frunze academy.[61] After attending the VII Congress as a guest, he reentered Spain with a Portuguese passport. Codovilla and the PCE leadership commissioned him to take over immediately the work of creating communist cells within the armed forces of Spain, work the party had been carrying out since 1932.[62] Lister writes that the party dedicated great impulse and resources to this work, setting up cells in barracks in many provinces. In 1935, hundreds of soldiers, NCOs, and officers were trained and managed by party representatives, and in Madrid the party had at least one cell in every barracks. Given this success, the party organized a clandestine conference in Madrid in January 1936 with delegates from multiple infantry and artillery regiments in attendance, as well as representatives of other branches of the armed forces. In a September 22, 1936, report,[63] Codovilla makes reference to the "Pacific barracks" (Cuartel de Pacífico), and to the fact that it had communist cells as of July 17, 1936. He added that in that location "communist and socialists were in a majority." Starting in late 1935, the clandestine organ of the PCE for the armed forces, Soldado Rojo, was distributed secretly in most military installations across Spain. The leader of the opposition, in an appeal to the prime minister, Mr. Azaña, famously denounced this infiltration of the armed forces while holding an issue of Soldado Rojo in his hands.[64]

Communist "work" in the Spanish Navy was equally extensive since at least 1932. In a forty-two-page report[65] produced shortly after the Spanish Civil War for the PCE leadership, Manuel Espada Peregrino details the extent of communist infiltration in the armada. Espada, navy NCO and later member of the communist fifth Regiment, begins his report with a note of sarcasm: "[i]s it true that the communist boogey man, as so often repeated by those on the right, had planted its royal behind on the navy's ships?" The report is Espada's own affirmative answer to the question, which includes his discussion of the masonic connections of officers and NCOs prior to and in the early years of the II Republic and the setting up of the first communist cells on the Almirante Cervera and other vessels. The aim of these cells was, writes Espada, the "call to armed insurrection and to organize the councils of workers and peasants, soldiers and sailors." The leaders of these cells referred to themselves in their agit-prop materials as "The red sailors of the navy." According to Espada, a majority of navy corporals were under the influence of these cells before the outbreak of war, a significant success that was, in Espada's words, the result of significant "seasoning" and "finishing."

The Comintern-mandated and -supported activities of infiltration and undermining of the armed forces had been a significant concern of western European governments, especially in the early to the mid-30s. The UK and French[66] governments' tracking of these subversive activities within their armed forces is of particular interest to us. In the case of the UK, the ongoing British experience of Comintern operations within its borders made the Baldwin government particularly determined to track and contain Comintern subversive activities in Spain, given its industrial and strategic interests there.[67] In the case of France, violent events just south of the border since 1934 caused consternation, especially as viewed in connection with parallel Comintern-supported events and activities in France, more on this below. The French minister of war, Jean Fabry, spoke about "the same revolutionary techniques" being deployed on both sides of the border and the implications of this for the national security of France.[68]

In the context of interwar Europe in which multiple and conflicting views regarding the source and nature of legitimate government coexisted, Soviet communism's traction among important sections of the population owed much to its alternative legitimacy based on a complete and violent break with the past.[69] For Stalin and the Comintern and for those who held the reins of power among socialists in Madrid, the UGT and the socialist youth as of January 1934, there was no parliamentary path to socialism. As we have seen, the revolutionary struggle for proletarian dictatorship remained the raison d'être of the Comintern throughout the period of our study. While stressing the need to modulate the tactics according to local conditions in each country so as to win over a majority of the "reformist" socialist masses, Comintern communications also reminded the sections that the coming revolution required constant preparation. The three primary terms used in Russian language Comintern documents to refer to the forceful capture of political power are coup (perevorot),[70] the German loan word putch,[71] and insurrection (vosstanie),[72] often accompanied by the qualifier vooruzhennoe (armed). Of these, armed insurrection became the standard term to refer to the Comintern-mandated means, as per Marxist-Leninist doctrine, of seizing political power. The Austrian and, shortly after, the Spanish armed uprisings of 1934 demonstrated to the ECCI that armed insurrections were indeed possible in modern countries with technically advanced armed forces. The Comintern urged all sections to draw the correct conclusions and use these two success stories to draw the proletarian masses away from reformist parties and intensify their implementation of the insurrectionary instructions given to them by Moscow. For the Spanish proletariat, Manuilsky told the ECCI in January 1935,[73] the Asturian insurrection would play a huge role. It showed the Spanish proletariat, he continued, the need to take up arms to overthrow the government the bourgeoisie. This was a big lesson, Manuilsky concluded. The coming to power of the Popular Front in February 1936 did not change the insurrectional plans of the Comintern for Spain, a fact that was made transparently clear in a February 21, 1936, ECCI directive to the Spanish section.[74] The instruction in that document was not to assume that parliamentary representation would break the remaining resistance of the enemy and to increase agitation of the broad masses, being alert to the "opportunistic waiting for the natural maturing of the revolution." The focus remained on a "conspirational method of organizing an uprising," for which a single proletarian party under a unified communist control was needed.

One of the key benefits the Comintern expected to draw out of the October 1934 armed uprising was a merger with the socialist union[75] and youth section who had led the insurrection. The Anti-Fascist Front (1933) and the Popular Front (its first version in January 1935, as we shall see) were the two strategic moves the Comintern deployed to achieve this end.

"We Must Have Our Hands Free": From Anti-Fascist Front to Popular Front

As early as March 1931, the Comintern had reprimanded the Spanish section for their inability to deploy the duplicitous Marxist-Leninist modus operandi of fronts, slogans, and tactics that are flexible even to the point of appearing to contradict the Comintern's true aims and actual underground work. The Spanish section was being transparent in their rejection of parliamentary democracy and boycotting of the municipal elections that would result in the installation of the Second Republic. Humbert-Droz addressed the naiveté of the Spanish party in no uncertain terms:[76] we consider the tactics of boycotting the election to be wrong. You must run with a complete program that is driven by slogans that incorporate those of the proletariat, soldiers, peasantry, etc. Yes, we want to smash democratic illusion, but the task at hand is to win over the proletarian masses. To this end, do not engage in a general criticism of parliamentarianism in toto, but rather, expose concrete inconsistencies in it in a manner that appeals to the desires of the masses. The Spanish leaders were failing to understand and deploy the most fundamental skills of a communist revolutionary: agitation and propaganda which identify, stir, and leverage human emotion to align it with the party's revolutionary aims. The Anti-Fascist Front of 1933 and the Popular Front which the Comintern set up in Spain on its basis represent the successful achievement of the Comintern's instructions to the Spanish section since 1931. This required an embarrassing U turn on the branding of the PSOE leadership as social fascists, a label that bore little credibility after the process of bolshevization of the key socialist leadership was complete in early 1934.

On March 5, 1932, the Spanish section presents a report to the Roman Lander Secretariat[77] in which it confesses its inability, up to the time of writing, to show the masses the reality of the "fascist-Bonapartist-monarchist-clerical danger" and its connection with the bourgeois government, let alone lead a fight against it. The left-wing socialist ideologue Luis Araquistain, writing to a foreign audience in English in April 1934, admitted openly that Spain lacked all the fundamental ingredients of fascism: "[o]ut of what could Spanish fascism be concocted? I cannot imagine the recipe."[78] In his speeches and writings to Spanish audiences that same year, however, Araquistain referred often to the fascist threat in Spain as justification for revolutionary, insurrectional socialism.[79] Exposing a fascist threat in Spain was indeed a tall order which required the full resources of the Comintern. A detailed survey of the press archives reveals how anti-fascism was born and eventually became the first platform uniting socialists and communists. In 1931 and 1932, all the references to "anti-fascist" in the press refer to events in Italy, Germany of other locations outside of Spain. The first mention we have found of an anti-fascist protest in Spain was a march organized by the left-wing student union FUE against the German embassy to protest Hitler's policies.[80] On March 16, 1933, the first and last issue of *El Fascio* was published with an immediate government-imposed shut down of its operation. This failed periodical seems to have become the local visualization of fascism that was needed for anti-fascism to become a potent force in Spain. From the outset, however, anti-fascist protests and campaigns, which turned violent on occasion, were directed not against the minuscule JONS or the publishers of *Fascio*, but against Catholics, monarchists, or members of the Acción Popular or CEDA.[81] On March 27, the Radical socialist agriculture minister warned anti-fascists to tone down their rhetoric and protests, since "it is not necessary to be anti-fascist where fascism cannot exist."[82] But the atmosphere lent itself to the funneling of anti-fascist sentiment into a formal political platform that would unite the left against a common enemy.

On April 1, 1933, *El Heraldo de Madrid* published a letter inviting all men and women to join "a powerful anti-fascist front," and among its signatories were José Antonio Balbontín, Pasionaria, and Eduardo Ortega y Gasset, Radical socialist and frequent representative of Socorro Rojo (International Red Aid) at rallies and other events. At the first official event of the new organization, delegates were invited to the first World Anti-Fascist Congress in Copenhagen. Registration was to be carried out by writing to the attention of Aksel Larsen, the leader of the Danish Communist Party. By July, Evaristo Gil, representing the socialist union UGT, was able to confirm that over 200 organizations belonging to the II International had attended the World Congress.[83] On July 8, the *Luz* newspaper announced the visit to Madrid, in support of the anti-fascist front, of the London-based duo of Ellen Wilkinson and Lord Marley of the Comintern-sponsored Relief Committee.[84] The socialist Luis Jiménez de Asúa was then mentioned as president of the Anti-Fascist Front. With Wilkinson and Marley came Henri Barbusse[85] and the three engaged in various media interviews and meetings with politicians over the following days. Barbusse, speaking at the Teatro Español on July 13, delivered the Comintern line on anti-fascism:

> The powers we fight against are not called Germany, Italy, and Japan, but imperialism, capitalism, and fascism ....There are no particular causes but all have a common cause ... which is today's capitalist organization.[86]

The Comintern and its Spanish section, with the support of the "Münzenberg trust," had achieved a significant success with the creation of this widely appealing political platform. The Anti-Fascist Front embodied the Comintern's united front concept and secured socialist participation while keeping under control significant remaining tensions between socialists and communists.[87] The anti-fascist platform was to serve an even greater purpose in early 1935. Drawing masterfully from Willi Münzenberg's propaganda toolset and with Stalin's blessing, Henri Barbusse created the World Committee against War and Fascism[88] in the summer of 1934. On February 8, 1935, the committee wrote a secret memo to the Roman Lander Secretariat of the ECCI[89] making reference to a series of reports the World Committee against Fascism and War received from its "Spain representative in the committee," comrade "Albert." The reports, dated January 16, 17, and 20, 1935, detailed the successful Comintern campaign to secure socialist and republican support for the establishment of a Popular Front in Spain. It is very likely that "Albert" is none other than Hugo Eberlein, a.k.a. (Max) Albert.[90] Hugo Eberlein was an extremely gifted Comintern financier and negotiator, involved in multiple international deals for the Comintern in previous years from China to France. He was often deployed as part of OMS operations, for example in Shanghai in 1930, in connection with the Comintern-created Metropolitan Trading Company, the Comintern channel for financing the military operations of its Far Eastern Bureau.[91] Eberlein was most famous as the protagonist of what soon became known as "the Eberlein Affair" in France in November 1935, ten months after writing these reports. Upon crossing the French border in possession of a false Danish passport in the name of Daniel Nielsen, Eberlein was arrested with cash and propaganda aimed at promoting the "liberation" of the "oppressed people" of Alsace-Lorraine.

In the introductory note, the Committee informs the Roman Lander Secretariat that, due to slow progress by the Committee and a number of missed opportunities, they had decided to send over a "friend," later referred to as an instructor and identified as "Albert," in order to move things forward. Upon arrival of the instructor, "our friends," continues the memo in reference to the PCE, decided together with him to lead a movement of the "Popular Front" (eine Bewegung der Volksfront). While the Committee has not yet confirmed independently the success of this initiative as reported by the instructor, continues the memo, "judging by the mood of the working masses ... we believe that on this basis a broad movement can be created ... [as] an instrument of mass revolutionary struggle to such a scale as has not been seen here before." Albert's reports, the first one from January 16, read like a sales manager's pipeline opportunity review. He gives a numbered list of the parties/unions and persons the Popular Front will consist of, detailing those whose participation is confirmed, and those with whom negotiations are still ongoing and results are expected by the following day. Those that are a done deal are Radical Socialist Party, Federal Republican Party, Federation of Agricultural Workers, Autonomous Union of Postal Workers, Autonomous National Telegraph Workers Union, Union of Anti-Fascist Students (a united front of socialists and communists), Republican Women's Union, and Cultural and Sports Workers Union. Under negotiation were still the top prize socialist party and its union, UGT Albert also mentions a number of leading politicians and intellectuals joining as individuals due to what he considers the current illegal status of their party or organization, including Victoria Kent, the socialists Luis Araquistain, Jiménez de Asúa,[92] and del Vayo (del Vayo is identified as left wing and part of the Caballero faction), Pasionaria, Eduardo Ortega y Gasset, Antonio de Lezama, Director of *La Libertad* newspaper, Franchy Roca, leader of Federal Republicans, and others. "Albert" adds that some of the individuals have also committed to participate in a founding assembly of the Popular Front (Gründungssitzung der "Volksfront") to be held on January 22 at the Ateneo or at the headquarters of the radical socialists (Ortega y Gasset's party). The proclamation of the Popular Front is to be based on the slogans: the struggle against reaction, the lifting of the state of siege (arising from the October 1934 armed insurrection), in defense of democratic and parliamentary freedoms, for the release of prisoners and the shutting down of military tribunals and for peace. Albert adds, revealing the highly flexible and pragmatic approach taken, that the slogan "against war" had to be dropped since the radical republicans could not agree to it. Of these, only the defense of democratic and parliamentary freedoms, struggle against reaction and defense of peace have been communicated to the government.

Albert's update dated January 17 gives additional details on the involvement of Victoria Kent, and of a large group of intellectuals who will be organized in support of the initiative following "the French model." In the evening of Sunday January 20, Albert breaks the news of those who have "officially joined." Along with other parties already mentioned above, "Albert" adds that a long meeting was held on Sunday with the secretary of the socialist party and with the chairman of the UGT. The result was the grand prize of Eberlein's campaign: the socialist party, he wrote, had officially joined the Popular Front. These were frank conversations, adds Albert, and he informed the socialists that this is the Amsterdam-Pleyel movement as well as the World Committee (against War and Fascism). On the basis of this trusted background and shared ideas and enmities, the UGT chairman informed Albert, he wrote, that he saw no obstacle to the joining of the (communist and socialist) trade unions. Finally, it is interesting to note Albert's comment on the status of the Ateneo. While they were not able to join officially because they received public funds, all the prominent intellectuals who had signed would be in the Ateneo's oversight committee, which secured, in effect, its participation. Understandably, Eberlein concluded that "our friends are very happy," in reference to PCE.

Contrary to the plans expressed in these reports, the negotiations and agreement around the Popular Front as detailed in the document did not become widely publicized in February 1935. *La Libertad* of March 17, 1935, did take note, however, of a meeting of the Federal Party led by Franchy Roca, one of the leaders highlighted individually in Eberlein's report, which discussed the proposal for "a popular front" in March 1935. The Comintern was not committed to specific formulas. The popular front concept had worked in France and was getting traction in Spain, in spite of some republican suspicions of its origins. In discussing the popular front and united front from above concepts Dimitrov advised to define them in general terms only because "we must keep our hands free."[93] It would take nearly a full year for a popular front-type coalition to take shape officially as an electoral platform with non-communists such as Azaña taking the leading role. In any case, several conclusions can be drawn from the content of this document. First, contrary to Juliá and Graham[94] among others, both the French and Spanish Popular Fronts can be traced back to the brilliant propaganda machine of Münzenberg and Barbusse in Paris. Specifically, both emerged out of the Comintern-organized anti-fascist platform in its various forms taken in 1933–5: Amsterdam-Pleyel, World Committee, etc. Indeed, in the Comintern strategy, Spain was explicitly following the French pattern, because the French section was stronger in thought leadership, positioning within the society as well as weight within the Comintern. Interestingly, the French Popular Front coalition published its program on January 10, 1936, just under a week before the Spanish Alianza de Izquierdas published their agreement, with slogans of peace and freedom reminiscent of those mentioned in the Eberlein report. Secondly, contrary to Rees[95] and Preston,[96] the Comintern and its Spanish section did have a leading role in the original design of the popular front as a mass movement, though

Azaña and others took the lead in the formation of the later left-wing electoral coalition. When Preston suggests only francoists believed the Frente Popular was a creation of the Comintern,[97] he neglects to mention the moderate socialist newspaper *Democracia*, which affirmed as much.[98] Thirdly, contrary to Preston, Graham, Juliá,[99] and many others, it is simply not true that "the PCE counted for almost nothing," and, therefore, it could not play a leading role in the formation of a Popular Front. As we have shown above, the Comintern and its Spanish section had a consistently applied strategy to infiltrate and control UGT-affiliated unions and to drive toward a merger or absorption into UGT. That final step was taken in November 1935 benefiting from substantial SRI funds and Comintern networking with socialist leaders in both Madrid and Moscow (see Chapter 2 on this). Interestingly, very shortly after the socialists received Azaña's invitation to join the left-wing electoral coalition ("coalición de izquierdas"),[100] Caballero asked UGT to enable the start of negotiations for the CGTU to join UGT.[101] The merger of the socialist and communist youth organizations took place in April 1936, but the discussions had started months before as socialist youth leaders met secretly with del Vayo *and* with the Comintern's representative Victorio Codovilla in del Vayo and Araquistain's prestigious apartment building on Espalter 5, a short walk away from Retiro Park.[102] The closure of the deal necessitated a visit to Moscow to meet the KIM leadership there, an organization the merged Juventudes Socialistas Unificadas (JSU) was later to join.[103] Juliá notes the cool reception Caballero gave to Azaña's offer in late 1935, and his insistence that the non-inclusion of PCE and UGT would be a deal breaker. Juan Simeón-Vidarte, the socialist representative tasked with negotiating the Popular Front platform, makes clear that his party's priority had been, from the start, to agree the content with the "workers organizations" (including the communists), before sitting down with the republicans.[104] The above Comintern report sheds light on Caballero's strategic alignment with the PCE as early as January 1935 and helps explain his unenthusiastic and conditional response to Azaña. All these achievements of the Comintern and its Spanish section amount to rather more than "almost nothing," and he ECCI's perspective on its success in Spain illuminates this point. Speaking on April 1, 1936, Ercoli addressed the ECCI Presidium[105] and asked an enthusiastic audience: "[h]ow did we reach a united front in France and Spain? What was the first step in organizing the popular front against fascism? Thanks to promotions ... campaigns, rallies, organized by our party we reached the popular front in France. It was the same in Spain ... we overcame the resistance of part of the socialist leadership." In Stalin's own words, democracy, "as the masses understand it," was the bridge to the Popular Front.[106]

Conclusion

In this chapter, we have begun our analysis of the subversive and illegal dimension of Comintern operations in Spain prior to the outbreak of the Spanish Civil War by introducing key elements of those operations that will be further detailed in later chapters. In the first section, we stablished the early financing and directive efforts of the Comintern that achieved its Spanish section's successful infiltration of Spanish unions, especially UGT, and of Spanish culture and society as a whole via its front organizations. This topic will be fully developed in our chapters detailing the communist revolutionary opposition groups within UGT from 1932 to 1935, Comintern publishing in Spain, and the organization of the Popular Olympiad in Barcelona. In the second section, we showed that Moscow's fundamentally revolutionary aims, inherent to Leninist doctrine, remained in place in Spain after the VII Congress of the Comintern. Further, we showed that the Comintern's perception that Spain was ripe for revolution also remained unchanged after 1935, and their training, financing, and directing of their Spanish section was consistent with that perception. Our third section, the heart of this chapter, demonstrates that the Comintern's illegal operations in Spain in our period were heavily focused on the preparation and promotion of armed insurrection. Military and "work in the army" training of communists and others in Moscow and Spain, constant reminders via letters and instructions delivered in no uncertain terms before, during and after the VII Congress of the Comintern, confirm there was in fact no change in strategy, the Popular Front tactic notwithstanding. This key topic will be fully developed in our chapter comparing communist army work in France and Spain in our period. Finally, our last section discusses a little-known Comintern document detailing the early (January 1935) recruitment by a mysterious figure we believe could be Hugo Eberlein of all the leading left-wing and republican parties to the Comintern's early vision of the Popular Front. The evolution from Anti-Fascist Front to Popular Front will be covered in greater detail in our chapter on the post-October 1934 victimization narrative as the cornerstone of the Popular Front platform. The Comintern archives reveal that tactical maneuvers like the anti-fascist and popular fronts never weakened the fundamental aim of the Comintern, essential to Marxism-Leninism: winning over the broad masses for armed insurrection and the dictatorship of the proletariat. The basic Comintern playbook for achieving these ends, together with the appropriate funding, training, and ongoing oversight, was fully deployed in Spain well before the outbreak of civil war. This chapter begins to complete a missing link in the literature by treating the early transition period to the Popular Front, never before fully covered from this angle.

2

Save the Children!

The Comintern Narrative of Victimization in Spain as the Cornerstone of the Popular Front Platform

Introduction

Social scientists, psychologists, and narratologists have long been aware of the frequent role victimization narratives play in the justification of political violence. Perpetrators of violence often construct "victimologies" focusing on an event as an injustice, "exaggerating the impact, minimizing the context and extending the time frame of the event backward and forward in time."[1] George Mosse studied the cult of the fallen soldier after the Great War and how myths of redemptive suffering were used to construct extreme nationalist ideologies, especially by defeated nations.[2] Using some of Mosse's insights, Brian D. Bunk explored the political propaganda in both revolutionary and anti-revolutionary texts produced after the socialist-led armed insurrection in Spain in October 1934. Bunk's conclusion was, in essence, that in the pro-revolutionary accounts "commentators hope to shift the perceptions of the revolt as a violent uprising to highlight instead a cruel repression."[3] Bunk suggests that the pervasive deployment of such narratives united all left-wing parties in a common cause as "victims of the repression" and became a major contributor to the campaign of the Popular Front in January and early February 1936.

In this chapter, we will examine the direct and leading role of the Comintern in the shaping and deployment of the left-wing victimization narrative as the cornerstone of the Popular Front tactic in Spain. To this end, the Comintern utilized the Moscow-based leadership and resources of International Red Aid[4] under Elena Stasova, the world-class agit-prop capabilities of the "Münzenberg trust" in Paris, and local assets in Spain including Comintern agents and a myriad of committees and front organizations. All these assets masterfully combined and generously financed resulted in the identification of all left-wing republicans and socialists with the victimization narrative as the most potent unifying factor of their individual visions and aspirations after October 1934. Thus, contrary to Juliá, substantial unity of action was in fact achieved among all the left-wing parties on the basis of aiding and vindicating the *victims*, as early as the winter of 1934–5.[5] Much of the archival material[6] we will discuss has not been covered in the literature until now. This material is combined with period press reports and other sources to demonstrate the step-by-step-leadership of the Comintern in building and deploying the victimization narrative to win over every major left-wing party in the country to the banner of the Popular Front. This chapter thus challenges the traditional view of the Popular Front in Spain primarily as a grassroots movement driven by a real threat of fascism.[7] We also challenge the common understanding of Manuel Azaña as the architect, not merely of the convergence of republican parties under his leadership, but of the entire Popular Front platform that was victorious in February 1936.[8] The data presented and discussed in this chapter suggest the Popular Front is not properly understood without a primary "history from above" interpretation. This interpretation takes full account of the masterful agit-prop leadership of the Comintern in drafting and securing widespread support for the victimization narrative, the linchpin of the Popular Front platform.

The Prisoners and Their Children: *Voilà* a Great Method!

"North of the Pyrenees they assume fascism is installed in Spain ... that I have become a reactionary, an ally of the monarchists," protested Alejandro Lerroux to a special correspondent of the regional French daily *L'Ouest Éclair* on December 6, 1934. The reality on the ground was rather different, insisted the Spanish republican prime minister. A double attack had been launched against the democratic regime and the unity of Spain, an explosion of anarchy in Asturias and a separatist attempt in Cataluña. In the face of such a threat, which resulted in over one thousand casualties among the armed forces and police, continued Lerroux, "I have not abused my powers. I have merely deployed the constitutional measures the framers of our constitution, *des républicains authentiques*, designed for the defense of our institutions. Could I have acted more liberally than I did?" Of twenty-seven death penalties, he concluded, only two have been carried out.[9]

Lerroux was right. According to Simeón-Vidarte's account of his conversation with General López Ochoa, the number of armed forces personnel executed for abuses in Asturias more than doubled the number of insurrectionists whose death sentences were actually carried out.[10] Immediately following the end of hostilities in Asturias, Cataluña, and elsewhere, the conservatives in the government coalition insisted on justice by the book ("justicia a secas"), while Lerroux admitted openly that when duty and feelings were in conflict, he would go with his feelings.[11] Simeón Vidarte admits openly that in the amnesty campaign he was a part of, Lerroux, was a key ally, thanks to whom "salvaríamos a todos los encartados por la insurrección."[12] A careful perusal of the period press reveals the widespread interest in the military tribunals and the sentences throughout the late fall and winter of 1934. Additionally, such a perusal reveals the build-up of frustration among the conservatives over the *impunismo* they perceived in the government intervention in the judicial process, a frustration which led eventually to the departure of the CEDA ministers from the government.[13] The repression that followed the October insurrection was, in fact, rather restrained by contemporary European standards, and it pales by comparison, for example, with the systematic execution of red prisoners after the revolutionary/counterrevolutionary civil war in Finland.[14]

In January 1935, with the destruction caused by the October 1934 armed insurrection[15] still evident in Asturias and elsewhere, socialist leader Graciano Antuña wrote a confidential letter to the Executive Committee of the Comintern. In this four-page document, Antuña, probably writing from soviet territory as one of many socialist exiles there,[16] mentions the full ideological and strategic alignment of the socialist leadership of the insurrection with the Comintern and its Spanish section. The Asturian socialist, secretary general of the SOMA, the Asturian miners' union, and of the regional socialist federation, had had a leading role in the technical preparation, financing and in the actual fighting that occurred from October 5 through 18, 1934. Antuña writes to the Comintern as an individual yet expresses what he considers to be the majority view shared by the PSOE's insurrectional leadership of Caballero in Madrid, González Peña in Asturias, and both UGT and the youth organization. The door to the unification of the proletarian parties, argues Antuña, has been opened wide by the "hecho insurreccional" of October 1934. As for the socialists, he continues:

> Once accepted, as it is by the Spanish socialist party, that violence is needed to bring about the revolution through armed insurrection in order to establish the dictatorship of the proletariat, moving the party from this stance will not be easy.[17]

Antuña then proceeds to propose a plan by which PCE and PSOE, together with unions and youth organizations will eventually achieve full unification into a single proletarian party and union, though, he adds, "without the desire to absorb." In light of this opportunity, Antuña asks the Comintern to halt their criticisms of the socialists and look to the future. In his final paragraph, the Asturian socialist tells the Comintern that the socialists have 40,000 insurrectional fighters in prison, a significantly exaggerated figure.[18] The prisoners are led by Caballero and Peña, Antuña continues, and the will of the proletariat is to free them. Any criticism of the jailed fighters will be considered, he concludes, a barrier to the proposal he puts forth in his letter. Thus, Antuña refers to the imprisoned socialists as the ultimate badge of insurrectional credibility which shields the party from any criticism as to tactical errors. Additionally, he presents the imprisoned socialists as the current focus of proletariat affections in Spain and the glue that holds together those who supported the violence as they await a new and finally successful insurrection. The February 1935 correspondence between Antuña and Caballero evidences the leading role of the Asturian among socialist exiles in the USSR.[19] Further, the Asturian socialist's view on the centrality of the prisoners in left-wing strategy soon became dominant in his party. Thus, UGT leader and socialist deputy Bruno Alonso, writing a few months later in reference to communists, socialists, and anarchists, affirmed that "… the only condition that can unite us and heal our wounds … is the prisoners!"[20]

With his emphasis on the prisoners and their families, Antuña was preaching to the choir. The Comintern had already grasped the agit-prop opportunity presented by the imprisoned rebels, their wives, and children, and all the left-wing *victims* of the insurrection. In an October 31, 1934, cable of the Political Commission of the Executive Committee of the Communist International (ECCI) to the English and Irish sections,[21] the Comintern leadership complained about the "extremely inefficient" campaign carried out to that date by those sections in support of the Spanish proletariat, adding that the non-execution of the death sentences was merely a fascist ploy to distract international attention.[22] To compensate for this inefficiency, the center instructed its English section to organize delegations to Spain and to "raise scientists, writers and radical bourgeois politicians." Less than two weeks later, the Willi Münzenberg-run World Committee against War and Fascism had arranged a delegation to Spain led by Lord Listowel (William Hare, the fifth Earl of Listowel), and a veteran Comintern envoy to Spain, the Labour MP Ellen Wilkinson. In addition to the British Labour politicians, Charles Bourthomieux, a French attorney, and Münzenberg's right-hand man Otto Katz formed the core of the group. The foreign delegation was a proven formula for the Comintern and a favorite in Münzenberg's agit-prop arsenal since its success in Madrid a year earlier. In a July 1933 telegram to Moscow, the Comintern's Roman Lander Secretariat had inquired about "which tactics comrade Barbusse should use in the Anti-Fascist Committee in Spain."[23] A year later, in his 1934 retrospective report on 1933 World Committee budget and activities, Münzenberg highlights the high impact the Barbusse, Wilkinson, and Lord Marley visit to Madrid had in July 1933. Although the trip was a "great expense" for the Paris office, the agitation that ensued in Spain made this a great success.[24]

The media, both in the UK and in Spain followed Listowel and Wilkinson's trip to Asturias closely, with interpretations split along party lines. On November 15, 1934, the Cortes President, the Radical Republican Santiago Alba, informed the media that he could not accept any foreign collective investigation of internal Spanish affairs and that he had communicated this decision to the visitors during their meeting at the Cortes that day. He added that several other violent events had taken place in Europe that same month, and neither Britain nor France had considered themselves entitled to investigate.[25] Meanwhile, the visit generated a substantial amount of correspondence within the Labour Party in the UK, evidencing growing doubts and concern regarding its legitimacy. The Labour Party enquiry led to the conclusion that neither Lord Listowel nor Ellen Wilkinson had any Labour credentials or support for such a trip, that Wilkinson did not understand Spanish, and that she was most likely working for a committee "to which members of the Labour Party are not allowed to belong."[26] Perhaps due to the language barrier, as well as the suspicion aroused in both Madrid and Asturias by the foreign visitors, they did not manage a single interview with local citizens. Nevertheless, the visit was a significant propaganda coup, as admitted years later by del Vayo.[27]

Meanwhile, Elena Stasova, the Moscow-based head of International Red Aid and its global network of sections and affiliated organizations, was already busy coordinating campaigns on behalf of Spanish "victims of fascism," especially from a fund-raising and aid distribution angle. In a November 14, 1934, letter to the Political Commission of the ECCI,[28] Stasova noted that "a whole series of committees" had already been created, ranging from women and youth to liberation of prisoner committees and others. Stasova expressed her concern, however, that while Red Aid was pursuing a unified approach to aid, assisting the socialists and others, she perceived a great danger of fragmentation as other groups seemed to be acting independently from Red Aid. In addition to recommending unification of all aid efforts under Red Aid leadership, Stasova asked the Political Commission to decide on who should distribute the funds, though she recommended the Paris committee be the first recipient of all the money collected. As we shall see below, the Comintern's effort to secure a socialist commitment to the unification of all aid committees under Comintern control would not reach a final breakthrough until October 1935. The Comintern's Political Commission stressed to the English section on November 19 the relationship of dependency that they saw between the united front and a joint effort in the campaigns on behalf of the "victims of fascism" in Spain. The Second International's failure to support the Comintern's campaigns was, therefore, a threat to the united front.[29]

Among the "whole series of committees" Stasova refers to in her November 1934 letter, few proved a greater success than those involving children and women. Immediately after the end of hostilities, the president of the Council of Ministers, Mr. Lerroux, had issued an order by which Clara Campoamor, the government's Director of Public Beneficence and Social Assistance, was to travel to Asturias to organize and deliver assistance to the orphans of both rebels and police and military, "without regard for political views."[30] Shortly thereafter, various alternative orphan committees were created by left-wing organizations following strictly the left-wing parties' narrative of fascist *aggressors* and proletarian *victims*. Thus, on October 20, the "Comité de Mujeres contra la Guerra y el Fascismo," together with Socorro Rojo Internacional, having gathered "the humanitarian feeling of all democratic women,"[31] announced the launch of a subscription to aid women and children from Asturias. The Committee appointed the radical republican Dolores Merás as the coordinator of this program. Two days later, *La Libertad* reported the creation of "Asociación Pro Infancia Obrera" headed by Dolores Merás and with no reference to Red Aid or the Word Committee, with office on Arenal 26 in Madrid. The aim of this association was to assist proletarian *victims* by hosting abandoned children in homes, "the only means of obtaining love." A month later *Heraldo de Madrid* reported on the activities of "Comisión Pro Infancia Obrera," the creation of sub-commissions and offices headed by local delegates in a number of locations. The piece included photos of several of the children and invited the public to contribute financially with a very emotion-laden appeal. The Madrid daily *La Libertad* followed suit on December 7 by opening its own subscription in support of Asturian children not covered by other initiatives. *La Libertad* added a note of suspicion in relation to the other associations, demanding proof of the "integrity and purity of their feelings." The Comintern's direct financing of the campaign included a 1.5 million peseta transfer to Red Aid in Spain in late 1934.[32]

Elena Stasova was following these activities in Spain closely. On January 9, 1935, she wrote a letter[33] to the Comintern's Political Commission in which she addressed weaknesses in the ongoing "campaign against terror in Spain" as well as opportunities that remained unexploited. Ever since Ercoli (in reference to Comintern Secretary Palmiro Togliatti) left Paris, Stasova writes, the whole movement has lacked direction and concreteness and has suffered from internal rivalries between the World Committee and International Red Aid. The World Committee had expressed the erroneous idea, writes Stasova, that Red Aid is a "very communist organization" and has attempted to replace Red Aid in the fight against terror. It is indispensable, continues Stasova, to work within the communist factions of all these organizations in order to dissipate any suspicion regarding the non-party character of Red Aid and to ensure the correct functioning of the movement. To turn the situation around, Stasova proposed to the commission several measures. These included a renewed Paris-based leadership including Willi Münzenberg of the World Committee and Raoul of Red Aid in France, with instructions to concentrate all efforts on the slogans against the death penalties, and to organize rapidly conference tours by Rafael Alberti and Margarita Nelken, the socialist deputy. Finally, Stasova addressed the topic of the orphans. Immediately, she writes, take practical measures to transport the Asturias orphans to Paris and bring ten of the children to Russia. Putting the Münzenberg team in charge of a campaign involving children made sense in several ways. In addition to his proven ability to deploy countless apparently independent organizations and to recruit and manage intellectuals and artists, Willi had already led a campaign involving orphans. Arthur Koestler recalled Willi's assignment to him to come to Paris and write a propaganda booklet based on "La Pouponniere," a Comintern-run orphanage near the French capital. While pretending to be open to children of German refugees of all parties and persuasions, in reality it served, with a few exceptions, those of German Communist Party and Comintern officials. The orphanage suffered from so many deficiencies that it had become, Koestler writes, a sort of "organized bedlam." Those deficiencies notwithstanding, Willi asked Koestler to come, take some pictures of the children and write 5,000 words, making them look "jolly but thin."[34] The utilization of orphans in the context of Comintern mass organizational campaigns against "fascist terror" was known to Comintern representative in Spain Victorio Codovilla from prior experiences in 1932 and early 1934.[35]

In late January 1935, the Comintern's Spanish section seems to have started implementing Stasova's recommendations. On January 22 *La Voz* reported that the leaders of a local chapter of a "Comisión Pro Infancia" were arrested in Oviedo. The charges involved an alleged attempt to bring orphans to Madrid and to deliver some to Russia. The leaders, including Dolores Ibarruri, the Pasionaria, were later released but instructed to return to Madrid that same evening. *El Día de Palencia* reported, a week later, that the Pasionaria-led group had traveled through Palencia from Oviedo, transporting children who were already receiving material help from the government's public assistance program. The report claimed the children were instructed to reject any government funds, since the funds "come from monarchists and fascists."[36] In his lengthy February 1935 report delivered in person to the Comintern's Roman Secretariat, Codovilla explained that Pasionaria was driving these efforts. The choice of Pasionaria made sense because of her great popularity, not only among proletarian masses but even among the petit bourgeoisie and republicans. The most crucial aspect of this work, wrote Codovilla, was the "moral effect" produced in the working masses who welcomed Pasionaria screaming "long live the revolution! long live the Communist Party! long live Pasionaria!" Once the children were taken to Madrid, Codovilla added, it was necessary to use the event to attract the attention of workers. Codovilla described the typical procedure followed in the many political events featuring children:

> The committee organizes many events in theaters and thus gathers large masses of workers to deliver the children in patronage. Each time a child is given in patronage we place a member of the committee on stage telling the story of the child, and with it the story of his father and of the revolution. The police, present at the event, do not know what to do, but they know that their brutal intervention in an event of this type will trigger the audiences' protest. So, they decide to do nothing. *Voilà* a great method for breaking free of our illegality![37]

The leadership of Infancia Obrera was later to include Clara Campoamor, the former director of the government aid program, and both Campoamor and Pasionaria would address a rally in Madrid in May. The rally, held at the popular theater Cine Europa, was advertised as a gathering in support of amnesty and against the death penalty, and all the speakers, including Red Aid representative Eduardo Ortega y Gasset, declared their support for the united front as the best means to achieve their stated aims.[38] In reference to the campaigns with children in late 1934, Codovilla was not too far off target when he wrote in his report that "all the left-wing press talks about this activity." Indeed, the Comintern understood and exploited the popularity of the "infancia obrera" campaign to target Spanish women nationwide. The legality of the children's committees enabled the Comintern and its Spanish section in March 1935 to use their offices and personnel to launch a larger outreach to women under the banner of International Women's Day. Moscow proposed a number of slogans for this campaign that connected women, children, and the challenges posed by the high cost of living with anti-fascism. These slogans "should demonstrate the impact of government terror" on bottom-line issues related to motherhood and family such as medical care, proletarian education, and the cost of milk. The campaign also involved bringing six women to the USSR and the slogan "Women in the USSR are happy mothers."[39]

As Stasova's communications with the Political Commission of the ECCI make clear, International Red Aid in Moscow, Paris and Spain was the driving force behind the campaigns in support of prisoners, families, and children. The World Committee, as well as the various Spain-based committees and sub-committees, was carefully implementing the recommendations of the Red Aid chief with the approval of the Comintern's Political Commission. The full alignment of the activities on the ground with the official aims of Red Aid is evident in a March 29, 1935, Comintern letter[40] to the Central Committee of its Spanish section, the PCE, detailing instructions for the work of Red Aid in Spain. The three-page letter starts by reminding the PCE leadership that the ongoing campaigns for the "persecuted peasant workers ... prisoners and their families, and the fight for the liberation of all proletarian political prisoners has in Spain the highest political significance." This requires, continues the letter, the full attention and support of the communist party to the Red Aid organization in Spain. The primary task of Red Aid in Spain, affirms the letter, is to utilize all the legal and semi-legal means necessary to carry out the aid to the prisoners and their families so as to contribute to create in the whole country "an environment of discontent and hatred towards the murderous regime." The press coverage of these campaigns in early 1935 indicates they were having the desired effect.[41] Further, the instructions from Moscow to Madrid stress the importance of using these activities to create a true mass movement that does not have a public communist façade. Depending on local and regional conditions, continues the letter, the movement can have the most varied forms. Where police presence makes creating a Red Aid branch impossible "it is necessary to organize under a different form and name, including sowing clubs to repair clothes for the children, patronage groups for specific Asturian villages, etc." Further, the PCE was asked to ensure that more non-communists are recruited for Socorro Rojo, especially socialists, anarchists, and individuals with no party membership. The aim of all of this, according to the letter, is to drive the united front project forward ensuring that socialists, anarchists, and nationalist parties in Cataluña and Basque Country follow the communist lead in this movement. Rallies and other activities should be used to explain to the leaders of these parties the central role of International Red Aid in the movement, demonstrated practically by the distribution of funds exceeding three million pesetas to that date.

The abundant resources of Socorro Rojo had a powerful impact on the socialists in 1935 as the need of the hour forced them to abandon earlier refusals to accept Red Aid Spain's regular outreaches to them.[42] Socialist leader J. Martinez Amutio wrote openly about the socialist leaders' trips to Paris in 1935 to request additional funding from Comintern agent Stepanov after "Contreras" and Codovilla made the introduction.[43] Codovilla informed the center in his 125-page January report that the Red Aid-funded campaigns and outreaches to the socialists were a resounding success, and the most solid basis for the achievement of the united front in Spain. As of January 1935, Codovilla continued, there were prisoner aid committees in every major town in Spain, with over 1,000 lawyers recruited for the cause by Red Aid. The merit of the communist organization, concluded Codovilla, is that "neither socialists nor anarchists were able to do for their people what we have done for them." The Comintern, its Spanish section and its conglomerate of front organizations, he concluded, ought now to focus on promoting a concentration of all anti-fascists into a single left-wing block. As for the socialists, if progress is not made toward the merger of unions, youth and, eventually, party, added Codovilla, the plan is to split PSOE from inside.

From del Vayo to Azaña: The Victimization Narrative and the Emergence of the Popular Front

The spring and summer of 1935 was a particularly busy period at Münzenberg's office on 83 Boulevard Montparnasse in Paris. Just as Stavova had requested, the socialists Margarita Nelken and Álvarez del Vayo were among the speakers secured for a "first European conference for the victims of fascism in Spain," held in Paris on April 13 and 14, 1935. The protocol and program reveal the content and aim of this event.[44] Beyond fundraising, the objective of the event was to unite "all anti-fascist forces without distinction of political party" in a single solidarity movement for the people of Spain. Interestingly, the Spanish delegation, made up of thirty-three delegates, is referred to as the Popular Front in Spain (Die Volksfront in Spanien). Nelken was introduced as the socialist member of parliament who would address the "reign of terror" of the "foreign legionnaires and the Arab troops," and the tortures suffered by the workers. Del Vayo was to address the unification of the solidarity movement as all anti-fascists were coming together, from the communists to the left-wing republicans. On the second day of the conference, Lord Listowel was to address the experience he gained in his trip to Spain, especially the heroic fight of the Asturian miners and the "poisoning campaign" Gil Robles engaged in against the foreign delegation. Del Vayo's close collaboration with the Comintern in 1935 developed significantly, when, in November 1935, on his way to the meeting of the Second International, del Vayo asked the Comintern for instructions via the Paris-based representative "Julius" (Gyula Alpári).[45] Ercoli replied explaining what del Vayo "should" do at the meeting. The Spanish socialist, instructed Ercoli, should stir up debate between left and right wings of the international socialist organization, ensure the communist united front tactic is discussed, and ask any supporters of the united front concept to reach out to the Comintern directly. It appears, therefore, that del Vayo was in fact operating as an "agent of Moscow" long before his taking over the wartime army commissariat.[46]

In the late spring of 1935 Henri Barbusse took over the leadership of the campaign in Spain. Using his own contacts from his 1933 Madrid visit and others provided by the Paris Comintern office, Barbusse proceeded to write every leading left-wing republican, socialist, and anarchist group to invite their participation in a movement he called the "Concentración Popular." Elorza and Bizcarrondo mention this recruitment effort by Barbusse but leave out an interesting accompanying report in the same RGASPI file.[47] The authors of *Queridos Camaradas* are also somewhat dismissive of this Barbusse campaign, suggesting its results were "minuscule" as was the case, they argue, with his visit in 1933. To begin with, however, Münzenberg had a higher estimation of the return on investment to the Comintern of the expensive 1933 trip, considering the agitation and awareness of the anti-fascism concept among the republican and left-wing parties. Münzenberg's continued successful leadership of the various Spanish campaigns brought him to Madrid in April 1936 for meetings with Caballero and del Vayo.[48] As for the Concentración Popular campaign, the outcome of this effort was, in fact, significant. First, Barbusse obtained positive responses from the socialist party, with a response letter offering active involvement from Enrique de Francisco. Further, Barbusse's efforts also achieved the support of Prudencio Sayagués, the leader of the youth branch of Izquierda Republicana, Azaña's party,[49] as well as from Felix Gordón (Unión Republicana) and Botella Asensi (Izquierda Radical Socialista). The youth of Izquierda Republicana led by Sayagués were far more radicalized than the rest of Azaña's party, had many members in prison or closely monitored by the police, and were a natural entry point for the Comintern's outreach into Azaña's organization.⁵⁰ In addition, Elorza and Bizcarrondo are failing to see the full context of the Comintern popular front outreach that begins with "Albert's" (probably Hugo Eberlein, see Chapter 1) effort in January 1935. A detailed comparison of the "Albert" and Barbusse campaigns reveals they are two stages of the same Comintern-driven effort to win over all republican and left-wing parties to the banner of the Popular Front. The slogans agreed in both cases are almost identical, with the addition in the Barbusse campaign of a rejection of constitutional reform, a key requirement of left-wing republicans like Victoria Kent in those days. The core of the slogans in both cases centers on the campaign to secure amnesty for the October 1934 insurrectionists, a stand against military tribunals and the death penalty, and for the cancelation of the state of siege. Interestingly, both versions of the campaign include slogans in defense of democratic and parliamentary freedoms, while at the same time demanding immunity for those who took up arms against the center-right republican government. The slogans "for peace" and "against war" are equally surprising for the same reasons. The Comintern's victimization narrative embedded in these slogans was fully shared from left-wing republicanism to PSOE and anarchist parties in 1935, though the Comintern leadership understood it was fundamentally at odds with the facts on the ground.⁵¹

Other republicans who eventually joined the leadership of Azaña's party and are mentioned in these documents are Victoria Kent, mentioned as a definite commit by "Albert," and Felix Gordón, whose response to Barbusse is included in the file of the Frenchman's campaign for the Concentración Popular. Sayagués and Kent participated together as speakers in multiple events in 1935, some promoting left-wing republican unity, and others various Comintern or PCE-driven agendas.⁵² Lastly, José Salmerón, whose commitment is listed by "Albert" in January, became secretary general of Azaña's party and a close advisor to him. When Azaña met with Caballero in an early and unsuccessful attempt to win Caballero's support for the left-wing coalition, the meeting was held at Salmerón's house.⁵³ The Comintern's Popular Front outreach to the republican parties in the first half of 1935, therefore, appears to have been more successful than Elorza and Bizcarrondo were willing to accept. This outreach effort toward the republicans continued after the summer when it finally reached the very apex of Izquierda Republicana's leadership.

In late September 1935, Manuel Azaña went on a European trip for about two weeks.⁵⁴ The press did its best to track him down and find out where he was and when he was coming back, given the pressing matters facing republican parties at that time. On September 20, the leader of the left-wing minority in the Cortes was asked where Azaña was, to which he replied, "I think he is in Brussels." On the 26th, a *Diario de Almeria* reporter affirmed Azaña was being "visitadísimo" in Paris. On the 27th *Diario Palentino* informed its readers that Sanchez Roman had traveled to Paris to meet Azaña. The press also revealed the former prime minister had met the socialist Prieto in Brussels and the Catalan Casanovas in Paris. Manuel Azaña, however, had another meeting on September 26, 1935, that went unnoticed by the press. A then unknown thirty-one-year-old Eastern European man, speaking French with a heavy German, or perhaps Polish accent, had also managed to sit down for a "very interesting conversation" with Manuel Azaña during his Paris visit.[55] In the course of that conversation, the Spanish leader had told the enigmatic stranger he was in fact "ready to talk to the communists," and gladly committed to joining and supporting one of the many versions of Willi Münzenberg's World Committee. The discrete and slow talking stranger, who breathed deeply and stuck out his chest when he walked, was a Galizianer from near Lemberg who used the aliases "Gilbert" and "Otto." His real name was Leopold Trepper, and he was in Paris as a roving, high-powered Soviet army intelligence agent who was also completing a Moscow-based course of study. Trepper would achieve global fame in the Second World War as the leader of the Red Orchestra spy ring. His file at The National Archives[56] is extensive and enables us to make this identification based on the alias he uses in this report, "Gilbert," and the alias used in a report produced less than a week later from Valencia signed "Otto." Both documents are part of the same RGASPI opis (inventory) and delo (file) within the 495 Comintern fond (collection).[57] Additionally, the German language of the report and the French he used with Azaña match what we know of Trepper, as do the family details we know of "Gilbert" from other RGASPI files.[58] Finally, the TNA file does place Trepper in Paris at this time already as technical Director of R.U. Intelligence, with responsibilities that overlapped those of the Comintern's OMS (see Chapter 1 on the OMS) and responsibility in Western Europe including Spain, Portugal, and France. "Gilbert" also signed a delicate report on Henri Barbusse sent to Moscow in July 1935,[59] advising Bela Kun that Barbusse was becoming unreliable and that the leadership should use the Frenchman's upcoming visit to Moscow to have a detailed conversation with him. Barbusse died in Moscow during his visit in August 1935 and received an official Soviet government funeral.

The "Gilbert" report suggests its author is a masterful networker and negotiator, capable of engaging deeply with powerful men of cultures different from his. "Gilbert" explains in his report how he navigated the conversation with Azaña, probing him effectively about his vision for the collectivization of land, about which, "Gilbert" adds, "he developed these principles on his own, without any suggestion from my part." Gilbert was very pleased and perhaps surprised to hear Azaña had a vision of land collectivization[60] that was far better aligned with Comintern tactics than that expressed by Caballero and other leading socialists.[61] "Gilbert" also highlights that Azaña did not utter a single negative word about the communists and answered with an unqualified "yes" when asked if he was ready to contact them. Azaña added, however, that he believed the PCE was a relatively weak force, and he was focusing on securing the support that would bring a left-wing coalition to power. When Azaña expressed his wish that the proletarian parties support the democratic course he wished to take, "Gilbert" requested Azaña's active backing for a new committee for a world peace congress, and to create a committee in Spain in which all forces who work for peace should be included. "Gilbert" brought up last of all the question of prisoners and death penalties. Azaña replied that be believed any further executions were ruled out, but that amnesty was unthinkable while the conservative coalition was in power. In conclusion, "Gilbert" wrote to the center that he believed Azaña could we won over for the Comintern's amnesty strategy, and that the Spanish section should increase their ongoing efforts to form a popular front in the direction of Azaña. "Gilbert" concluded: "[w]e are constantly trying to orient the Concentración Popular toward this task."[62]

We cannot attribute a major shift in Azaña's political orientation to this encounter with Soviet military intelligence. We can, however, establish that the Spanish republican leader was no longer asking "where can we possibly go with the communists?"[63] as he had done in his April correspondence with Prieto. Azaña's agreement to join and promote the Comintern's World Committee to unite "all the forces who work for peace," that is, the anti-fascist united front under another name, was a major achievement of this meeting for the Cominern, which Azaña would later attempt to deny.[64] In all probability, Azaña's pragmatism led him, already in September of 1935, to relax his earlier commitment to exclude the far-left socialists and communists from his planned electoral alliance. For the Comintern, it was clear that Azaña had the charisma and the appeal to the masses that was absolutely required for the Popular Front to be successful. Once it became clear that he was also on board with the victimization theme as the basis for left-wing unity, the communists gave him their full support as the visible head of the Popular Front. Three weeks after Trepper produced his report, the PCE shouted their endorsement from the rooftops: ¡Todos al mitin de Azaña!, declared the leading headline on *Pueblo* on October 19.[65] In his famous Comillas speech the following day, Azaña fulfilled at least the essential requirements of socialists and communists by identifying true republicanism with the *victims* of the October insurrection. Further, he declared that the "revolution" had been the just exasperation of the popular masses whose rights had been sacrificed and referred to the advent of the II Republic in April 1931 as the coming of the Spanish revolution. With the 1933 electoral victory of the republican and conservative coalition, he concluded, *that* republic had disappeared. Azaña's final words, a sample of his most potent rhetoric, were a command for the audience to be silent and remember "the martyrs of the republic." While the silence of the people, he added, declares their indignation, the people's voice can sound as terrible as the trumpets of judgment. ¡People!, ¡all in one voice for Spain and the republic!.[66] Thus, the rhetorical spearhead of Azaña's message was fully satisfactory to socialists and communists and was sufficiently aligned with the Popular Front slogans promoted by "Albert" in January and Barbusse in June. A comparison of Azaña's words in Comillas and the wording of the Popular Front platform published in January 1936 with the April 1935 republican declaration reveals the radicalization of the republican amnesty message in this period of five months.[67] The victimization narrative, including the commitment to turn the tables on the *aggressors*, resonated fully with a majority of the 400,000 people who had come to the banks of the Manzanares that Sunday morning. That core message enabled the many socialist and communist attendees to ignore the constitutionalist elements in the republican's speech. Indeed, much of the press took note of the clear disconnect between many of Azaña's political speeches and the slogans and banners displayed by his audiences.[68] As Francesc Cambó had said five days before the speech, Azaña's democratic references are the lyrics of the song, but the music is provided by the far-left radicals and the anarchists. Everyone knows, Cambó added, that in Spain the music overpowers the lyrics.[69] In its front-page editorial the centrist republican daily *Ahora* wondered whether, when the time came, Azaña's enthusiasm would be able to contain the overwhelming impetus of the revolutionaries in his audience. "Albert," Barbusse, and the Comintern's Spanish section were counting on a negative answer to that question.

Five days after the Paris interview with Azaña, Trepper (using this time his "Otto" alias) appears in Valencia, Spain, to report on the recently concluded national plenary meeting of the prisoner aid committees, an organization with socialist and other left-wing presence. The meeting had taken place on September 14 and 15, 1935, and, though endorsed by PCE, PSOE, Red Aid, and a number of left-wing parties, the event had been open to all republican parties and cultural organizations.[70] The report is signed "Otto," and is forwarded to Ercoli via the Red Aid organization with a cover note from Stasova that reads: "[s]ince Victor is coming soon and will give the summary report on Spain, we send you the business report that has already arrived for preliminary inspection."[71] Victor is a reference to "Contreras," that is, Vittorio Vidali, Stasova's man in Spain in 1935 and early 1936. "Otto" starts his account with a reference to Victor, who was present at this even and at a parallel Socorro Rojo conference in Sevilla and will report on both.[72] However, "Otto" wishes to add his own commentary over two and one half typed pages. His insights into the event and why it was successful for the Comintern, as well as the intelligence he gathered through his on-site networking with Pasionaria and others, confirm, once more, the value of Trepper's involvement.

To begin with, "Otto" expresses his surprise at the fact that the Valencia event was legal. The government had originally banned the conference, probably because of its obvious connection with Socorro Rojo and the Comintern. The large media campaign, explains Otto, together with the widespread protests, forced the government to lift the ban, and this has a great impact on the continued legal status of "RH" (Rote Hilfe, Red Aid) in the province. But legality could be maintained only to the extent that the organizers did not reveal their true identity, and "Otto" laments the mistake made by the editor of the party newspaper who had published the names and addresses of the central committee members, all of which, he adds, are party members. Despite this, Otto celebrates that of the sixty-two participants, eighteen were socialists and two anarchists, and that the program and discussions demonstrate that Socorro Rojo had "tremendously strengthened its authority as a non-partisan aid organization in the last few months and that it has real mass popularity in key parts of the country." The effective reach of Red Aid throughout Spain, continues Otto, is evidenced by the many regional meetings held to select delegates for the plenum, even in Asturias, though the meeting there was held illegally.

The unprecedented success of this event, concludes "Otto," is seen in the fact that PSOE and UGT have committed to the creation of a unified aid organization and this commitment is reflected in the adopted resolutions. These resolutions also affirm the commitment to extend the scope to "all forms of solidarity," including assistance to the prisoners, fight against death penalty, and support for political emigrants. This achievement, continues "Otto," dramatically changes the standing of the Comintern with Schevenels and Adler, the leaders of the Second International. Otto met with Dolores (Dolores Ibarruri, "La Pasionaria") after the event, and he was happy to hear she felt as satisfied as he did with the outcome. Immediate steps should be taken, the Spanish communist agreed, to initiate the implementation of a unified aid organization where the situation is ripe for this. Barely two months later, Elena Stasova was able to affirm that in some countries, including Spain, Red Aid had grown to such an extent that it had received within its ranks the socialists, not only isolated individuals, but the organization as a whole.[73] In her country-by-country status summary, Stasova refers to the Red Aid event in Sevilla, and sums up the joint achievement of that event and its partner plenum in Valencia by concluding that a new united organization was "created." That new organization, Stasova concludes, brings into the Red Aid ranks the socialists, unions, and other organizations belonging to the Popular Front.

The consolidation of the many comités de ayuda in Spain under communist control, agreed to in the Valencia plenary meeting, was a substantial return on the investment made by Red Aid in the country since October 1934. Thanks to this investment, the International Red Aid, the World Committee, and multiple organizations created by them since October (orphans, women, students, anti-death penalty, for peace …) succeeded in driving the narrative of *victims* and *aggressors* from October 1934 to February 1936. The unification of aid committees was the fourth leg to the unification chair, the others being unions, youth, and single party, but its role from an agit-prop perspective in the creation and success of the Popular Front was fundamental. With its unification program on track, the Comintern focused heavily on the Popular Front campaign, pouring substantial sums into the country in January and early February 1936.[74] According to Socorro Rojo's own assessment of the content of their campaign after victory was declared on February 18, the heart of the message had been amnesty and justice.[75] That is, in full alignment with the "Albert" (January 1935) and Barbusse (June 1935) campaigns, the Popular Front program was fundamentally about the full vindication of the October *victims* and the punishment of the *fascists* who repressed them. With the Popular Front in power, a thoroughgoing settling of accounts could begin, and Red Aid made sure socialists, anarchists, and republicans understood who had invested the most to bring this about. Meanwhile, Red Aid operative and PCE member Lucía Barón spoke in Moscow to the MOPR commission about the spectacular success of her organization, which entitled her to interpret the victory as a victory for Dimitrov and for Moscow.[76] The deep wells of resentment, dug skillfully over fourteen months, were full to the brim. La ansiedad popular, declared *La Libertad*, demands immediate action.[77] In Caballero's own words, "nothing will happen" if the new government moves fast to deliver justice to the people.[78] On February 18, with votes still being counted, *La Libertad* placed a large cartoon of a republican citizen holding the tricolor flag on page three. He smiles as he stands on top of a large pile of bodies, the faces of opposition party leaders clearly discernible in it. Just below, a brief report on the hurried departure from Spain of well-known anti-revolutionaries, including the former interior minister Salazar Alonso,[79] "the man who provoked the October revolution." The article suggests that if their crimes were merely political it would be best to simply let them go. That was certainly not the case, the article concludes.

¡Viva la senda de Octubre! The Emigrants Return … with a Vengeance

As news of the Popular Front victory reached Moscow, Margarita Nelken, José Laín, Adalberto Salas, and the rest of the 200 socialist, communist, and anarchist[80] immigrants in Moscow understood their time to return home had arrived. At an ECCI secretariat meeting held on February 21, 1936, the outcome of the elections in Spain was discussed, with Manuilsky as reporter and Florin, Dimitrov, and Gere as the panel. Based on that discussion, the stenographic protocol (A) Number 29[81] indicated that Manuilsky was to draft a set of directives for the Spanish party, and Dimitrov would approve the final text with a deadline of two days from the date of that discussion. In a follow-up meeting that same day, it was agreed, in relation to the Spain topic, to produce both a directives document and an accompanying "letter of the Spanish emigrants" in Moscow. The content of both documents is fundamentally the same, but the "letter from the Spanish emigrants" is significantly expanded and includes an introduction and conclusion related to the status of the signatories as fighters having escaped "fascist terror." The version of the letter in Spanish that contains the hand-written signatures of twenty-seven socialist, communist, and anarchist October fighters bears several minor corrections that required a final, clean version in Spanish.

The directives document begins by alerting the Spanish section to the fact that, although the Popular Front coalition is now in power, reactionaries and fascists in Spain are still strong. The Spanish party should, therefore, take immediate action to wrest the masses away from the opposition parties and prepare to undermine their economic and sociopolitical base until they are "completely destroyed." The document covers the familiar tactics of extra-parliamentary militias and worker and peasant alliances through which to "paralyze" the hostile actions of the moderate elements within the People's Front government. Systematic agitation should be carried out for full unification with the socialists, on the basis of the five conditions for unification detailed by Dimitrov at the VII Comintern Congress.[82] A final set of requirements are listed, and these include the "cleansing" of rightists and centrists from the ranks of the PSOE, as those are the elements that disrupted the October insurrection. Lastly, the Comintern recommends its Spanish section to agree with Largo Caballero a joint manifesto based on these directives and initiate a campaign on *Mundo Obrero* and other media.

The "letter of the Spanish emigrants" covers the same material but expands it at various points. The letter is addressed to the "comrades of the socialist and communist parties and those of the CNT, and to all the workers of Spain." In the first draft of the Russian original dated February 21, the anarchists are not included in the typewritten text of the title, but this omission is corrected by hand by Manuilsky (adding "and National Confederation of Labor") in the February 23 Russian draft. The introduction presents the signatories as the Spanish socialists, communists, and anarcho-sindicalists who, "in the fateful days [of October 1934] managed to escape the claws of fascist terror and were fortunate enough to find refuge in the USSR." Having heard the news of the Popular Front victory, the emigrants rejoice at the immediate prospect of returning home to re-join the fight against the enemies of the people. Before launching into an expanded commentary of the directives, the letter establishes the authority and legitimacy of the emigrants. Having lived and studied Soviet communism in situ, they advise their readers that any true revolutionary, regardless of affiliation, must take advantage of the "formidable experience of the Bolshevik party." When addressing the pursuit of full unity with the socialist party based on Dimitrov's five conditions, the Spanish version of the letter which bears the signatures, as well as the French translation, spells out the conditions in a footnote. These include "complete break of the social democrats with the bourgeoisie, and recognition of the need to remove the bourgeoisie from power revolutionarily and establish the dictatorship of the proletariat in the form of soviets." The letter concludes with a brief reflection on the need to learn from the October 1934 insurrection and be better prepared both politically and technically. The signatures are preceded by a list of vivas: long live the October path, the USSR, etc. Among the twenty-seven signatures many are easily recognizable: the socialists Virgilio Llanos, José Laín, Margarita Nelken, Adalberto Salas (Margarita Nelken's son-in-law who married her daughter in Moscow), and others. Among the communists Rubén Ruiz was Pasionaria's son who would be killed in the battle of Stalingrad. Manuel Zapico, an anarchist, and other less known names are identifiable thanks to the lists in Elpátievsky's book cited above.

The Spanish version of the letter is based on the first edited Russian draft, dated February 23, 1936. However, as we have already mentioned, only the Spanish and French versions contain the fully spelled out five conditions for unification with their explicit statement on dictatorship of the proletariat and soviets. The corrected version of the Spanish language letter, bearing the footnote with the five conditions, is followed in the RGASPI file by a cover letter from Manuilksy to "Medina," that is, Victorio Codovilla, the leading Comintern agent in Madrid. Manuilsky writes in his note:

> For Medina. My dear friend, I attach a letter-platform produced by certain political emigrants. The [political] line presented in it corresponds entirely with the position we ourselves defend. I beg you to examine it with Pepe [Díaz]. It would be good for you to discuss it with [our] friend Caballero and then use it as the basis for a joint political platform .... such a platform will render great services for the political orientation of the masses. The letter should not be published as it is, and doing so would create great inconveniences for us, for you, and for the objectives we pursue. Its political value depends on the condition that it be presented in the name of the local militants in the country who have worked the whole time in country and not from outside, from the emigrants. Fraternal greeting, your, M.

In summary, though we ignore the authorship of the Russian draft used as a basis and mentioned in the protocol, both the directives and the letter were edited and completed in Russian and with the direct editing responsibility of Dmitry Manuilsky. Evidently, the Spanish emigrants did get an opportunity to add their edits to the working Russian draft, and their most distinctive addition is the footnote with the detail of the five conditions for unification, as well as the introduction and final exhortations. Directives and letter together were the output the ECCI decided was needed to address the situation in Spain after the February elections. The "letter from the emigrants" was believed likely to have the greatest impact on Caballero, given the leading socialists who signed it, all having maximum insurrectional credibility. However, for the larger audience in Spain, the ECCI wisely instructed that its content be presented only as coming from local militants so as to hide any connection with the Comintern and Moscow.

Much of the letter's contents were published by José "Pepe" Diaz on Mundo Obrero in June 1936.[83] However, the returning emigrants, socialists included, would work effectively as the primary promoters of the agenda it contained. The

RGASPI file contains an interesting two-line note confirming that the Spanish language documents were sent to Spain via the Comintern's OMS ciphering infrastructure. Later that same month, the ECCI secretariat met again, declaring that, due to the amnesty declared in Spain, the Red Aid leadership had decided that "all Spanish political emigrants" should return to Spain immediately, even those attending the International Lenin School and other training programs.[84] The same RGASPI file contains a farewell letter to Stalin, in which the Spanish October fighters, "with absolute unanimity and devoted enthusiasm" thank the leader of the proletariat for the privilege of having witnessed the glorious soviet project.

The arrival in Madrid via Irun of the main group of emigrants was the focus of media attention and reveals the key role they played in acting out the final act of the victimization narrative. The extensive photographic reports in *Mundo Gráfico*, *Ahora*, and on *Transporte*, the UGT's transport organ, together with the description of the event in the press,[85] are a window into the sociopolitical meanings and impact of that event. Nelken, De Francisco, and others had been in Spain since March 15 or earlier to start work in the Cortes under the new government.[86] The journey of the main group of 121 immigrants from Leningrad via London, and their arrival by train, however, was carefully staged, with media and the public becoming a part of the pageantry and procession through the heart of Madrid.[87] The leader of the Asturian socialist insurrectionists, Ramón González Peña stood on the platform at Estación del Norte together the press and the Red Aid leadership awaiting the train carrying the emigrants from Irun via El Escorial. Socorro Rojo had carried out a significant campaign inviting the public to attend the welcome ceremony and parade. Based on the photographs in *Transporte* and *Mundo Gráfico*, the campaign was a success. The train cars carrying the group had the windows down with red flags and UHP banners sticking out, matching those held by the crowds at the station. The 121 October fighters proceeded to march toward Calle Segovia and then up the steep hill toward the Almudena Cathedral, Calle Bailén, and Calle Mayor, for a carefully planned stop at City Hall. Ahead of the crowd were a group of cyclists warning cars to make way. After the cyclists a group of children, the communist "pioneers," and then the communist and socialist youth parading in uniform. Finally, a car filled with women carrying the flag of the Soviet Union just ahead of the group of exiles and their entourage. At City Hall on Calle Mayor, González Peña went out on the balcony and saluted the crowds with a raised fist as the mayor of Madrid stood, immediately to his right, to welcome the group to the capital. When the parade reached the Ministry of Gobernación (Interior) on

Puerta del Sol, the crowd stopped again, sang the International and chanted slogans in favor of the rule of workers and peasants. The former exiles had now become celebrities. Being a former "refugiado político" became so attractive and profitable that the left-wing media warned about false refugees coming out of the woodwork in those days.

The message conveyed by this carefully choreographed procession through the capital of Spain that spring evening was reasonably clear. The vindication of the *victims* of October was acted out for all, especially local and national government to witness. For anyone who failed to grasp the meaning of that procession, Largo Caballero would spell out that message in one of several rallies held at Cine Europa in the following weeks: "[i]t is because of October that the Popular Front has triumphed."[88] In the same rally, also featuring PCE's José "Pepe" Díaz, Margarita Nelken declared to the enthusiastic crowd that Spanish workers had to follow the path of October, and added:

> We cannot allow that men who exercised the violent and unjust October repression walk the streets and sit in Parliament ... if they executed (fusilaron) our comrades we can do nothing less with them. This measure is urgent and necessary for public health.[89]

In another rally held in the same theater in March, Nelken had started by delivering a proletarian greeting Comintern boss Dimitrov had personally given to her for the workers of Spain. She went on to say that sentimentalism was the worst enemy of Spanish proletarians. Because of sentimentalism, she continued, the great cathedral in Oviedo was not completely destroyed. She went on to address the judiciary and put forth the Soviet justice system as a model for Spain. Following the Soviet example, she added, it is preferable to have a baker in the judiciary than a monarchist. The baker knows nothing about laws, but he does know the revolution.[90] The tables had been turned.

Conclusion

In an April 1935 *Pravda* editorial entitled "Agitation, a great art," the writer explained that, given its importance, agitation could not be entrusted to low-level operatives. The communist agitator, continued the *Pravda* piece, must know, and understand people, "what worries them and interests them, in order to find paths to their consciousness."[91] The *Münzenberg*—Barbusse led anti-fascist front campaign of 1933 had been reasonably successful for the Comintern, yet it did not galvanize all the left-wing masses to an extent sufficient to bring about unity of action. The October 1934 insurrection delivered what had been missing. Substantial bloodshed, destruction, and suffering, adequately interpreted within a victimization narrative of proletarian *victims* and fascist *aggressors* enabled the Comintern to bring all the left-wing forces together under a single banner. Although the post-October repression had been rather mild by contemporary European standards, revolutionary historical memory, crafted and deployed successfully by the Comintern and its allies, successfully contradicted that narrative and became embedded in left-wing identity throughout 1935. In this chapter, we have discussed archival material, largely ignored thus far in the historiography of the II Republic and have detailed the step-by-step leadership of Red Aid and other Comintern organizations in deploying the victimization story as the cornerstone and "banderin de enganche"[92] of the Popular Front from late October 1934 to February 1936. The powerful "network effect" of all the Comintern organizations, working in unison while appearing to be independent of one another in the achievement of Moscow's goals is a theme we will develop fully in the following chapters. The material we have discussed requires a significant revision of the widely held notion that the Popular Front in Spain was "born of pressure from the grassroots" and driven by an "overwhelming need to oppose the advance of fascism."[93] In the larger context of Comintern operations in Spain from 1931 to 1936, the successful Moscow-financed and -led campaign to own and exploit the post October 1934 narrative is further evidence that the beginning of significant Soviet influence over the affairs of the Spanish Second Republic must be dated much earlier than the outbreak of civil war.[94]

3

A Vast and Concrete Ideological Penetration

The Comintern's Publishing Conglomerate in Spain 1931–6

Introduction

The decade of the 1920s in Spain witnessed an unprecedented growth in literacy rates throughout the country, for both girls and boys in school age.¹ Additionally, important advances in technology, corporate praxis in the printing and editorial business, and government initiatives turned the 1920s into a golden era of book publishing and reading in the country.² Thus, the number of corporations dedicated to printing and graphic arts grew by nearly 50 percent from 96 in 1920 to 143 in 1931, with the growth rate declining to just under 26 percent during the II Republic period.³ As to the number of titles published in Spain, the decade between 1920 and 1930 saw a 70 percent growth rate in the number of books received by the intellectual property registry.⁴ As Guillermo Gil Mugarza has shown, however, the statistics on numbers of titles during the II Republic differ widely depending on the source, and this makes comparison with earlier periods and detailed analysis challenging.⁵ Among the primary beneficiaries of this publishing boom were a number of politically oriented publishing houses which saw the light in Spain in the late 1920s. With a strong focus on revolutionary books, often by Soviet authors, these companies achieved a steady growth in titles and print runs in those years that was considered newsworthy.⁶ José Antonio Balbontín of Ediciones Oriente, Cesar Falcón of Historia Nueva, or Rafael Giménez Siles and Wenceslao Roces of Editorial Cenit, all acquired their skills and networks of contacts as revolutionary publishers in the final years of Primo de Rivera's dictatorship. By 1933, they would all be a part, with varying degrees of responsibility, of the Comintern's publishing network in the country.

During his April 1933 visit to Madrid as part of a lecture tour, Alexander Kerensky expressed a degree of surprise at the number of books promoting the Soviet Union as a model state he found at the *Feria del Libro*. During various interviews with journalists, the former leader of the Russian provisional government was asked to comment on the rumors of "Moscow gold" financing communist revolutionary propaganda in Spain. "Eso no es ninguna fantasía—translated the reporter from the French—los comunistas han manejado enormes cantidades para las revoluciones extranjeras."[7] In this chapter, we will turn our attention to the large volume of archival material covering the full history of the Comintern publishing effort in Spain, from the move to Barcelona of Ediciones Europa América in late 1931 through to the spring of 1936. Our focus will be on strategy, personnel, financing, and on the evolution of publishing operations in the context of the tumultuous events in Spain in those years. To our knowledge, this is the first detailed analysis of the operations of the Comintern's publishing department (Redizdat, Redaktsionno Izdatelskyij Otdel) in one country, and one of very few to cover Redizdat in any detail.[8] Elorza and Bizcarrondo dedicated a couple of pages to the topic and mention two of the RGASPI files on Redizdat, but make a number of mistakes and leave out a vast majority of the relevant material.[9] Rafael Cruz's brief treatment of PCE publishing in the early to mid-1930s was based almost entirely on Enrique Matorras's dissident memoir and has important lacunas and factual errors.[10] A better treatment of the Comintern's publishing network in Spain was produced by Gustavo Bueno Sánchez in a series of online articles, though it also has a number of errors and blind spots.[11] None of these writers take full account of the vast information on Redizdat's Spain operations in Fond 495 Opis 78 of the Comintern archives,[12] and therefore, ignore the strategic and tactical, personnel, financing, and other crucial aspects we will detail in this chapter. As we will show, the documentation confirms the formal roles of both Wenceslao Roces and Rafael Giménez Siles within Redizdat Spain and, in the case of Giménez Siles, within the Comintern's World Committee as well. Further, this chapter details once more the Comintern's powerful network of organizations in Spain, always ignored by those who insist on communist influence in Spain being merely a function of communist party membership. In the following pages, we will detail how Redizdat Spain was a pioneer of Comintern publishing best practices in 1932 and 1933, managed to seize significant opportunities in the wake of the socialist-led October 1934 insurrection, and reached its peak of power and influence in the spring of 1936. Our analysis will demonstrate that, fully in line with the rest of the Comintern's network of organizations in Spain in our period, Redizdat engaged in a masterful game of duplicity. On one hand, it maintained a "bourgeois-friendly" educational and scientific front which fed into an existing mythology around the Soviet Union and Marxism-Leninism. On the other hand, with law enforcement attention focused on its legal operation, Redizdat Spain was careful to build and expand its illegal, conspiratorial, and insurrectional apparatus which it saw as the true essence of its work.

Setting up Shop: Ediciones Europa-América Moves to Barcelona

Redizdat, the editorial and publishing department of the Comintern,[13] was established in 1921 by a decision of the Third Comintern Congress. Its original manager was Bela Kun, with Mikhail Kreps taking over in 1926 and remaining until his execution in the purges of 1937. A key department of the ECCI's central apparatus,[14] Redizdat fulfilled the fundamental Comintern aim of delivering its training and agit-prop materials in the form of books, pamphlets, and periodical publications in all the languages of its sections. In a 1935 ECCI reorganization,[15] Redizdat was placed as a "sector" under the Propaganda and Mass Organizations Department led by Klement Gottwald and mentioned in ninth place after the Wan-Min Secretariat and before the Cadres Department. Redizdat and Gottwald's Propaganda and Mass Organizations Department were a perfect fit, since the latter's mission was "the propaganda work and the ideological struggle of the ECCI" which included, for example, "the popularization of the Soviet Union ... in capitalist countries."[16] In the October 2, 1935, reorganization report, Kreps is mentioned as the sector's continuing manager, and two *referents*[17] are named as overseers of publishing in the Roman Lands Secretariat's territories, Moriens and Heinrichs. As we shall see, however, it was "Ozrin" (the Czech polyglot Dragan Müller) who would soon start to work as referent for Redizdat in Spain. As of June 1935, Redizdat had a total of sixty-five workers, of which only eight, the Moscow-based management team including Kreps himself, were paid from the ECCI's budget.[18] Kreps had the highest salary in the sector at 500 rubles plus a 20-ruble food (lit. "bread") supplement. The management of salaries within the budget became a complex matter for Redizdat as its administrators attempted to reduce operational expenses and report balanced budgets. For the Spanish team this would require, as we shall see, the transfer of a particularly well-paid employee from Redizdat's budget to that of the Moscow-based VEGAAR (Verlagsgenossenschaft aus- ländischer Arbeiter in der Sowjetunion) publishing house.

As of 1930, the Comintern's single publishing house fully dedicated to producing material for Spain and Latinamerica, Ediciones Europa América (EEA), was based in Paris at Rue de la Roquette 75, a site shared with the Fédération du Théâtre Ouvrier Français. The move of EEA to Barcelona at the end of 1931 was a logical first step in the localization of Comintern publishing which Redizdat would soon consider a best practice.[19] Redizdat's Spanish delegation proved to be a pioneering organization in more significant ways. A December 1933 resolution on publishing work in France[20] exhibited important tensions between Third Period and emerging Popular Front tactics. While Libert Cical, the manager of Bureau d'Editions, had reported a financially successful operation and a steady increase in titles, the Roman Secretariat objected that a heavy dependence on "petit bourgeois" book buyers had injected confusion into its political line. Additionally, the secretariat perceived a need to establish close links between the various elements of the publishing organization, the local party agit-prop organization, mass organizations, and the Comintern. The full capabilities and network effect of all those elements could not be realized without effective control from headquarters. By April 1934, the "use" of both bourgeois publishing houses and social-democrat and other left-wing intellectuals and writers, as well as the production of material that would be suitable and interesting to all types of left-wing readers, had become a requirement. Redizdat's Spanish operation from early 1932 to June 1936, under the able leadership of Ettore Quaglierini ("Klavego" see below), provides a fascinating demonstration of successful implementation of these best practices, with a steady pioneering effort in the years 1932–4, and significant momentum after October 1934.

EEA's move to Barcelona was announced to readers and business partners in a letter which is undated, but most likely written in January 1932.[21] The letter informed readers of its new address, Apartado de Correos 890, Barcelona, and of its continued commitment to remain their source for Marxist and international proletarian publications. The May to November 1932 correspondence and documentation, most of it authored by "Klavego,"[22] reveals the deep fracture that took place between the Spanish and French Redizdat management teams as a result of the move, the significant challenges faced by Klavego to set up Spain-wide operations, and his notable achievements in that first year of work in country. For our identification of "Klavego" with Ettore Quaglierini, we have direct confirmation in a December 1933 letter from "Pierre" in Barcelona to "Ireneo" in Paris or Moscow. In this short letter, Pierre, another alias used by Quaglierini, conveys the data requested of him on "Ettore Quaglierini, 40 years old and an Italian national." "Pierre" adds that he can supply further data but suggests to Ireneo he can gather more biographical details from, among others, Ercoli (Comintern Secretary Palmiro Togliatti), who "know[s] Klav quite well."[23]

One of the most surprising aspects of the November 1932-dated nine-page report from Klavego and Raoul to their superiors is the devastating set of accusations they make against the head of the Bureau d'Editions in Paris, "le confrere Cic.," that is, Libert Cical.[24] Klavego suggests Cical had objected to EEA's move to Barcelona purely on selfish grounds, as he had been profiting from scandalous fees charged by the Imprimerie Centrale for work done for EEA. Since the move to Spain was decided, complains Klavego, Cical never stopped boycotting the Spanish operation. Cical's behavior, argued Klavego, was unheard of even among bourgeois printing houses and was more aligned with "capitalist cynicism than with revolutionary fraternity." Particularly damaging was the legal demand for payment of 3,480 francs which Cical sent to the new Spanish company via a notary public, thus potentially opening the Spanish EEA firm to police investigation in an act of "outright sabotage." Klavego requested the urgent mediation of his superiors in the resolution of this crisis.

These and other birth pains notwithstanding, the Spanish publishing operation used its first year in country to lay a solid foundation for the achievement of Redizdat's objectives in Spain. Fundamentally, Klavego's efforts in 1932 centered on the set-up of a distribution network in the leading Spanish provincial capitals, for which he received no support from his "former friends," a clear reference to Cical and his organization in Paris. The account is interesting because it gives us a fascinating "out of the box" perspective on the level of training, vision, and efficiency of provincial PCE organizations in the tumultuous year of 1932. Klavego was dismayed to find, he recounts, local party cadres which were severely lacking in organizational control, political training, revolutionary zeal, and overcome by "an incredible state of inertia." As Klavego and team traveled through Zaragoza, Andalucia, Valencia, and other regions, he writes, rather than finding needed support in the local party, he had to invest in putting together a set of political training materials to enable these provincial cadres to rise to a minimum level of competence. With the manuals and a new team of instructors in place, Klavego was able to rally local members for a new network of book, booklet, and periodical distribution based in factories, fields, and worker's homes. He was hopeful, he wrote, that the "new friends" that were "currently heading up the organization" would cooperate with his efforts going forward. This is surely a reference to the dramatic leadership change in the PCE in the late summer and fall of 1932 when Bullejos, Adame, Vega, and others were removed from the leadership and replaced by José Diaz, Jesús Hernández,

Hurtado remaining as Organization Secretary, and others.[25] It is particularly interesting, in the context of our discussion in this chapter, that printing, in particular, the inclusion of "bourgeois" printing shops in the network of communist publications in Spain was at the heart of the bitter debates that led to the break-up with the old leadership team.

When "Medina" (Victorio Codovilla) arrived in Spain in late July 1932 as Comintern delegate to the Spanish section, his focus turned quickly to publications, noting that printing presented "almost insurmountable difficulties."[26] As early as the end of July, Medina found himself in a head-to-head confrontation with PCE leaders Bullejos, Vega, Marcelino (perhaps UJCE leader Marcelino González), and others who insisted on the need for the party to acquire its own printing infrastructure. Medina argued multiple times that using a bourgeois printing shop made more sense for economic, operational, and security reasons, even if the printers required some financial guarantees upfront. When Marcelino argued no bourgeois printer would be willing or able to take the job, Medina investigated the market independently and, to Marcelino's dismay, came up with two candidates ready to get to work on the periodical *Mundo Obrero*. Following the resignation of Bullejos, Adame, and others in the late summer and their dramatic last stand in Moscow, Medina writes in an October 1 report to the Comintern that Vega, Ángel Pumarega ("A. Puma") and Marcelino took advantage of the confusion and proceeded with the purchase of the printing shop at a cost of 71,000 pesetas. This, Medina argued, amounted to the sabotage of *Mundo Obrero*, which could not be printed on time, and was a direct challenge to the instructions received from the Comintern's representative in Spain. This insubordination, Medina believed, was not simply more of the same sectarian, dissident spirit that had led to the expulsion of the Bullejos team. Those who had pushed so hard for the party to buy its own printing house had done so because they stood to gain financially from the transaction, through opportunities to hire friends and other corrupt practices.[27] In order to manage this fait accompli in the best way possible, discussions were ongoing, continued Medina, to place the printing machinery within the facilities of a friendly printer who had already agreed to support the relaunch of *Mundo Obrero*. The accounts of the purchase and set-up of the new printing infrastructure in *El Financiero*[28] and in Enrique Matorras's dissident memoir[29] agree as to the basic facts and shed additional light on what transpired. Matorras wrote that Ángel Pumarega drove the purchase operation and both Matorras and *El Financiero* affirm the shop, Imprenta Rotativa/Imp-Rot, was purchased in the name of Editorial Cenit's director Rafael Giménez Siles with Comintern funds that were transferred from

Paris. Matorras adds, in line with the suspicions expressed by Medina, that the transaction earned Pumarega a 15,000 pts. commission. From that point on, Cenit begins to print some of its books at the Imp-Rot facilities on Andrés Mellado 4 in Madrid,[30] in a move that delivered operational cost efficiencies for both the Comintern and Cenit.

The deal between the Comintern's publishing organization in Spain and Giménez Siles led shortly after to a meeting between Medina and the Cenit Director in which wider publishing synergies were explored. After the discussion, Medina wrote to Klavego enthusiastically about Cenit, urging the EEA team to roll out the red carpet. Not only are they technically excellent, he wrote, but they have specialized in editing material "of our genre." More importantly:

> Both the directors and administrators of the publishing house very much look forward to ("están deseando") establishing permanent contact with you and, on this basis, begin editing based on a plan and <u>under your direct political control</u>. It is, therefore, necessary to reach an understanding with them ... I repeat, do not neglect Cenit as the company is a friend of ours ("empresa amiga") [emphasis original].[31]

It is not surprising, therefore, that, as Gonzalo Santonja indicates, we see a considerable increment of Marxist-Leninist works in Cenit starting in 1932.[32] By this time, however, Rafael Giménez Siles was already part of the Comintern's network of organizations in Spain as head of the "communist fraction" in the Comintern-run World Committee against War. His report to Paris in August 1932, detailing how the fraction had managed to marginalize "reformists" and Trotskyists, securing the leadership of the Spanish committee in communist hands (Red Aid, OSR groups, etc.), is very revealing.[33] With Cenit, however, Giménez Siles's value to the Comintern grew exponentially from 1932 to early 1936 when, as we shall see, the Comintern decided Cenit was no longer needed. In a 1933 report to his boss "Bertrand" (Austrian communist Johannes Wertheim), Klavego begins his account of the latest titles in Spain with a new edition of *Das Kapital* in thirty-two-page installments forthcoming from Cenit.[34] Moscow would also order sets of books from Cenit through Klavego,[35] and in February 1935 Klavego reports to Bertrand that the kiosks in Spain are "inundated" with Lenin, Rosa Luxemburg, and other books published by Cenit, as well as their short booklets such as *Lenin, Illegal Activist* (*Lenin, Militant illegal*).[36] In his letter to Klavego, Medina had indicated that if Cenit had published certain materials "from our enemies" (in reference, for example, to the works of Trotsky) it was only because they had been operating outside of Comintern control, a situation that would change if Klavego followed Medina's instructions. When we read through the Cenit catalogue, we observe that the publication of Trotsky's works does indeed cease in 1932, a fact that Santonja fails to note, together with the rest of the data we have just discussed.[37]

An April 1933 German language report on Redizdat operations in Spain has a legal and financial focus which helps us complete the picture of the growing network of Comintern-run publishing enterprises in Spain after a full year of local operations. The report is signed by "Franz," a pseudonym used in 1936 by Willi Münzenberg's right-hand man in Paris Otto Katz. In addition to his responsibilities in the Relief Committee, Katz held in 1933 a senior role within the Bureau d'Editions. His background in finance and publishing makes this identification likely, though by no means certain. The most interesting part of the report is the details it provides on the Spanish corporate entities and their financial connection with the European-wide Redizdat network. Franz mentions three separate Spanish companies, EEA, Edeya (Ediciones Europa y América), and *Mundo Obrero*, all three being fully independent and isolated from each other legally, politically and having separate bank accounts to avoid police action. Immediately after the EEA name, Franz writes in parenthesis "Lipo," a reference to the Comintern-operated publishing house Verlag für Literatur und Politik, based in Vienna and registered in 1924 by Redizdat operative Johannes Wertheim ("Bertrand").[38] Franz states EEA was established in Barcelona on November 1, 1931, with its three leading shareholders being Ricardo Marín González with a 25,000 pts. investment, "Pedro Bono Piombo" (another of Quaglierini's aliases, though in his letters and reports he usually signs Klav. or Klavego), with a 15,000 pts. share, and "Antonio Aragón" (probably Antonio Buendía Aragón) at 10,000 pts. Buendía Aragón had been the 1930 translator of Henri Barbusse's *Le Feu* for Editorial Cenit. Marín González and Buendía Aragón were both among the socialist party members who left the PSOE in 1920 to form the Spanish Communist Party (Partido Comunista Español in 1920, later Partido Comunista de España, Sección Española de la Internacional Comunista), becoming members of the PCE's first National Committee in 1921. Klavego would soon call upon another former socialist and member of that first PCE National Committee with publishing experience to join his management team, Rito Esteban Novillo.

Franz makes clear that Edeya and EEA are set up as separate legal entities, both independent from *Mundo Obrero* as well. While connecting EEA with "Lipo," as we have seen, Franz connects Edeya, using the same parenthetical formula, with "Hoym," that is, the Comintern publishing house Carl Hoym Verlag, based in Germany until 1933. Lastly, Franz makes the same connection between

Mundo Obrero and "Partei." The abundant Redizdat documentation covering its operations in several European countries reveals the role of Carl Hoym, Lipo/LitPol, Interbook, Litag, VEGAAR, and other Comintern-owned and operated publishing houses in the financing and set up of new local publishers.[39] A number of writers on book publishing in the Spanish II Republic seem oblivious to the true nature of these enterprises as they discuss, for example, the distribution agreements Cenit signed with "editoriales de ámbito europeo" such as "Verlag fur Literature und Politik" [*sic*] or Malik Verlag. It is not surprising, therefore, that Gonzalo Santonja goes on to argue:

> It is not gratuitous to state that Giménez Siles was not a member … of the Communist Party nor of any other Marxist group … thus falls apart the manipulative and deceptive theory promoted by the right-wing press regarding the communist control and promotion of the progressive and ground-breaking publishing movement characteristic of that period.[40]

The topics covered in the books and booklets of EEA and Edeya were, naturally, fully aligned with Redizdat and the Comintern's guidance on training and agit-prop subjects for European countries such as France or Spain. These subjects were, fundamentally, Marxist-Leninist classics and Stalin's works, locally focused revolutionary books covering the urgent concerns of the proletariat written in simple language, and the popularization of the Soviet Union. While EEA's catalogue, as detailed in Franz's 1933 report, focused on the Marxist-Leninist classics and the works of Stalin, Edeya's offering delivered shorter, cheaper, and locally focused titles such as "The National Question," "The Communist Party in the Spanish Revolution," "Lenin and Religion," or a series on the lives of revolutionaries in the Soviet Union, with a total of twenty-four titles planned for 1933 versus thirteen of EEA. The thematic focus on the land question, and specifically, on the popularization of the myth of "land for the peasants" in the USSR is central to both Edeya's and *Mundo Obrero*'s offering, with titles such as "The consolidation of the Kolkhozes," "Stalin's Speech to the Kolkhoz Congress," or "The Agrarian Problem and the Fight of the Peasants."[41] This theme of happy and land-owning peasants in the Soviet Union was central to the popularization of the USSR directives of Redizdat, a theme which was already being popularized in Spain by Cenit and other similar publishers since at least 1932.[42] In the course of an interview during the Feria del Libro he had launched in 1933, Giménez Siles was transparent as to the overall editorial focus of Cenit:

> Cenit represents Russian literature. [conservative publishing house] Fax presents a pathetic vision of a Russia adrift … the Russia that Cenit offers its customers

could hardly please the devote readers of father Laburu ... our two best-selling books at the fair have been History of Lenin's Russian Revolution and Results of Stalin's first Five Year Plan.[43]

The total number of titles Klavego's organization planned for 1933 was impressive at fifty-nine when we compare that number with the just over sixty titles published by Redizdat publishers North of the border that same year.[44] Franz presents a balanced budget with expenses and income of 78,000 pts., but with a heavy reliance on the loans received from the Comintern companies mentioned above. Among the measures for reducing operational costs is the move of Ricardo Marín, whose salary was 9,999 pts. to the budget of VEGAAR, the Moscow-based Comintern publisher dedicated to the translation of Soviet works. The successful operation as detailed by Franz in this report relied heavily on a sales and distribution network which was made up, fundamentally, of 1,300 "bourgeois" bookstores and 6,000 "bourgeois" kiosks, who received attractive sales discounts. The challenge remained, noted Franz, in line with Redizdat guidance, to develop a distribution apparatus aimed specifically at left-wing intellectuals, writers, and Giménez Siles's fellow Ateneo members. Franz noted the potential of individuals such as the Chief Editor of *La Estampa*, who was to publish a special number dedicated to the Soviet Union with half a million copies, and was allowing the Redizdat team to review and edit the text.[45] Bolshevik pragmatism and complete tactical flexibility thus enabled Klavego's team in 1933 to outsource distribution to a large network of bourgeois businesses and to pursue remunerated collaboration with leading bourgeois intellectuals, many of whom were already avid readers of the Marxist-Leninist classics.[46] Among those intellectuals was a doctor in library science and communist, Juan Vicéns, who served as inspector of the Patronato de Misiones Pedagógicas of the republican government from 1933 to 1936. Vicéns saw himself as a "petit bourgeois intellectual" whose mission was to apply in Spain the best practices in library science he believed should be copied from the Soviet Union.[47] Vicéns believed that the Soviet Union and Spain were on a parallel path toward culture and enlightenment, and communism was central to that vision. Among the original board members of the *Misiones* was the socialist Rodolfo Llopis who shared Vicéns's vision of the Soviet Union as a Mecca of culture and books, and who defended a revolutionary approach to education reform.[48] Not surprisingly, among the many volumes the *Misiones* regularly sent to schools throughout Spain was Editorial Roja's *El Origen de la Familia, la Propiedad Privada y el Estado*, by F. Engels, and Llopis's own book, *Como se Forja un Pueblo*.[49]

The fundamental aim and raison d'être of Comintern publishing, however, was not a bookish knowledge of Marxist-Leninist ideas, but the promotion of Bolshevik revolution. As we shall see in the next section, Klavego and team will insist on keeping EEA alive in 1935 because it served as a legal front which "distracts the attention" from the main operation of Redizdat in Spain which was, in his words, "the clandestine publishing and distribution of our agit-prop material."

October Blessings: The Potent Unifying Force of Armed Insurrection

In the morning of November 6, 1934, a month after the start of the socialist-led armed insurrection across Spain, a captain of the Guardia Civil, accompanied by a number of agents, showed up at EEA's main bookstore on La Rambla.[50] In his account of the arrest, written in January 1935, Klavego informs his superiors that the authorities inquired about the ownership of the store and were looking for illegal, clandestine propaganda materials. After a first week spent in crowded holding cells, Klavego, Ricardo Marín, Rito Esteban, and Juan Moñino[51] were transferred to the prison ship Argentina, where things started looking up for the group. For the following forty-five days, the Argentina provided a captive audience of 4–500 revolutionaries belonging to CNT, UGT, ERC, and other organizations who, in Klavego's words, listened to the EEA managers discuss topics such as class struggle and life in the Soviet Union "with an interest that bordered on enthusiasm." The EEA team spent much of their time preparing the interrogation by a military tribunal they knew was coming, rehearsing stories and roles among them to avoid contradictions. Surprisingly, the interview with the judge, an artillery major, was conducted "in an atmosphere of extraordinary cordiality" and that officer assisted them significantly in their efforts to secure a dismissal of the case against them: "[y]our activity is completely legal," he concluded. In order to accelerate the bureaucracy and obtain their release, a creditor printing shop hired a lawyer who successfully pursued the transfer of the EEA case to civilian justice. The lawyer communicated to them the final conclusions of the military tribunal: "I have read all the publications of EEA from beginning to end and did not find a single line that can be considered illicit propaganda." Even allowing for a degree of hyperbolic embellishment in Klavego's report, the outcome was highly surprising in the context of a supposedly brutal government repression.[52]

The rest of his report is, fundamentally, Klavego's argument in favor of the full continuation of EEA operations, as he believed the following months presented unprecedented opportunities for them in Spain. The almost judicial style of Klavego suggests the management in Paris and Moscow wanted EEA to shift into a cautious, undercover mode of operation while the government repression was ongoing. In response, Klavego, claiming Bertrand's support, argues that the situation was in fact optimal, with full legal status for their company ("as if nothing had happened") while the political situation in the country was becoming "rapidly radicalized." To exaggerate the difficulties and underestimate the huge opportunities that lie ahead in the country amounted to a "dangerous opportunism." The arguments Klavego provided for his "full speed ahead" approach were first, economic. Redizdat would lose all the funds already invested, would forfeit a significant number of new orders already received, and would lose face with customers, partners, and enemies. The notion that EEA should be "astute" and disappear, leaving its printers and other creditors in the lurch was simply infantile, argued Klavego, as this would immediately trigger a police investigation of their books. Lastly, if EEA went underground, it would forfeit an expected 200,000 pts. in damages that the lawyers were pursuing from the government. The strongest arguments in favor of staying put were, however, of a strategic and political nature. The October insurrection and its aftermath had facilitated for the Redizdat team an unprecedented level of inter-party collaboration and support, with great distribution and sales synergies that could be achieved with little effort. Additionally, the full legal status of EEA had government and police eyes fully fixed on that bourgeois-friendly visible front, while the "special apparatus" for printing and distributing illegal, revolutionary material could continue to operate undisturbed.

Klavego and Betrand also made several recommendations to Kreps for increasing the security of their work in Spain, such as the set-up of a temporary shadow office in Paris, where Klavego had moved in January. Nonetheless, they urged the immediate resumption of illegal publishing work, as well as the relaunch of the party newspaper under a new name. By March 1935, Klavego had returned to Barcelona and was reporting the publication of "From the Strike to the Insurrection" and other works, and an immediate tour of the country to relaunch sales and distribution networks. As of September 1935, the number of titles published had grown significantly to 142, though a number of these were not new, with 72,000 copies sold in the summer trimester alone.

The celebration of the Comintern's VII Congress in Moscow in July and August 1935, with a strong delegation from Spain, forced a fresh rethink of the editorial pipeline in Spain, France, and across Europe. Suddenly, the instructions from headquarters were to put the focus on the urgent and massive-scale publication of all the materials of the "VII International Literary Festival," as the Congress was referred to in the early reports. In November 1935, Klavego wrote directly to "Bruno," that is, Redizdat General Manager Mikhail Kreps[53] in Moscow, detailing a plan which included 10,000 posters in support of the edition of Dimitrov's speeches ("Disc. de Dim."), 2,000 of which already covered the walls of working-class quarters in Madrid. In addition, Klavego's team had printed a large number of leaflets promoting the speeches of the Comintern's general secretary, bound in a single volume with the title of "Toward the Popular Front in every Country." By December, and utilizing all of the party organizations in Spain, Klavego was able to announce the distribution of 100,000 copies of the summary of Dimitrov's speeches, 10,000 copies of the full set of Dimitrov's orations, and 145,000 copies of the speeches of other Comintern speakers including those of the Spanish delegation.[54] No longer using code to refer to the congress or its speakers, Klavego reported the collaboration of the socialist party[55] in the promotion of the congress documentation, which, together with an advertising campaign in the left-wing press, ensured true nationwide marketing of the materials. Cenit had refused, probably on commercial grounds, to publish all of the congress materials in a single volume as requested by Klavego, a matter he mentioned to his management as a concern. In the end, however, the congress campaign was a significant success, one fifty-cent booklet or issue of *Internacional Comunista*[56] at a time. The visibility of Dimitrov and the Comintern as a whole across Spain from November 1935 to February 1936 as the Popular Front campaign got under way was very substantial. Hundreds of thousands of booklets, posters, leaflets, and books seem to have had an impact in public discourse and consciousness for both right- and left-wing voters. The moderate socialist daily *Democracia* complained in October 1935 that Marx himself was "out of fashion" since only Dimitrov had fans, the "dimitrovistas." Perhaps only Besteiro, it mused tongue-in-cheek, would remain a Marx reader.[57] For the right-wing press, the ever-present Dimitrov images and publications suggested that a vote for the left in the February 1936 elections was a vote for Dimitrov. Voters who did not wish to have Dimitrov as their "boss" should vote for the anti-revolutionary parties such as Acción Popular.[58] After a Popular Front victory was declared on February 18, International Red Aid (Socorro Rojo Internacional in Spain) operative Lucía Barón referred to that conservative slogan during her oral report in Moscow. She concluded: "[n]ow the people have responded: [w]e are with Dimitrov, we are with Moscow."[59] When socialist leader Margarita Nelken returned from the Soviet

Union in March 1936, she opened her speech to the crowd with greetings "from the leader of the world's proletariat, comrade Dimitrov."[60] Lastly, the Dimitrov iconography also played a central role in the popular front victory march of March 1.[61]

The final element of the ongoing publishing project mentioned by Klavego in detail was the recruitment of Spanish intellectuals and writers for a new set of revolutionary publications written in popular language and targeting the large masses of peasants and workers. Klavego's team, together with party leaders, had conducted a series of interviews in order to come up with a list of collaborators that went beyond "more or less platonic" support for communism. The names in that list, affirmed Klavego, were people the party could seriously count on, and whose ongoing remunerated work it could judge and guide. The objective was the "nationalization" of the publishing work, that is, the anchoring of the Comintern's revolutionary topics in the history and culture of Spain. For this task, Klavego drew up a list of Madrid-based committee members who would have editorial oversight in the major categories of political brochures, popular publications, historical, social and economic monographs, and popular literature. Additionally, he included a list of the selected contributing writers ("collaborateurs"). The names in both of these lists are highly popular figures who had already appeared in the press as founders or supporters of other Comintern-run organizations, such as Socorro Rojo Internacional, Amigos de la Unión Soviética, Comité Español contra la Guerra y el Fascismo, and Comité pro Liberación Thaelmann. There were communists such as Rafael Alberti and Cesar and Irene Falcón,[62] socialists such as Álvarez del Vayo, Republicans such as Eduardo Ortega y Gasset, anarchists on a steady path to the communist party such as Ramón J. Sender, and others. At the heart of the new effort, wrote Klavego, was the utilization of leading characters and stories of Spanish history, literature, and folklore which were felt to belong to the working class and which proletarians would soon wrench from the hands of their class enemies:

> The great characters that appear magnificent and immortal in the works of Cervantes, Calderón, etc ... naturally we will re-edit these classic texts but with a class criterion skillfully disguised and amplified.

Within the category of "popular publications" was the series Hombres y Hechos de Hoy under the brand of Publicaciones del Frente Popular, which was meant to have a "pamphlet" (ton pamphletaire) and agitational style. *El Escándalo de la Telefónica*[63] was the second volume in that series published in January 1936. The plan to rewrite the classics of Spanish history and literature with a "skillfully disguised" Marxist angle only saw the light during the Spanish Civil War, and became educational policy as detailed in the manual for teachers written by Isidoro Enriquez Calleja circa 1937.[64] According to the new policy, for example, *El Lazarillo de Tormes* was an anti-fascist novel in which the blind man was a "burguesote de la miseria." In his 1937 *Crónica del Pueblo en Armas*, Sender contrasts "la gorda Isabel" (Queen Isabel II of Spain) with the purity and goodness of the "socialists" she opposed in nineteenth-century Spain. A wartime publishing brand fulfilling the vision detailed by Klavego and named "Nuestro Pueblo," would also publish a new edition of Galdós's classic *Episodios Nacionales* with a strong proletarian flavor in 1938. The Klavego report reveals that these examples of the utilization of literature and history as part of an agit-prop toolset were not the product of wartime radicalization, but rather the implementation of a plan that was put together in late 1935.

Among the few names appearing as both committee members and individual contributors is Wenceslao Roces, close collaborator of Giménez Siles at Cenit and leading salaried member of Klavego's team as of early 1936, if not before. As of January 1936, Roces appears in Klavego and Bertrand's reports as an absolutely central figure, as we shall see in the next section, who follows closely the instructions he receives from Redizdat management, including his divestment from Cenit in early 1936. As early as April 1935, however, a note from Bertrand to Red Aid boss Helena Stasova mentions that "Ramón" (also "Klavego," that is, Ettore Quaglierini) was to give the literary editor of Cenit a key role in his organization. A handwritten note identifies this person as "Roces."[65] Wenceslao Roces, Professor of Roman Law at the University of Salamanca, historian and translator, was a perfect example of the committed revolutionary intellectual the Comintern was intentionally targeting in the early to mid-1930s. As is the case with his partner at Cenit, Giménez Siles, Roces's career is often shrouded in clouds of polemics and politically motivated apologetics.[66] While the formal role of both in the Comintern's publishing organization in Spain is clearly established by the archival data we discuss in this chapter, Roces may have also been the victim of false attribution. The twenty-first-century POUM, as well as Javier Marias, Victor Alba, Michael Alpert, and others have argued that "Max Rieger," the author of *Espionaje en España*, the 1937 communist pamphlet justifying the murder of Andreu Nin and other POUM leaders, was in fact Wenceslao Roces. However, while Roces remained a part of the Comintern organization in Spain during the war and would have certainly supported the official view on the May 1937 events, the identification of Roces with Max Rieger has not taken all the data into account. Among the Austrian members of the Comintern-run

International Brigades, arriving in Spain in October to November 1936, was a Lenin School graduate, veteran of the 1934 Austrian insurrection, and army lieutenant named Franz Loschl. Loschl had a background in publishing and used the alias "Max Rieger."[67]

The active involvement of Giménez Siles and Roces in the Spanish publishing organization under Klavego's leadership was a key to Redizdat's success in Spain in 1935 and 1936. Yet, it was the October insurrection and the radicalized sociopolitical atmosphere in its aftermath that facilitated the recruitment of a veritable who-is-who of Spanish writers for the next phase of revolutionary publishing. With these collaborators on board, representing all the major parties in the Spanish republican left, Klavego and team were well positioned to achieve "a vast and concrete ideological penetration of the masses which should make up the Popular Front."[68]

1936: The Sky Is the Limit

In late February 1936, Mikhail Kreps requested budget approval from ECCI General Secretary Georgi Dimitrov for an ambitious publishing plan by which 5 million copies of "communist and revolutionary literature" would be distributed in Spain.[69] To enable the plan, Kreps asked Dimitrov to sign off on a 75,000 pts. advance of a total of 228,000 pts. as an initial estimate. The Comintern had invested heavily in the Popular Front electoral campaign[70] and, with the left-wing coalition in power and full legal status for the Redizdat companies in country, the time was right for significant additional investment in publishing. Among the new books and booklets were further Lenin and Stalin works, as well as some produced by local socialists and communists including: a collection of articles by the "Spanish immigrants," that is, the large group of socialists, anarchists, and communists who had participated in the October 1934 insurrection and were hosted in Moscow until March 1936 (see my chapter "Save the Children …" on this); a book on women in the Soviet Union by socialist leader Margarita Nelken; Dolores (Ibarruri, "Pasionaria") on Spanish women; and Diego and Laín (socialist youth leader José Laín[71]) on Spanish youth and its future, among others. Kreps's assessment of the publishing opportunities in Spain with a government under pressure to implement the full Popular Front platform was communicated to Klavego and Medina in no uncertain terms:

> In view of legal possibilities, it is imperative immediately to increase publications. Publish at once the most important previous publications. Accelerate the

creation of new literature and translations in SPAIN itself. Develop circulation on the widest lines so that there may be enough of our literature in every factory, home, and village in the shortest time possible.⁷²

The intensification of Redizdat operations and investment in Spain after the government change in February 1936 is just one piece of a larger Comintern trend that becomes very visible to us when we study, for example, the MASK intercepts as archived in TNA from September 1934 through July 17, 1936.⁷³ Thus, the number of individual communications between Moscow and Spain and vice versa between September 1933 and end of 1934 were fifty-five. The number goes down in 1935 with a total of thirty-four. In 1936, between January 1 and February 16 elections there were thirty communications. After the Popular Front comes to power, from February 18 until July 17, 1936, we have a total of 149 communications, several of these being multi-page, that is, nearly three times the amount for 1934, and roughly five times the amount of 1935. It is important to note that the Comintern leadership saw Azaña and his republican government as useful insofar as it would implement the full Popular Front platform as negotiated with the left-wing parties in December and January. The government itself, however, was not, in the eyes of Moscow, the PCE, and most of the socialists, a Popular Front government. Thus, in line with Comintern resolutions of late February 1936 we will discuss in the final chapter, Moscow instructs Codovilla on February 26 that "this is not a Government of the Popular Front." Yet, the party should support Azaña insofar as he applies the Popular Front platform to the letter. Simultaneously, though, "do not slacken agitation."⁷⁴ This was the attitude expressed by the PCE's Dolores Ibarruri, "Pasionaria" in an interview with the Madrid illustrated magazine *Crónica* after the elections. The party had no intention of legislating but would be "taking advantage of parliament to … carry out propaganda that will reach every corner of Spain."⁷⁵

The set of 1936 reports detailing the latest status of Redizdat Spain's operations reveals very significant changes beyond the intensification of its work. First, much of the communication is conducted at a higher level in the Comintern hierarchy, with, as we have seen, Kreps writing to Dimitrov about the publishing effort in Spain. Further, "Bertrand" takes center stage as he travels to Madrid and Barcelona to bring about a reorganization of the team and its operations and reports back to Kreps on his findings and achievements. Interestingly, Klavego appears somewhat marginalized as he is required, originally by Medina and later by Kreps, to move to Madrid where his power is curtailed.⁷⁶ In parallel with Klavego's move to Madrid, the documentation reveals the emergence of a local Spaniard who becomes the star of the Redizdat team: Giménez Siles's partner at Cenit Wenceslao Roces. The primary aim of this reorganization is made evident in the repeated emphasis Bertrand places on control[77] throughout his report. Fundamentally, this involved the shifting of Redizdat's center of gravity to the seat of the country's new government where a new office is opened, the integration of the leading cadres within the PCE's agit-prop department based in the capital, and the clarification of roles and reporting structures. Once these tasks were carried out with fresh financing from Moscow, Bertrand was able to commit to the completion of the aggressive 1936 publishing plan, already well under way in June.

Throughout this book, we have stressed the strategic and tactical importance of the "network effect" of Comintern resources and organizations in Spain, a fact not appreciated by those who insist the communist party was marginal in Spain based on party membership numbers alone. The network effect, a concept I am borrowing from the world of high-tech business, means that when a set of networked elements are properly linked, the value and power of the network is greater than that of the sum of the individual parts. In his report Bertrand mentions at the outset that, after his visit and reorganization, the linking of the publishing department with the various instances of the party was guaranteed. As of the late spring of 1936, both Klavego, as manager, and Roces, as chief editor, had become members of the PCE's central agit-prop organ led by Vicente Uribe, with "Red" being another member, probably in reference to Izrin, see organizational chart below. Mutual control between party and publishing organization was enabled in large measure by the presence of Roces himself, a far better organizer than Klavego, argued Bertrand, since Roces's return from Moscow in April. In the new Madrid office, located on the central Calle Rodríguez San Pedro, Roces exerted the correct amount of managerial control over the team, which PCE veteran Ricardo Marin feared and resented. Bertrand suggested that, in the previous organization, Klavego was unable to provide the strong leadership that Moscow required. Bertrand also introduces a new name as belonging to the EEA Madrid team, a woman referred to as Pauline, or Lina. This is none other than the Argentinian Paulina Abramson,[78] who had worked with Roces in VEGAAR during his Moscow exile and became one of his direct reports since April 1936. Paulina also traveled to Spain with her husband, PCE youth leader and leading organizer of the July 1936 Popular Olympiad in Barcelona, Andrés Martín. Paulina's salary was 300 pts. per month, and Roces's 700 including his compensation as chief editor of EEA (500 pts. equal to Klavego's manager pay) and an additional 200 pts. under a separate heading, illegible in the document. The total monetary compensation, as per this budget dated June 1936, was the same for the top employees of Redizdat Spain at a very generous[79] 700 pts. per month: Klavego, Roces, Marín, and Rito Esteban, who remained in Barcelona. Finally, "Ernesto" completes the team under Wenceslao Roces with a monthly salary of 450 pts. "Ernesto" is most likely a reference to Felipe Muñoz Arconada, member of the PCE's Central Committee, journalist, and with responsibility over the PCE's youth periodical *Juventud*,[80] who often signed messages to Moscow in conjunction with "Evaristo," that is, Trifón Medrano.

The report also updates Moscow on the four separate companies making up the Redizdat network in Spain as of the spring of 1936: EEA Madrid, EEA Barcelona headed up by Rito with a new Catalan employee, and Ediciones Nuestro Pueblo, focused on the nationalization of Comintern content via the editorial committee and list of collaborators we have discussed in the previous section. This entity had a significant budget for salaries, at 900 pts. monthly for each of the contributing writers in the list, and 500 and 400 pts. for chief and assistant editor, respectively. Finally, Bertrand lists a new company with "Valdez" appearing as sole proprietor of the legal entity incorporating "Ediciones Mundiales" and the official Comintern periodical *Internacional Comunista* of which Valdez had already been an administrator. Bertrand drew up a simple diagram detailing the correct communication and reporting of the management and each of the entities to Moscow ("M"), and to Bertrand in Paris: a box labeled "M" to the far right, Bertrand as an intermediate box immediately to the left and "Leitung/Red" (referent Izrin) as a large box on the far left to which EEA and its "filiales" are connected below. In the text of the report Bertrand clarified that the management can reach "M" direct or through Bertrand, and Red "im Wesentlichen direkt."

After a brief discussion of sales during the Madrid Feria del Libro (book fair), an event launched by Giménez Siles in 1933 with building blocks from pre-republican practice,[81] Bertrand announces the end of the working relationship with Cenit. It is clear from the 1935 and 1936 Redizdat reports that, by the spring of 1936, the Comintern's publishing operation was a force to be reckoned with in Spain which did not need Cenit. Although both Giménez Siles and Roces were an integral part of the Comintern organization in Spain, as the documentation demonstrates, the Cenit management was not always entirely aligned with Moscow's priorities and way of working. As we saw in the previous section, Cenit had refused to print all the Comintern VII Congress materials in a single volume, probably on commercial viability grounds. In his 1936 report, Bertrand mentions that EEA was more successful at the book fair than Cenit that year, and that Cenit's "ambiguous medical literature," cheap prices, and product marketing were at odds with the reputation EEA wished to maintain. Therefore, Bertrand recommended that Redizdat not enter into purchase negotiations with Cenit, adding that Roces had already agreed to move his investment in Cenit to EEA, with a variable compensation based on sales. Thus, the archival documentation reveals the full story of the relationship between Comintern publishing in Spain and Cenit, from the enthusiastic endorsement by Medina in 1932, through the three years of close collaboration until the decline and end in the spring of 1936.[82] It seems fair to argue that this falling out between Moscow and Cenit, including Roces's divestment, played a direct role in the demise of the Spanish publisher in 1936.

Finally, Bertrand reviews at some length the plans for the nationalization of content via an editorial committee and group of Spanish intellectuals and writers. At the time of writing, in June 1936, Bertrand sees the plan materializing in the form of an "Illustrated Weekly of the Popular Front" named *Nuestro Pueblo*, having a format similar to the monarchist daily newspaper *ABC*. The themes and overall plan remain the same as we have already discussed, though the names vary somewhat. Ramón J. Sender has dropped out of the list of editors due to party concerns. On the advisory board remain Alberti, Lorca, Álvarez del Vayo, Cesar Falcón, and Javier Bueno, the editor of the revolutionary socialist Asturian newspaper *Avance*. The "faktische," the real or executive editorial committee, includes the key Redizdat managers in Madrid, Roces, Klavego, as well as Uribe. Finally, the long list of collaborators and contributors includes Eduardo Ortega y Gasset, Margarita Nelken, Antonio Machado, and others, with topical experts including Buñuel ("Numuell") for Cinema, and Maria Teresa León for women and children. Interestingly, Bertrand had to deal with a potentially serious conflict when Willi Münzenberg showed up in Madrid in April 1936 with a plan to launch a magazine of almost identical characteristics to that envisioned by Klavego and Bertrand since 1935. Witnessing to the importance Spain had acquired for the Comintern after February 1936, this incident suggests multiple Comintern organizations were pursuing projects in Spain without proper communication with all the teams working in the country. On March 22, an unsigned message from Moscow[83] informed Medina that it had been decided to publish an illustrated paper together with "a group of syndicates or parties represented by Caballero," enabling the socialist leader to have a degree of say in the details. In order to support this effort, Medina was informed Willi was coming to Madrid and told to make arrangements. The message was repeated on March 26, adding that Willi would be in Madrid on April 15 and that Medina should do everything to support the launch of the publication, the details of which Willi would negotiate with Caballero and Del Vayo. Bertrand, however, saw the visit as an encroachment from Paris on his work. In his report, he comments, inserting a "nota bene" to draw attention to the fact that Willi was in Madrid, claiming to have been commissioned to publish the illustrated paper and to already have the funds to do it. To the bewilderment of the Spanish Central Committee at this "double assignment," Bertrand clarified that it was his team which would carry out this task. In the spring of 1936, Moscow gold was flowing into Spain from multiple sources and everyone in the large and confusing Comintern organization wanted a piece of the pie.

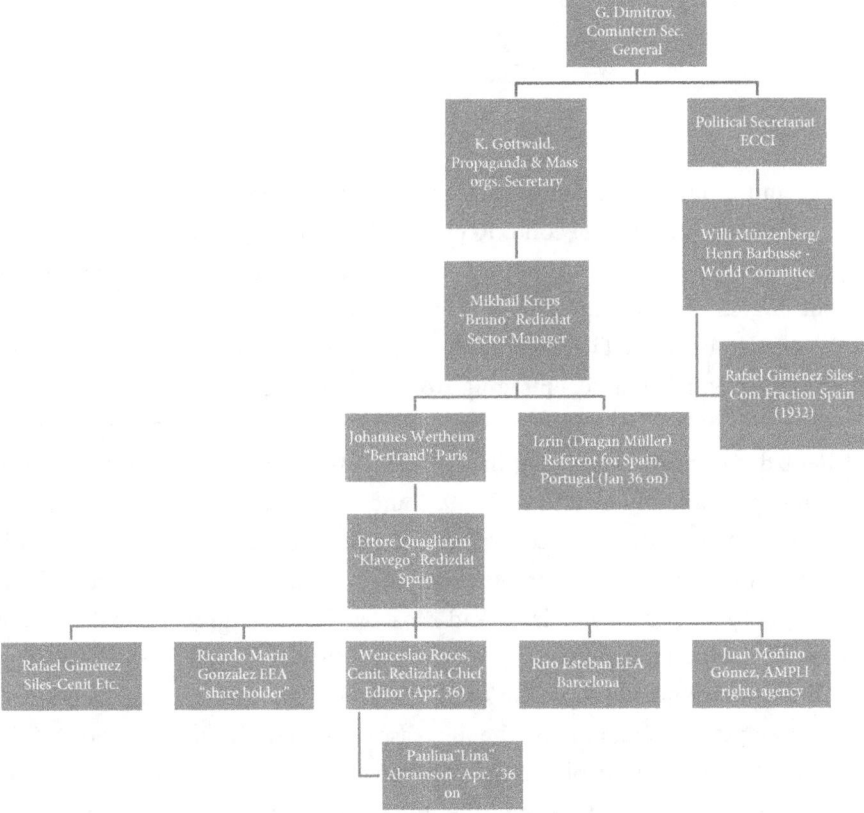

Figure 1 Organizational chart of Redizdat's Spanish organization and part of the Political Secretariat of the Executive Committee of the Communist International (Comintern ECCI) based on author's research. As of the spring of 1936, Ricardo Marín and "Ernesto," Felipe Muñoz Arconada, were also based at the EEA Madrid office reporting to Roces, together with Paulina Abramson.

To Spaniards outside of the Popular Front coalition, the topic of a near omnipresent revolutionary propaganda of foreign origin was on the forefront since at least 1935. We have discussed briefly the public perceptions of Dimitrov iconography in late 1935 and early 1936. In January 1936, the centrist Madrid daily *Ahora* reported the seizure by the police of ninety-five packages of "communist propaganda sent from Moscow," including Stalin portraits and a booklet on the production of bread in Moscow.[84] In March, centrist republican leader Felipe Sánchez Román explained the reasons why his party decided to pull out of the Popular Front coalition two months earlier. It was the refusal of the left-wing parties to reject a revolutionary path, which Sánchez Román wanted excluded even in its propaganda form.[85] In the spring of 1936 in Spain, that revolutionary propaganda seemed ubiquitous and unstoppable, as communists and socialists openly promoted the "October path."

Conclusion

As we and a number of others have shown before, many of the political and cultural leaders of the Second Republic thought of the regime change of April 14, 1931, in strict revolutionary terms. In relation to culture and book publishing, the facts of the 1920s in Spain notwithstanding, cultural leaders such as Wenceslao Roces, Rafael Giménez Siles, or Rodolfo Llopis believed Spain was, with the Second Republic, emerging from the dark ages into an era of Soviet-inspired cultural and political renaissance. That was an ideal setting for the work of Redizdat in Spain beginning in late 1931. As we have seen, Codovilla saw the great potential of Cenit in early 1932 and urged Klavego and team to bring its management under their control as Giménez Siles and Roces desired. With substantial financing and a complex web of corporate entities that spread from Barcelona to Paris, Berlin, Viena, and Moscow, Redizdat grew in Spain on the basis of a strong and thoroughly "bourgeois" distribution network. In Steven Spielberg's monumental *Schindler's List*, Oskar is overwhelmed with excitement as he attempts to explain to his wife the reasons behind his success in Poland. In previous businesses, he explains, there was always something missing. "You can't create this thing. And it makes all the difference in the world between success and failure … war!" For Klavego and team, it was the October 1934 bloodshed that made the difference between meeting and substantially exceeding their targets. Specifically, it was the masterful agit-prop role played by the communists, late comers to that insurrection, together with the surprising institutional weaknesses of a government that was fundamentally divided. After October 1934, Klavego found nothing but collaboration among socialists and left-wing republicans in his effort to popularize the Comintern's VII Congress, including the Comintern's unchanged revolutionary tasks. Immediately after his return to Spain in March 1935, Klavego reported the reopening of his illegal apparatus and the publication of a work entitled *From the Strike to the Insurrection*, a defense of the "October path" as the way forward for communists and socialists alike. With the Popular Front platform in the driver seat of the new government in February 1936, all of Redizdat Spain became legal. With unprecedented levels of financing, distribution, large print-runs, and connections in the government, Redizat Spain rightly saw itself as a fundamental enabler of the Comintern's larger revolutionary goals for the country. Klavego's optimistic assessment in late 1934 had been proven correct.

4

Star Pupils

A Transnational, Comparative Approach to Comintern "Army Work" in France and Spain 1932–6

Introduction

In his speech to the VII Congress of the Comintern on August 2, 1935, General Secretary Georgy Dimitrov addressed his international audience on the unity of the working class in the fight against fascism. Right at the outset, Dimitrov mentioned the *sitz im leben*, the historical setting for his speech: the ruling bourgeoisie in the capitalist countries was preparing imperialist war against the Soviet Union.[1] In his talk, Dimitrov often used fascism interchangeably with bourgeoisie, capitalism, and imperialism and asserted that war was a natural outcome of bourgeois imperialist regimes, not only in Germany, but also in Britain, France, or the United States. When imperialist or bourgeois war breaks out, affirmed Dimitrov following Leninist doctrine, the duty of proletarians everywhere was to work within their countries' armies to cleanse them from fascists and prepare them to join the side of the proletariat. Spain and France were among the nations singled out for detailed instruction in the matter of army work: communist work within (*au sein de*) the army was required since the army was, in Dimitrov and the Comintern's narrative, a key pillar of fascism in both countries.[2]

Contrary to Georges Vidal's thesis, communist army work in France was not "unparalleled in the rest of the world" nor was it phased out starting in mid-1934.[3] Rather, as we began to show in Chapter 1, "work in the bourgeois armies" was part and parcel of the Comintern-directed operational playbook for its sections from Greece to Brazil throughout the 1920s and 1930s. Working to turn the bourgeois armies red was standard Comintern operating procedure in our period, a natural consequence of the enduring Soviet obsession with the threat of imperialist war against the Soviet state. The fundamental aim of army work, the decomposition of capitalist armies through "fraternization" and insubordination, was meant as the primary means of pursuing the Leninist mandate of revolutionary defeatism, a mandate which remained in place and undiluted after the VII Congress of the Comintern.

A transnational, comparative approach[4] to our topic makes particular sense in relation to the French and Spanish parties, in light of the long history of collaboration between them. Since the early 1920s, when the French party began sending emissaries to Spain in support of army work during the conflict in Morocco, the PCF often assumed the role of guide and teacher, a role often resented by PCE leadership during the tenure of José Bullejos. After October 1934, however, the PCE's participation in and skillful utilization of the socialist-led armed insurrection enabled the Spanish Communist Party to be recognized as an example north of the border. The internal reports we will study in this chapter reveal that, starting at least in mid-1934, the PCE was applying a French template in much of its army work. At the same time, the language and the intensity of the Spanish directives reveal how the proximity of the October armed insurrection moved army work away from the realm of theory and turned it into a key piece of communist insurgency planning. Victorio Codovilla's two assessments of the status of army work in Spain in January 1935 and January 1936 reveal the quantitative and qualitative growth in army work achieved in the wake of and thanks to the October violence that had gripped Asturias, Catalonia, and other regions of Spain. As celebrated by *L'Humanité* in November 1934, the "civil war" in Spain was deeply meaningful for all communist parties across Europe: "L'Insurrection armée pour le pouvoir dans un des pays de l'Europe capitaliste! ... les soviets victorieux."[5] For the most part, communist army cells failed to rally their units against the officer corps and government in October. Further, the deployment of professional forces from the Spanish legion and the *Regulares* as the backbone of the government response effectively sidelined the most successful communist cells in several infantry regiments. However, the insurrection yielded for army work leaders valuable experience not obtainable from textbooks like the "A. Neuberg" classic (see Chapter 1 on this). Further, the October fighting uncovered military, political, and institutional vulnerabilities, and opportunities the leadership believed could be exploited in future insurrections, in both Spain and elsewhere. The French Communist Party was perceived by the Comintern as a star pupil in communist army work and received the lion's share of the praise at the VII Comintern Congress, as we will see. Our research reveals, however, that the Spanish party successfully implemented French best practices in this domain in the run-up to the October 1934 insurrection and soon after became a model for its counterpart north of the border. This transnational approach to communist army work reveals continuity, rather than an intentional phasing out of this key building block of Bolshevist revolution in late 1934 and beyond. Additionally, this approach helps us see, on one hand, the cross-border collaborative network of communist cadres, best practice and resources, and, on the other, the application of these, true to Leninist principles, in a manner that is sensitive to local opportunities and conditions.

Communist Military Work in the Armée: From 1917 to the 6 *Février* and the Popular Front

In order to understand the prevailing attitudes of the French officer corps toward communism in the interwar period, we must start at the beginning. Since at least 1916, the French General Staff was well informed of the military situation in Russia thanks to the presence in Petrograd and elsewhere of the eighty officers and other personnel who made up the Mission Militaire Française (MMF).[6] The objective of the MMF had been, first and foremost, to provide the best up-to-date intelligence on the Russian forces so as to ensure the overall sustainability of the Eastern Front. Any weakening of the Entente's eastern campaign was expected to have adverse consequences in the West by enabling the Central Powers to reallocate at least some of their divisions to France. As early as 1916, the MMF commanders observed with unease the massive casualties the Russian army suffered during its otherwise successful Brusilov offensive, and the impact of those losses on troop morale. The February 1917 revolution was received by the French General Staff and government with mixed feelings, but the primary criterion for evaluating the new regime was still its ability to sustain Russia's war effort. In the eyes of the MMF, however, the Bolshevik coup in October to November was the start of a rapid deterioration of the situation that would culminate in the March 1918 Brest-Litovsk Treaty and the collapse of the Eastern Front. Between October 1917 and March 1918, leading French banks and corporate investors began to voice grave concerns over the Bolshevik regime's inability or unwillingness to honor the substantial Russian financial commitments to them. On the ground, the military situation began to look dire. "This is the most complete mess. Everyone commands and no one obeys," wrote Colonel de Renty, who was in Moscow at the time of the October Revolution, to General Berthelot.[7] Meanwhile, the MMF witnessed the formation of the Trotsky-led Red Army, whose mission was both to protect the soviet regime and to support revolution everywhere else, including in Western Europe. Further, the MMF had first-hand information on the first Bolshevik-inspired mutinies and desertions in Crimea, as well as in France.[8] For the French, the Brest-Litovsk Treaty was fundamentally a betrayal, and the French officer corps initially saw the signing of a separate peace as a classic stab in the back deal initiated by the Germans and enabled by their Bolshevik clients. For the Entente powers, including France, a naval blockade of Russia seemed the best way of both containing the Bolsheviks and ensuring German POWs in Russia were not able to move to the Western Front. A *cordon sanitaire* against Bolshevism remained in place and became a key piece in the French and allied support for white forces in the Russian Civil War. In the words of Marshall Foch to Wilson:

> Against an infectious disease, a cordon sanitaire is established … the whole system I have submitted to you tends to organize a barrier against Bolshevism. This is not an offensive, but a defensive barrier, behind which the necessary mopping-up operations can be carried out.[9]

After the armistice in November 1918, strategic considerations and pragmatism no longer held back the French military and government's profound loathing for communism. Indeed, upon his return to France in January 1919, ambassador Joseph Noulens was able to affirm that "France is in a state of war against Bolshevism."[10] Among the allies who supported the anti-Bolshevik forces during the Russian Civil War, the French were the most consistent in their determination to see the downfall of the new regime, as seen in the uncompromising statements of Noulens and Foreign Minister Stephen Pichon. In meetings and correspondence with the allies, both affirmed that the Bolshevik regime was holding on to power by terror alone, was intent on exporting revolution across Europe and Asia, and that no lasting peace was possible if Russia was left in its hands.[11]

After the victory of the Bolsheviks in the civil war, the attention of the French high command turned to the home front. As the war was entering its final phase, most of the French socialist party broke away to form the French Communist Party (PCF), the French Section of the Communist International. Capitalizing on strong pacifist sentiment in post-Great War France, and to the dismay of the security forces, the PCF began to deploy antimilitarist propaganda and tactics, following faithfully the Comintern's instructions regarding "work in the bourgeois armed forces." In fact, among the twenty-one conditions set by the

Comintern in 1920 for the acceptance of the French socialists into the Third International, the fourth condition affirmed:

> [T]he special obligation of forceful and systematic propaganda in the army. Where this agitation is interrupted by emergency laws it must be continued illegally. Refusal to carry out such work would be tantamount to a betrayal of revolutionary duty and would be incompatible with membership of the Communist International.[12]

The French text of that fourth condition was printed as a header in the communist newspaper dedicated to the promotion of army work among communist organizations in France, *Notre Bulletin*. Given France's standing as the world's leading military power, the Comintern, as Georges Vidal has argued, expected its French section to excel in the essential Bolshevik task of army work. As the hierarchical and financial links between the Comintern and the PCF became evident, and police and military surveillance revealed the existence of communist cells inside army barracks in Paris and elsewhere, a twenty-year-long process of systematic surveillance of PCF activity by the French Ministry of Interior began.[13] In the words of Albert Sarraut, minister of the interior in April 1927, the conclusion of the French government was clear: "Le communisme, voilà *l'ennemi!*."[14] It is important to note, a point made by Vidal, that this consensus opinion extended also to many in the socialist party including its leader Leon Blum, who, in line with his moderate and constitutional socialism, saw the communists in 1931 as a "professional army of insurrection."[15] Thus, the Interior Ministry's National Security Directorate began gathering surveillance data on all PCF and Comintern activities in France, including some related to propaganda within the armed forces and other illegal operations of the Comintern's French section.[16] Additionally, as of 1932, the French army began producing detailed analyses and mitigation plans of the threat posed by the systematic communist infiltration of military bases and strategic arsenals, and the communist promotion of armed insurrection in capitalist states. Thus, in his report entitled "La Défense de la Région Parisienne contre l'Ennemi Intérieur en Temps de Guerre,"[17] General Voiriot discussed in detail the vulnerabilities of key military installations in Paris, and the evidence of existent communist cells and strategy to infiltrate the army and generate insubordination in the ranks. Voiriot was primarily concerned with the danger posed by these communist subversive activities to French national defense in time of war, given the explicit and consistent Comintern tactics of using states of war to generate armed insurrection in the home front.[18] In May and June 1934, this time writing in a public medium,

General Niessel addressed the armed insurrectional threat posed by "socialism" and the French military's response to that threat.[19] The questions must be asked: what was the nature and extent of communist work in the Armée in 1932–6? Was there, as Vidal has argued multiple times, a progressive turning away from these subversive activities starting in the summer of 1934? Finally, how much of the army work carried out by the PCF was replicated by its sister party south of the Pyrenees and how did the two implementations of this key Bolshevik task differ in application and relative success?

In a meeting held in Moscow on June 2, 1934, PCF representative to the Comintern Albert Vassart presented to Dmitry Manuilsky the status of communist "work in the army" from 1929 to June 1934.[20] In true Bolshevik fashion, Vassart began with a self-critical assessment of the "deviations" that the PCF was plagued with in their army work prior to 1933. In the earlier period, Vassart affirmed, the leadership had a tendency to politicize the work at all costs. Ignoring the real needs and interests of soldiers, the party launched preposterous "machine guns for the Red Army" and other similar campaigns conscripts showed little interest in. Additionally, Vassart continued, communist agit-prop in the barracks had been exposed as a fraud when the slogans promoted with the soldiers were too grand to be attainable: two months leave and six months of total service, for example. The party then went to the other extreme and promoted slogans that were "too economical" to have any real impact on the "immediate demands" of the troops.

Starting in 1933, however, Vassart affirmed, the party carried out a profound analysis of strategy and tactics, improving their understanding of the real needs and desires of the troops, and deploying slogans that matched those needs without being either too ambitious or too conservative. In terms of numbers of cells, Vassart explained that, while total numbers for the whole country were not available to him at the meeting, he was able to report positive figures for Alsace-Lorraine. There, the party had access to eighteen regiments through nine cells and nine other groups of soldiers not constituted as proper cells. Thanks to this presence, the party was able to distribute 5,000 copies of *La Caserne*, the communist newspaper for soldiers, out of a total of 20,000 copies nationwide, as well as five regiment-specific pamphlets. Additionally, 200 soldiers from Alsace-Lorraine supported the communist-run "Youth against War" Congress, with one of those soldiers addressing the audience in Paris. The focus on the "oppressed nation" of Alsace-Lorraine is consistent with PCF and mass organizational strategy in our period, as we shall see, and was also in itself a major concern of France's national security agencies.

In terms of organizational structure, Vassart explained that army cells were organized under three-person "troikas," similarly to communist cell structure in factories and villages, for example. One party member, one member of the communist youth, and one "technician," that is, an expert in subversive operations within the armed forces, made up this three-person team, designed for secrecy and conspiratorial excellence. Only one soldier per barracks had access to the troika. The objective of these cells, was, first, to build relationships and engage in constant and active listening for problems, challenges, and short-term needs among the soldiers. The troikas and higher-level organization depended on these insights for the creation of relevant pamphlets and other material, as well as for the deployment of higher-level agitation through national communist media like *L'Humanité*. Additionally, the cells were the spearhead of the communist effort to agitate, to capitalize on anything soldiers may find objectionable to generate discontent, dissention, and insubordination. Thus, relatively trivial issues such as "bad food" or having to pay one's train fare to the barracks, or more fundamental ones such as the need to go on "tiring" military maneuvers or to be trained to endure cold and heat were masterfully turned into campaigns deployed simultaneously by *La Caserne*, *L'Humanité*, and communist youth press, for example.[21] In the words of a booklet published in 1935:

> Within the army, as within the enterprises, it is necessary to capitalize on (il faut profiter de) every instance of dissatisfaction, every claim made by the soldiers, to organize the revolutionary struggle. The fight for good food, for comfortable barracks, against the brutality of officers, all of it will give us the chance to educate, to gather together, to organize the revolutionary elements in the army.[22]

The fundamental ideas present in all of these campaigns were core communist topics: soldiers are sons of the working class and officers are war-mongering bourgeois oppressors; the Soviet Union alone stands for peace and fraternity, while all capitalist countries serve or enable imperialism and fascism; military discipline and chain of command are fascist ploys but soldiers learn their real duty when they follow their proletarian brothers; France is an imperialist oppressor of the people of Alsace-Lorraine, among others, and only the communists will enable the liberation of that nation, etc.

In the higher-level agit-prop of *L'Humanité* and mass market booklets, as well as internal documents, insubordination and the breakdown of the chain of command were given a happy face. The political interpretation of events in which soldiers disobeyed orders and went along, instead, with the instructions or actions of fellow proletarians was "fraternisation." Although the tactic was first implemented in the Armée in 1922,[23] in 1934, starting with the February 6–12 events in Paris, fraternization became a mantra encapsulating the desired outcome of communist work in the armed forces of France. Addressing the topic of fraternization, Vassart detailed a number of potent examples in the 1933–4 period. He began by highlighting the courage of both young and adult communists in the recent strike in Strasbourg, who, despite significant police measures meant to prevent the infiltration of the army, showed great initiative in reaching and influencing the soldiers. Further, during the canal boatmen strike, Vassart continues, when the government deployed the navy to remove the barges the boatmen had blocked the canals with, the striking boatmen succeeded in getting the sailors to understand their duty. The communist youth also had a leading role in this effort, both young men and women. The report details how, understanding the importance of this anti-militarist work, communist youth members used a variety of means, including the proverbial honey trap, to influence the soldiers.[24] Vassart explains that the importance of fraternization became clear during the "February [1934] events" in Paris, and a booklet was produced on this subject, the communist best-seller "Les Soldats aux Côtés des Travailleurs."[25] The sixteen-page tract was attributed to A. Mortier, most likely a pseudonym of André Marty, PCF leader who would be deployed to Albacete, Spain, in October 1936 to lead the Comintern-recruited International Brigades. Fundamentally, Vassart continues, fraternization enabled the party personnel deployed with the marchers in Paris to win over enough of the soldiers sent to support law enforcement to exercise a degree of leadership over both and control the narrative. The fact that, as soldiers arrived in the vicinity of the Chambre des députés, some of the workers were able to engage with them, sing their regimental song and the Internationale, and, having taken some of their rifles, march alongside them was symptomatic of what was achieved that day, suggests Vassart. Mortier booklet's narrative of the February events ends with an inspirational quote from Lenin and a summary of lessons learned: the revolution will not come without the "disorganization of the army." The armed forces of a bourgeois country, affirms "Mortier," are the surest column sustaining its capitalist regime, but, thanks to the February events, the column is now shaking and the entire structure with it. The fight carried out by soldiers and sailors to sap and disorganize their ranks on one hand, and the support delivered by workers to what was done in the barracks are keys to this success. The tract ends with some slogans that point the way forward in army agitation: against the murderous training and forced discipline, for healthy and abundant food, for frequent vacations with free travel and food allowances, etc.

Lastly, Vassart's report mentioned the work being carried out among conscripts, that is, draftees on their way to boot camp or barracks. A serious improvement in the penetration of conscripts has been achieved, he asserts, as a result of both the publication of Le Conscrit, with 20,000 copies distributed with the help of the communist youth, and the setting up of a school to train youth in work among conscripts and cell work. Additionally, the party has come up with creative and engaging means of reaching the young men as they get ready to board their trains: "[t]he good-bye wine." As glasses of wine are handed out, relationships are built, and contact is established for follow-up with both the soldiers and their families. Manuilsky is impressed and comments: "[i]t is cheerful and French!." It was also Spanish. The goodbye wine was to be eagerly copied south of the border starting in 1934, along with other culturally relevant tactics. As late as August 5, 1936, the French Federation of Communist Youth was ordering its members to "perpetuate" the goodbye wine accompanied by parties and other entertainment as the best means of obtaining contact details of the recruits for further indoctrination on "the dangers of war," with special focus on socialist, nonreligious, and republican recruits.[26]

The Vassart report was not triumphalist and admitted openly that numbers were not what they were desired to be. Work in the army was fundamentally a communist network-wide effort, with communist youth, Red Aid, the communist-controlled veterans' organization ARAC, and others supporting the on-site work of cells within the barracks. If communist youth numbers are down, Vassart argued, he could not be expected to deliver on army cell numbers. However, the work in Alsace-Lorraine was wisely highlighted as a success story given the centrality of the "national question" to both Comintern strategy and French national security. The loss of Alsace-Lorraine as a result of the Treaty of Frankfurt in 1871 had inflicted an unforgettable wound on France, and the recovery of the lost province was central to the country's justification of the massive cost of the Great War. Not surprisingly, when France's internal intelligence service[27] began to confirm that the PCF's political statements on Alsace-Lorraine in the Chambre[28] were matched by large-scale subversive activity on the ground, it made the surveillance of this activity a top priority. Much of what was secret, underground communist work in the region, however, was blown open with the "Eberlein affair" of September 1935.[29] Communist work among officers in Alsatian regiments remained, contrary to Vidal's thesis, active through late 1936, and Deuxième Bureau surveillance implemented a mitigation plan that was to be triggered in case of a "communist putsch" in the region.[30]

A key insight we may draw from Vassart's speech is the multiplicity of communist organizations that were involved in army work. He mentions explicitly the contributions of the communist youth organization (Fédération des Jeunesses), of cells (factory, village or army), sports clubs (see on this the final chapter in this book), unions, publishing, and anti-fascist committees. As Vassart mentions, success depends on the full utilization of all these resources. The arsenal of communist "mass organizations" in France in the period also included the 50,000-strong (by 1936) and Duclos-led Association Républicaine des Anciens Combattants, ARAC.[31] This organization, part and parcel of the larger PCF army work strategy, was deployed successfully in the February 6, 1934, marches in Paris, infiltrating the Union Nationale des Combattants (UNC) group and yelling pro-Soviet and other revolutionary slogans (see Appendix to this chapter for details).[32] The effective channeling of the anger of the masses after the "Stavisky affair" was one of the great achievements of PCF agit-prop in 1934. In the words of Doriot:

> Those who lived through the demonstrations of Tuesday and Wednesday will long remember the extraordinary dynamism of that crowd, its hunger for action. What a lesson for revolutionary organizations![33]

Failing to take account of the full network of communist resources deployed in the context of French army work leads Vidal to significantly underestimate the real impact of this work in our period. Additionally, his assumption that the objective of the communist cell network in France was primarily to distribute propaganda in the barracks misses the point of "army work," point made abundantly clear in the Comintern archival documents, as well as in the published materials. As we have seen, insubordination, the breakdown of the chain of command and its replacement with proletarian fraternization were an absolutely central set of performance metrics for army work. Lastly, Vidal's thesis that the PCF and Comintern anti-military work was significantly reduced by mid-1935 flies in the face of the documentary evidence we will detail in the section that follows.

In this chapter, we are discussing and comparing the parallel efforts carried out by French and Spanish Comintern sections to deploy "army work" in their respective countries, as detailed in several internal Comintern reports and other sources. We have discussed the highlights of the French report as presented by Albert Vassart in Moscow in June 1934. The Spanish report is dated August 1934 and mentions explicitly the valuable French experiences the Spanish party was to copy and apply. This continuity of Comintern army work south of the border suggests there was in fact no communist turning away from the infiltration and subversion of bourgeois armies after mid-1934. Vidal has argued that a June 1934 speech by André Marty signaled a fundamental French communist shift away from anti-militarism. The quote Vidal selected to make his point is this: "[o]n the attitude of the army depends, in the final analysis, the victory or defeat of fascism in France."[34] Thus, since the defeat of fascism depended on the attitude of the army, so goes the argument, and fascism is ultimately based in Nazi Germany, the French party and the Comintern as a whole were turning away from the decomposition of bourgeois armies and beginning to support their strengthening and alignment with the collective security policy of the Soviet Union. The problems for Vidal's thesis begin with the document itself. In his speech, Marty goes on to affirm that communists must relate the entire struggle of the working class with the "immediate claims of soldiers" and the support of their political rights. More agit-prop in the army, not less, was the order of the day. Further, the rest of the September 1934 document is a faithful restatement of the same set of "army work" strategy and tasks referred to in the Vassart report we have discussed. The revolutionary boon of the masses, begins the Cahiers du Bolshévisme article, finds its continuation in the barracks and camps of French imperialism. Marty goes on to celebrate the dramatic increase in the participation of soldiers and sailors in communist-led marches in which slogans such as "long live the Red Army" and "soviets everywhere" were used. He goes on to cite various infantry regiments in which fraternization led to insubordination and concludes that we communists know that the bourgeois army constitutes the last defense of capitalism, with senior officers being the enablers of fascism in the ranks. The activity of soldiers and reservists is, therefore, important for us insofar as they break the discipline of the bourgeois army.[35] The article, it appears, is affirming the very opposite of what Vidal suggests. That is, in the fall of 1934 there was full continuity with rather than turning away from the traditional Bolshevik understanding of work in the army.

In the summer of 1935, the PCF believed it was reaping the benefits of the anti-fascist campaign it began on February 6, 1934, in Paris. The agreement of the socialist youth organization to join forces with the communist youth under the banner of Unité d'action was a major milestone for the Comintern which was formalized as the VII Comintern Congress was being held in Moscow. The unity pact signed by both parties confirmed that, in the summer of 1935, many socialist leaders were supportive of the long-standing communist vision for work in the armed forces of the French republic. Point 4 of the agreed action plan affirmed that it was necessary immediately to "win over the popular layers of the army ... that the claims of conscripts and soldiers be secured, that committees be created for the 'goodbye to the conscripts' together with the working populace."[36] Further, the plan stated that the united youth federation "repudiates *all national defense* in case of imperialist war [emphasis mine]." In case of war against a proletarian country, continues the document, the young workers shall refuse to fight and shall join the efforts of the revolutionary army. This is a crucial point. Contrary to Vidal's thesis, Bolshevik doctrine, as applied by both French and Spanish Comintern sections in 1935–6 did not support national defense per se, not did it see fascism as its single global enemy. Quite the contrary, when it came to what the Soviet Union understood as imperialist or capitalist war, members of the communist party and affiliated organizations were to use the chaos of armed conflict to unleash civil war and armed insurrection against their capitalist governments. Revolutionary defeatism in such a scenario was defended by PCF leader André Marty as late as 1939.[37] The PCF booklet on war we have mentioned above, published in 1935, detailed the correct communist understanding of armed conflict. Imperialism reigns in all capitalist countries, France included, and, naturally, these countries wage imperialist wars. Although many tensions exist among the capitalist nations (Britain, France, the United States, Japan, Germany, etc.), an all-imperialist war of them all against the Soviet Union is inevitable. Thus, affirms the booklet, in preparation for the unavoidable conflict, the proletariat in these capitalist nations must prioritize active work within the armies of their nations. Without this work, according to Leninist doctrine, it will be impossible to turn imperialist war into civil war and proletarian revolution when the opportune time comes. In December 1935, Jacques Duclos addressed a joint gathering of socialists and communists and reaffirmed the same principles in no uncertain terms receiving what the booklet describes as a "storm of applause."[38] As Stephen Kotkin has argued insistently, and we have affirmed in our thesis put forth in the introduction, this vision was essential to Soviet geopolitics from the 1920s to 1941.

Vidal's thesis of a Comintern and PCF fully converted to "republican military policy"[39] by mid-1935 falls apart when we consider the secret instructions distributed to all sections during the VII Comintern Congress, the very event Vidal attributes this final shift to. We have already mentioned these instructions in earlier chapters. However, the fact that the French section is mentioned explicitly in them makes a brief review of that material worthwhile. As the congress was winding down on August 19, 1935, ECCI Organizational Committee secretary Boris Vasiliev addressed the topic of army work.[40] Slacking off on communist army work is inexcusable, affirmed Vasiliev. As per Lenin's words reflected in the twenty-one conditions for joining the Comintern, failing to perform this task is tantamount to treason. Vasiliev warns the sections they should all act, immediately after returning home from the congress, to ensure work in the army is strengthened and turned into an activity involving every communist, rather than an only an elite of specialists. In his June 1934 report, Albert Vassart highlighted the French party had already shown great progress in relation to this objective. Vasiliev adds that the time had come, thanks in part to the tactics of united and anti-fascist fronts, to turn army work into a task for the masses, as the French and Greek parties were doing. While developing cells remained the best practice for infantry or cavalry regiments, he argued, radio communications and other specialist units required individual connections to avoid special police surveillance of these units. Finally, Vasiliev addressed what was one of the key objectives of army work, realized with significant success in France during the February 1934 events. When army units were deployed to support law enforcement in times of general strikes or large-scale unrest, revolutionary workers and soldiers were to work to isolate the reactionary officers and ensure the army could not carry out its plans effectively. The French success story, as detailed in Mortier's booklet, should have the widest distribution among Comintern sections, he added. Interestingly, Vasiliev's analysis was handed over for discussion by each section, following which the ECCI was to give special proposals to each party for local implementation.

Finally, a brief survey of period French press yields additional insight into the continuity of communist army work in 1935 to 1936. On the first anniversary of the February events, *L'Humanité* ran an ad for recommended books ("read them and make them read") which could be ordered from one of the local PCF publishing houses in Paris.[41] Interestingly, all the titles are related to communist army work, including the "A. Mortier" booklet, Fraternization by "Michael Marty," and Le Travail des Bolsheviks dans l'Armée. Among the non-communist press, sporadic reports of communist cells in the armed forces continued to be reported in late 1934. On December 28, 1935, local daily *Le Mayenne* covered the discussions in the Chambre des Députés between the minister of war and the opposition. In the context of a discussion on the need for strengthening the army in light of German rearmament, the minister affirmed that "the communist cells are working within the military units," and that he was not prepared to allow the anti-military propaganda that aimed to sap the organization.[42] In November 1936, the minister of war in the Popular Front government Édouard Daladier was engaged in a heated debate with the communists on the subject of national defense. This debate is interesting, first, because of the unimpeachable progressive republican credentials of the minister, author of the "two hundred families" slogan embraced by both communists and right-wing leagues in 1934. Two hundred families, so went this popular myth, controlled the financial levers of French power and were a symbol of what needed to be changed in 1934 to restore power to the people. Secondly, the debate is relevant to our topic because it highlights the controversial stance of the communist deputies in fundamental matters of national defense in 1936. Lastly, the debate takes place at the height of what Vidal and others see as the pragmatic and moderate period of PCF support for French national defense. In this debate, Daladier defended the impossibility, given the needs of the French military in late 1936, of reducing the two-year military service, a reduction that was demanded by the communists.[43] In addition, Daladier argued that the strategic importance of national defense factories meant strike action could not be allowed in them, communist demands in this direction notwithstanding. Slamming the table, according to *Le Figaro* reporter Paul Camus, Daladier responded that he would never agree to such a right for workers in weapons factories. Lastly, the minister went on to affirm the continued threat posed by the penetration of French army barracks by communist propaganda promoting insubordination and the anonymous slander of officers. When communist deputy Gaston Cornavin insisted that it was urgent to "republicanize" the army, Daladier countered that the true intention of the communists was not the promotion of republican ideals but of their party politics, for which they could never count on his assistance. Thus, as Vidal himself has suggested,[44] the PCF's frequent use of terms such as "republicanization" or "democratization" in relation to the army in 1936 were, in reality, slogans masking traditional communist class warfare categories of purging the "fascists" out of the armed forces and making them "proletarian." These slogans also masked the PCF's lack of any substantial, technical military program, and their continued commitment to traditional communist army work.

All the above make Vidal's detailed chronogram of a supposed communist move away from subversion of the bourgeois armed forces starting in mid-1934 difficult to accept. In what appears to be the latest version of Vidal's proposed chronology of progressive phasing out of communist army work in France ("le long tournant"),[45] the first step in the communist retreat from subversion of the Armée takes place in the second half of 1934. This is the period, according to Vidal, in which anti-fascism reaches army work, propaganda focuses on junior cadres and the slogan of the "republicanization" of the army is deployed. Yet, as we have seen, army republicanization and democratization, meaning purging of "fascists" and a proletarian turn, were communist slogans at the heart of communist propaganda in the second half of 1936, that is, in Vidal's fifth phase. Additionally, Vidal offers no evidence of a certain moderation in antimilitaristic propaganda in this period, beyond evolving and ever utilitarian communist rhetoric. He is also dismissive of Vassart's June 1934 report and barely covers its content, since he believes communist army work was being phased out. Further, Vidal does not take into account the fact that the French "best practice" in army work was applied south of the border beginning in the second half of 1934.

Vidal attributes the greatest impact to the VII Comintern Congress and its application in the second half of 1935. This is the third phase in Vidal's timeline, and in these six months, he argues, the turn away from anti-military work accelerates, as Soviet collective security strategy is implemented, the military apparatus in the barracks is reduced, and the propaganda shifts to the hand of friendship extended toward the army cadres. According to Vidal, a new communist attitude which is decidedly pro-armed forces is embraced and retained through 1936. Yet, Vidal's fair discussion of the duplicity inherent in the use of republican and democratic slogans by the PCF in 1936, together with his admission that "some" communist cells remained in place until 1937, make his thesis that communist antimilitarism in 1936 was moderate and being phased out hard to accept. Daladier and his radical republican colleagues in the government did not see communist army work in 1936 as a minor issue, and nor did the French security establishment. Vidal also fails to consider the secret military tasks handed out to the sections at the end of the VII Congress, with the French section put forth as an example to follow. But what is perhaps the greatest weakness in Vidal's thesis is his failure to engage with PCF and Comintern war doctrine published in France throughout 1935 and 1936. In these texts, as we have seen, the Bolshevik understanding of imperialist war, revolution, and the attitude of communists toward capitalist and bourgeois armies in the type of war that was expected in 1935 remained unchanged.

Communist Army Work in Spain 1932–6: The Lessons of October

The immediate impact of the Russian revolutions of February and October 1917 upon the Spanish army has been covered in great detail in Roberto Villa's 2021 tome, *1917. El Estado Catalán y El Soviet Español*.[46] This is an important book for a number of reasons. First among these is Villa's careful narrative of the progressive convergence of unlikely partners upon a shared project of forceful change of the political and institutional status quo in the Spain of the *Restauración*. The strange alliance of PSOE and UGT, "libertarian communist" (the anarchist CNT) unions, left-wing republicans, Catalan separatists, and a politized and insubordinate military junta became a coordinated and radically disruptive force that put the constitutional democratic regime of the Restauración on a path to authoritarianism. The military element in that alliance is worth discussing in some detail, as it provides a necessary background for our treatment of communist army work in 1932 to 1936.

The Juntas de Defensa began as an association of artillery and engineering officers who wished to channel their concerns over promotions and destinations jointly, but always legally and respectfully of the chain of command. That initial commitment to the maintenance of military discipline was dealt a severe blow in December 1916 with the publication of the Junta's statutes, which asserted for the first time the autonomy of the Juntas vis-à-vis any military or civilian power. Fully conscious of the weakness of the government, the Infantry Juntas in particular began to exert their power in the political realm. This led the Juntas in June 1917 to the "limits of a power coup," according to Ángel Bahamonde,[47] though he later sees threat and ultimatum only in the "semantic fields" of the document they sent the government that day. Military justice, however, had already arrested the top Junteros under a charge of sedition on May 28, 1917. Undiluted sedition was made manifest in the instructions sent by the Barcelona Junta to their counterparts throughout Spain: if the government does not yield to the ultimatum by June 2, occupy the provincial army headquarters. From that point on, and until the defeat of the insurrection, socialists and republicans believed the Juntas were, at least potentially, on the side of revolution and engaged in regular communication with its leaders, mainly through Colonel Benito Márquez. At the very least, socialist leader Pablo Iglesias asserted, the Juntas evidence that the officers "no longer love" the regime,[48] and that was something he could work with. As Villa has shown, while socialist and republican leaders began negotiating with Márquez and other Junteros, other socialists and anarchists initiated a steady effort to reach NCOs and soldiers with Soviet-inspired revolutionary messages.

Colonel Marquez notwithstanding, a significant number of the officers in the Juntas was unwilling to sit down, let alone negotiate with revolutionary and separatist parties. To the dismay of PSOE, UGT, and Republicans, when the fires of insurrection started burning, many of the Junteros decided to break their promise to Lerroux and stood behind the regime.[49] Yet, the mutinous nature of the path taken by the Juntas, coupled with their liaisons with revolutionary parties, led many to be unsure of the eventual outcome. A careful foreign observer of these events was the French military attaché, General Denvignes, who informed Paris that a summer 1917 meeting had been "an officers' soviet like the one in Petrograd ... usurping the powers of Parliament."[50] A far more faithful implementation of the Soviet model was attempted by the NCO Junteros who had copied the concept, as well as the embrace of insubordination from their superiors and gained substantial numbers throughout 1917. The Sargentos Junteros, led by their openly revolutionary Madrid branch, planned a nationwide insurrection for January 4, 1918, that would result in the arrest of the king, the handing over of power to the revolutionary parties and the establishment of a republic. Socialists, anarchists, and left-wing republicans were in contact with the leaders and promised their support. The agile reaction of the ministry of war, informed of the seditious plans and working with the support of the king, enabled the arrest of the leaders and the dismantling of the "golpe de los sargentos" just before its planned launch. Of the NCOs that were discharged and remained separated from the army by the summer of 1918, most remained committed to a revolutionary and republican project that would remain dormant until December 1930. Five of them founded *El Soviet*, an openly Bolshevik newspaper "written for intellectuals, workers and soldiers" and possibly financed with German funds.[51] Three others were arrested in January 1919 for distributing an equally subversive pamphlet entitled *La Chusma Encanallada*.[52] The embrace of mutinous insubordination was the central feature that connected both NCO and officer Juntas with the Russian revolution. As McMeekin has shown, the February revolution in Russia began as a series of army and navy mutinies which continued to spread from February to October. This was a faithful application of Marxist doctrine reflected in the words of the Internationale: "[l]et the armies go on strike, guns in the air, and break ranks ... soon they will know our bullets are for our own generals."[53]

The Crisis of Annual and the war which continued for years in Morocco would expose the Spanish armed forces once more to revolutionary influence. This time, the source of such influence would be the Comintern through its French section and the able leadership of Jacques Doriot. The July–August 1921 defeat of the Spanish army at Annual and the slaughter of the surrendered troops delivered a shock to the nation that brought down the government. While the strategic, logistical, and other failures that led to the disaster were investigated, the nation's commitment to the conflict was increased in terms of budgets and numbers of troops sent to turn the war around. In 1925, when Abd-el Krim's forces moved into the French protectorate and inflicted some 6,000 casualties on the French, France became heavily involved in close coordination with Spain. From the start of the French counteroffensive in the summer of 1925, the PCF began a concentrated effort to apply the Comintern's directives in support of oppressed nations in the context of colonial wars. On one hand, the PCF organized rallies and promoted mutinies in several French vessels. On the other, a decision was made to send an agent to Spain in support of the PCE's own illegal work targeting the Spanish army.[54] Emphasis was to be placed upon propaganda at the ports of embarkation of the Spanish forces and upon the promotion of fraternization with the Moroccan guerrillas. For the Spanish party, this was a first taste of revolutionary defeatism: the deployment of open as well as secret support for the enemy while Spanish and French forces were dying on the battlefields.[55]

An interesting document dated February 1926 reveals the links between the revolutionary elements in the Juntas and the earliest efforts of the Spanish section of the Comintern to set up its army work. The document is a letter from PCE leader José Bullejos, in Paris at the time, to the ECCI on February 13, 1926. The letter details the set-up of the PCE's illegal infrastructure during the dictatorship of Primo de Rivera and its early contacts with Catalan separatists and members of the armed forces. On the situation among the military, Bullejos writes that a significant revolutionary ferment remained present among the officer corps and added that, among the keys to this ferment were:

> The former defense *juntas*, restored, now wish to provoke a fundamentally republican movement [and are] an organization that has entered into relationship with us, an organization that determined with its position the last change in Government.[56]

That "fundamentally republican movement" would have to await its realization until the Pacto de San Sebastian and the December 1930 revolutionary uprising in Jaca, preambles to the proclamation of the II Spanish Republic. One of the outcomes of the regime change brought about in April 1931 was the readmission of all the revolutionary junteros dishonorably discharged thirteen years earlier.

When studying communist work in the army in Spain in the early to mid-1930s, we benefit from a more substantial amount of archival documentation than in the French case. The documents include a March 28, 1934, status report, an August 14, 1934, set of directives taking account of both the earlier status report and the experiences of the French section, and a January 1935 report by Victorio Codovilla which is both retrospective and forward looking. All three are part of the Comintern archives held at the Russian State Archive of Socio-Political History (RGASPI). Lastly, 1934 through early 1936 issues of *Soldado Rojo* and various regimental and barracks-specific communist pamphlets are available at both the Comintern archives and the Archivo Histórico del Partido Comunista de España (AHPCE).

The first report dated March 28, 1934,[57] is fundamentally a review of the shortcomings in the management of nationwide army work by the prior leadership and a detailing of actions and achievements by the current boss. The writer identifies the prior leader, from whom he took over on January 7 as "Alfredo" and identifies himself as "Julio." The reporting of Julio's activities covers only the period January 7 to March 7, 1934, the date, we are told, in which he was arrested. The date of his arrest has enabled us to identify Julio with a high degree of certainty. In the March 9, 1934, edition of *Ahora*, a brief note was published detailing the arrest, two days earlier,[58] of six communists who were meeting at the Café de Platerías on Calle Mayor in Madrid. According to the police report, the six were "communist liaison agents" and were armed. Among them was Julio Suárez Rodríguez, a twenty-nine-year-old communist party member who would later hold the rank of Captain in the popular militias and would be shot by a firing squad in Zamora in 1937. Julio Suárez's report details the state of relative neglect in which he found the work, blaming "Alfredo" explicitly for failures to conduct regular meetings with troika and cell leaders, failures to report with the required accuracy and frequency, and for losing contact with soldiers after they finished their military service. Suárez goes on to report on the turnaround plan he put in place and on the results he achieved on that basis, in spite of significant challenges and limitations he was forced to operate with. Among these achievements was the setting up of weekly meetings with the specialist members of the troikas, in which he required them to report on their work regiment by regiment. For these meetings, Suárez placed special focus on the locations with high troop concentrations such as Montaña and Campamento barracks in central and southwest Madrid, respectively. Additionally, he secured training for the specialists which included technical as well as agitational education: immediate demands of the soldiers, "merciless fight" against the senior officers, etc. Of these troika meetings, the Madrid one was particularly important, since it covered the work both in cells in key barracks and in the Ministry of War, of great significance, wrote Suárez, due to the plans, maps, and other documentation held there which was of interest to the national apparatus. Clearly Madrid was by far the most successful province for army work during Suárez's brief tenure. In his numbers section, he lists contacts or cells in seventeen barracks, of which seven were located within the 31st Infantry Regiment (31 Regimiento de Infanteria "Asturias" in 1934, later renamed "Covadonga"). In his account of army work during his tenure as overall leader in 1935–6, Enrique Líster mentions the leading participation of the cells in this regiment in the first "congress" of communist army cells held in Madrid January 1, 1936.[59] Suárez also mentions, among the reasons for the success in Madrid, the effective collaboration of the full network of communist mass organizations which included communist youth, Revolutionary Opposition Groups (Oposición Sindical Revolucionaria, OSR), and factory cells. He also mentions the Atheist League (Liga Atea) to which belonged a number of officers known to Salinas and Galán, in reference to Francisco Galán who became military instructor the MAOC militias prior to the outbreak of the Spanish Civil War. In order to ensure a positive development of the work, Suárez mentions the PCE leadership should re-prioritize army work in all the provinces, and make sure the youth organization trains recruits and provides detailed reporting.

The directives document[60] is a handwritten letter addressed to all regional and local party committees in regions where military installations are located and is unsigned. We know the date thanks to the Russian translation, which mentions "Orig. 14.8.34" as the date of the original Spanish text. The writer appears to have overall leadership of the Spain-wide army work operations and writes with full party authority instructing the local committees to make full use of lessons learned and best practices in army work. Enrique Líster mentioned in his book that, when he was appointed by Codovilla and Uribe to this role in September 1935, he took over from a young comrade named Mariano Calvo.[61] Calvo could, therefore, be the author of this letter.

The directive begins by addressing one of the key weaknesses identified by Julio in his report, namely, the failure of many provincial committees outside of Madrid to place army work at the heart of their agitational and conspiratorial work. Every local party committee with a military installation in its region, should, instructs the letter, pursue army work throughout the full lifecycle of the soldier, and deploy legal, semi legal as well as illegal communist tactics to this end. The communist factions in all of the organizations that prepare young men for military service, for example, the sports associations, should carry out systematic agitation among the youth ahead of their call-up and deployment. A second phase, work among the conscripts is particularly important, and it is this phase in which the writer mentions the need to follow French party best practices. The "goodbye wine," the set-up of apartments for meeting recruits, the purchase of clothing and food items to be paid by municipalities or enterprises should be carried out following the French template. Once the recruits become soldiers, cells are to be created under the guise of sports clubs or clubs of boys from the same province of village, for example. The primary objective of these cells, similarly to the French model, is to drive discontent and agitate on the basis of "bad food," "tiring manoeuvres," etc., so as to promote insubordination. Cells should be particularly alert to the deployment of their regiment to repress protests, strikes, or rebellions. In such cases, cell members must lead in fraternization with the workers, and, as needed, "liquidate the officers." The local party organization, continues the directive, should support the raising up of courageous agitators to cause the disaffection or breaking down ("descomponer") of specialist soldiers such as snipers so as to liquidate reactionary officers in the critical moments. This instruction and the one concluding the letter suggest the party was very much focused on preparing for a period that would test the level of preparedness of army work, requiring maximum alertness and conspiratorial excellence: for the immediate future, concludes the letter, managing the troikas directly from the center is strictly prohibited. The socialist-led October 1934 armed insurrection was in its final stage of preparation at the time of writing, and Codovilla had been in touch with the socialist leadership as the Comintern debated the convenience of joining the Alianzas Obreras.

The third and final piece of the puzzle of communist army work in Spain is provided by Codovilla's January 1935 report, which we will refer to throughout in this book due to its relevance to a number of topics we discuss. Thirty-three pages into his report, Codovilla moves to the topic of the "state of revolutionary decomposition of the army" and its role in the insurrection. If we judge this, argues Codovilla, only on the basis of the weak communist cell participation alongside the insurgents, we might conclude that the army is only mildly affected by revolutionary propaganda. For a correct assessment of the status of the army in Spain before October, Codovilla continues, one should simply read the book written by the former minister of war, ¿Por qué Fui Lanzado del Ministerio de la Guerra? a copy of which Codovilla had shipped to Moscow to illustrate his report. Codovilla affirms that in his book, Diego Hidalgo admitted he was forced to cancel military maneuvers in a hurry, once he realized the military units were undermined by communist infiltrators.

Diego Hidalgo y Durán, radical republican minister of war in 1934, was a politician who suffered in equal measure the attacks of the left and the right in the months that followed the October 1934 insurrection. Hidalgo certainly challenged easy stereotypes: he inherited aristocratic titles yet had to work to support his mother and brothers; early member of Friends of the Soviet

Union and investor in communist publishing houses yet pursuing a political vision of wealth creation and individual freedoms; committed republican yet widely considered by socialists and communists to be its enemy and ally of the fascists. Hidalgo's book is a frank defense of his work as minister of war during the tumultuous eleven months of January to November 1934, based largely on the official records of the Cortes and his own notes and recollections. Hidalgo touches upon the communist infiltration of Spanish armed forces in several of his very brief chapters. A careful reader of his book[62] will notice the author's struggle as he attempts, on one hand, to defend his management of the armed forces in this period, and is forced, on the other, to admit the continued infiltration of key units that had resulted in the canceling of major maneuvers a year earlier. Contrary to Codovilla's statement, Hidalgo takes pride in detailing the significant efforts he made to ensure that the military maneuvers planned for September 1934 were in fact carried out as planned.[63] Yet, due to the fears of insurrection in Asturias, Hidalgo gave orders in the last minute for the local infantry regiment to remain in place in support of law enforcement. For the deployment of the remaining units to the training grounds in Leon, he faced constant threats and intense subversive activities in the barracks and in the railway network which was to transport the troops.[64] The significant effort was worthwhile, argued Hidalgo, because to simply yield to the pressures would have been tantamount to admitting the breakdown of state institutions. Finally, Hidalgo dedicates a chapter in his book to the government decree emanating from his ministry in July 1934 which forbade active military personnel from joining political parties or trade unions. This decree, incapable of stopping communist army work which was by definition and intention illegal, was motivated by Hildalgo's realization, a few months after taking over the ministry, that radical politics had "invaded" the barracks and that a number of officers, NCOs, and soldiers were using military installations to make proselytes.[65] In the November 1934 parliamentary debate that led to Hidalgo's departure from the ministry, the government's struggle to remain in control of the armed forces became evident, even as units were deployed to supress the armed insurrection. The foreign legion and the Moroccan Regulares were called up when fighting broke out because these were professional and war-tested forces far more likely to succeed in guerrilla-style fighting than eighteen-year-old conscripts, argued Hidalgo. Yet, even as these units were being shipped to Asturias, the report that a North Africa-based Lieutenant Colonel had recommended to his battalion of Regulares fraternization with the insurgents resulted in a frantic, hours-long attempt to locate the vessel and order the officer to shore.[66] Although the report, Hidalgo argued in response to the opposition, was only partially true, the intensity of the effort to locate and neutralize the officer, while fighting already raged in several provinces, was indicative of the level of perceived threat at the highest echelons of government. Contrary to the minister of war's apologetic in the Cortes, Antonio Espada's report on communist activity in the Spanish navy confirms López Bravo had in fact met with communist cells on board the Almirante Álvarez Cervera while sailing to the Asturian coast.[67] Codovilla was, therefore, correct when he affirmed that communist army work had palpably impacted the perceived reliability of the armed forces as of January 1935, a situation reminiscent of the August 1917 events across Spain.[68] In his report, Codovilla celebrated the significant success achieved among NCOs, a number of whom were leaving socialist cells to join the communist army organization. A year later, back in Moscow with José Diaz and others, Codovilla was able to report significant success among the officer corps in the nation's capital, including liaison with eighty officers in various Madrid-based regiments.[69] This work, and the expansion "little by little" into the other regions, had led Gil Robles, argued Codovilla, to attempt two or three times a coup, a coup being resisted by the communist officers "upon the wide basis of defense of the republic."

October 1934 had yielded potent insights and know-how to the leaders of communist army work in Spain. By 1936, the student had become a teacher to its neighbor north of the border as revealed by Edouard Daladier in his prison memoirs. Some time that year, Daladier was handed a document by General Gérodias, Sub-Director of the Deuxième Bureau, that detailed communist tactics for neutralizing the French army in times of crisis. The document was a translation of a Spanish original produced by the PCE, with the added statement that these tactics "would soon be used in France."[70]

The October Watershed: The Military and Republican Legality in France and Spain in 1934–6

The Spanish Ministry of War's effort to neutralize communist infiltration in the armed forces in the run-up to the October 1934 insurrection included, among other measures, the passing of a law forbidding participation of active military in politics, the removal of "many commanders who did not inspire the least confidence,"[71] the removal of rifle bolts from bases storing large amounts of these, the removal of critical aircraft equipment to avoid them being taken over by insurgents, non-inclusion of key regiments in maneuvers, deployment of professional legion force and North African troops, and the frantic effort to neutralize Col. Lopez Bravo and others as the fighting began. Yet, throughout 1935 and early 1936 communist army work experienced qualitative and quantitative growth, as we have seen. Among the key enablers of that growth was the Comintern-financed and -directed campaign to craft and exploit a narrative of the Insurrection that became the single most potent rallying point uniting all the left-wing parties in Spain. According to this campaign, the police and armed forces had not been the constitutional and legitimate means of restoring order in Spain but the repressive arm of fascism which had enabled the murder and imprisonment of thousands of innocent proletarians. Army work post-October 1934 was part and parcel of this narrative. Socialist, communist, and left-wing republican delegitimization of the army in anti-fascist and class warfare terms became, throughout 1935 and, especially with the arrival of the Popular Front government in February 1936, a key enabler of disaffection and insubordination in the barracks. In parallel, the growth and legitimation of paramilitary militias, many of which had been active participants in the October 1934 insurrection, demonstrated a Bolshevik commitment to a red peasant and worker army operating outside of the Constitution and parliament.[72] In early 1936, calls for the "republicanization" of the Spanish army and its purging of "fascists" were coming, primarily, from the socialist party leader Caballero and the socialist union UGT.[73] What this republicanization looked like became apparent when, on one hand, army personnel who had joined the October insurrection were readmitted into their units by government decree, and General Lopez Ochoa, who led the government's repression of the insurrection, was imprisoned.

The appropriation of the republic as the exclusive property of the left and the submission of all state institutions and constitutional checks and balances to a Marxist framework of class warfare were, in early 1936, expected by the left-wing coalition to be thoroughly applied to the armed forces. The fates in 1936 of the two leading republican government ministers who had resisted both communist infiltration of the armed forces and the insurrection itself are indicative of the different paths taken in Spain and France by the respective Popular Front governments. While Diego Hidalgo, the minister of war in 1934 managed to flee to Paris after the outbreak of war in July 1936, Rafael Salazar Alonso, the interior minister in 1934, was captured by militias in August 1936, and shot by a firing squad shortly after.[74] The February 1936 issue of *Soldado Rojo* expressed unbridled optimism as it celebrated the first conference of army cell leaders held in Madrid the prior month, and the expected victory of the

Popular Front, with whose platform it fully identified. It was perhaps that same issue of *Soldado Rojo* that opposition leader José Calvo Sotelo held up in a heated debate in the Cortes in April 1936 in which he alerted Azaña to the systematic communist infiltration of the armed forces. Calvo Sotelo warned the president that a divided and undermined military was incapable of carrying out its role as guarantor of constitutional order for all Spaniards.[75] His fate three months later confirmed his assessment was not far off target.

In France, radical republican leader Édouard Daladier had been an outspoken critic of communist demonstrations in February 1934, and, as we have seen, stood firmly against communist infiltration of the Armée in 1936. His party's support for the Popular Front, materialized by November 1935, did not change the fact that the radical republicans saw the Popular Front, similarly to socialist party leader Leon Blum, as a constitutional expression of progressive republican values. When Daladier joined the Popular Front government in 1936, he did it as a defender of the large and upwardly mobile French middle class.[76] Later that year, he felt compelled to warn the left-wing maximalists in the Popular Front that "… we gave our signature to a program and expect its fulfilment and nothing more … we accept reforms but only within [a context of] interior order and peace," and "social peace is the indispensable condition of an efficient national defense."[77] But the champion par excellence of *légalité républicaine* in the French Popular Front government was none other than socialist leader Leon Blum. While Caballero, Nelken, de Francisco, and many other Spanish socialists had, by their own admission, fully embraced Bolshevik ideology and strategy by 1934, Blum never abandoned "legalistic scrupulousness."[78] His Popular Front cabinet, with Daladier in defense, served as an unbreachable barrier around republican institutions, especially the army. Additionally, although he joined the communists in an "anti-fascist" movement in February 1934 which led to "unity of action" by 1935 and to the Popular Front shortly after, he never abandoned his conviction that the PCF was, fundamentally, an insurrectional force serving the interests of a foreign power. While the French communists spoke in 1936 of republicanization and democratization while referring to the same Bolshevik program they had always defended, Blum often used revolutionary language to draw socialist voters to his thoroughly constitutional platform of social change achievable through legal means and the ballot box.[79] The wall of republican, constitutional order did not crack in France with the February 1934 events, and even less so with the arrival of the Popular Front in 1936. In his 1945 book, Blum summarized the views on war and revolution he had always held: war and bloodshed do not trigger true revolution. For a transfer of power to be consolidated,

> ... it must be acceptable to the conscience of mankind no less than to human emotion and to human reason. It must call forth from every sincere man the spontaneous tribute: "[i]t had to be", but not that alone. He must also say; "It is right, it is good and it is beautiful."[80]

Appendix

"Fascists" for a Day: A Fresh Look at the *6 Février* 1934

Communist agitation and propaganda were deployed with significant success by the Comintern and its sections in Europe throughout the interwar period. Driven by the old Leninist principle of "chem khuzhe, chem luchshe," the worse it is, the better it is, any instance of popular frustration and discontent was exploited in order to "expose the contradictions of the capitalist bourgeois system" and lead the masses to a revolutionary exit. A good Bolshevik was to be, fundamentally, a good listener and interpreter of the sentiment of the masses and Comintern leaders did not hesitate to put forth examples of excellence in such a skill from the most unexpected sources. Addressing the ECCI in April 1932,[81] Dmitry Manuilsky shared with admiration the story of how the NSDAP's brown-shirted militia, the Sturmabteilungen, had exploited the indignation of the German masses at the Sklarek corruption scandal. In a very timely and emotionally compelling manner, a local S.A. leader demonstrated that the Nazis had understood the gravity of the scandal and offered their party as the only truly revolutionary cure for German society's ills. The trial of the three Sklarek brothers was costing the German taxpayer 17,000 marks daily, claimed the S.A. agitator as quoted by Manuilsky. If the Nazis were in power, they would put an end to such a bourgeois democratic process. What then should we do with the Sklarek brothers? "Shoot them!" responded the crowd. Manuilsky concludes admiringly: there is a vivid picture! The Nazis had, the Comintern secretary reflected, understood and exploited the national socioeconomic moment and demonstrated they were men of timely, radical action. The French section of the Comintern would get their opportunity to apply this tactic in France, with spectacular success, less than two years later. The outcome of this effort would become a Comintern success story of "fraternization" the Comintern offered as a template to all its sections in the context of communist work in the army.

Serge Alexandre "Sasha" Stavisky, a Ukrainian immigrant in France who had tried his luck at various trades, ended up running a successful municipal bond scam in Bayonne in the early 1930s. By December 1933, the police investigation revealed Stavisky's clientele had reached the highest echelons of political power. His flight and mysterious death in the Alps in January 1934 triggered a frenzy of press attention and rapidly escalating popular indignation that would fuel violence on the streets of Paris on February 6, 1934. Scholarly discussion of the 6 *février* events[82] has been heavily influenced by the larger debate over whether fascism existed in France before the outbreak of the Second World War. Thus, the traditional view put forth by Serge Berstein, Michel Winock, and others is that the ideology of the leagues who marched in Paris on February 6 involved various shades of authoritarianism but certainly not fascism matching the Italian or German models. Since the late 1990s, that traditional view has been challenged, with a growing amount of literature arguing the leagues were fundamentally fascist and that the received denial of this fact amounts to wishful thinking, if not outright negationism. Brian Jenkins and Chris Millington have become the champions of the new perspective in the last twenty-five years.[83] It seems to me the intensity of this debate is a major contributor to the perpetuation of a significant elephant in the room, namely, the carefully planned and successfully implemented communist infiltration of the right-wing marches on February 6, 1934. Berstein argued the participants in the marches were politically heterogeneous within the right, a notion Jenkins attempted to dismiss in favor of a thorough fascist reading. The evidence we will present in this appendix underscores the heterogeneous nature of the marchers by demonstrating the effective communist infiltration and exploitation of Union Nationale des Combattants (UNC) and Croix de Feu crowds that historic evening. The carefully orchestrated communist involvement in both groups of marchers was designed to utilize and inflame anger over corruption, the inadequate social benefits of veterans and a perceived dilution of traditional values, in order to promote "soviets partout," that is, revolutionary regime change.

Our narrow focus in this appendix prevents us from engaging with Jenkins and Millington on the question of fascism and its alleged presence in France before 1940.[84] It is clear, however, that their desire to overturn the traditional view as presented by Berstein and Winock clouds their vision of the events of February 6, 1934. Jenkins has argued that the "orthodox" view downplayed what actually happened on the streets of Paris in favor of focusing on origins or outcomes.[85] Yet, both Jenkins and Millington chose to ignore a fundamental strand in the complex web of actors and agendas that were at play that historic evening, in order to present a fully coherent narrative that supports their thesis. The role of the PCF and its mass organizations, including the Association Républicaine des Anciens Combattants (ARAC), in the marches on February 6, 1934, in Paris is essential to any sound interpretation of the events, as we will show. Yet, Jenkins and Millington's insistence that authoritarian, radicalized, extra-parliamentary, and insurrectional approaches belonged only to the political right[86] forces these authors to relegate their few references to significant communist involvement to their footnotes or to quotes from other authors.[87] Further, in his effort to place France in the context of German and Italian fascism, Jenkins proposes a more transnational approach to the study of February 6, 1934. Yet, Jenkins fails to engage with the potent transnational agenda and resources of the Comintern in 1934, intent on making its French section a model in revolutionary decomposition of bourgeois armies and state institutions. Interestingly, Millington dedicated a full journal article[88] to discuss the communist-run veterans' organization ARAC but had nothing to say about its subversive involvement in the 6 *Février* marches.

As of January 1934, the leadership of the PCF's Political Bureau and Central Committee was tracking public reactions to the Stavisky scandal and what it saw as an effective channeling of public anger by the right-wing parties. On January 2, 1934, the Political Bureau met to discuss the status of various projects and actions taken by the party. The "affaire Stavisky" was addressed as an opportunity for the party to profit from its parliamentary participation in the debates and to appeal to the civil servants regarding their rights, as well as those of the unemployed. Further, Pricat suggested that the tribunal who had "buried" the Stavisky affaire was the same tribunal known for its prosecution of communist anti-military activities and that the party should make the connection clear in its appeals.[89]

Two weeks later, Coquelin and Cadet noted the party had taken too long to react to the scandal, while the "reaction," that is, the conservative and republican parties, was steering popular sentiment in their direction.[90] The Central Committee of the PCF met on January 23 and discussed in detail how this situation might be corrected. In his speech, Marcel Cachin noted that, thanks to the Stavisky affair, both the proletariat and the middle classes were "more receptive" to radical messages, a fact that had been intelligently and skillfully exploited by the reaction. The communists had the duty, he concluded, to participate more vigorously in that movement so as to not leave all the benefits to the reactionaries and future fascists of France. Interestingly, Cachin added that the entire bourgeoisie, including the socialists, cooperated in the fascistization of the army and the country. The Stavisky affair, the PCF leader continued, had provided a valuable supplement to PCF agitation, and had resulted in the doubling of the sales of *L'Humanité* in Paris. Among the tasks of the party were highlighted the redoubling of efforts to build the United Front by recruiting socialists into communist mass organizations such as ARAC, Red Aid, or Friends of the USSR. Croizat suggested that the Stavisky scandal had created an opportunity to organize large rallies: dozens of thousands instead of five or six thousand, and for the communists to seize the initiative on the streets. Finally, Dupuy detailed the best tactic going forward. In order to mitigate the threat posed by the cohesiveness of the fascist organizations, argued Dupuy, the party should plan on joining a "chauvinist" army veterans' march with a fascist character. Within that march, while supporting the demands of the veterans, the PCF should "try to make trouble and penetrate in this way this fascist veterans organization which is the Croix de Feu."[91]

Dupuy's proposal to infiltrate "fascist" marches was implemented for the first time in late January 1934. At the meeting of the Political Bureau of the PCF held on February 1, 1934, the party discussed the best means of reaching "fascist" leagues which had the same petit bourgeoisie and peasant memberships the PCF was aiming for. Pricat shared a communist youth success story from the previous week:

> At the time of the marches on the boulevards last week, the communist youth entered the line of fascist marchers with our slogans. The fascists mixed with them and told them: Fine! let's bring down the Government and after we shall settle our affairs.[92]

The challenge was clear. The PCF saw fascism or fascistization everywhere in France. In fact, there was, according to Piervi in the February 1 meeting, a "systematic fascistization of the regime," with the socialists actively supporting it. Given the strong internal cohesion of the fascist organizations and the fact that their slogans appealed widely to the same masses the PCF claimed as their natural proletarian base, the correct approach for the short term was infiltration. The tactic proposed by Dupuy on January 23 and implemented successfully by the communist youth a few days later was to become the PCF's modus operandi on February 6 on the streets of Paris.

Shortly after the UNC announced the meeting point for their march on February 6, the PCF made its move from the front page of *L'Humanité*. Following the standard "united front from the base" playbook, the communist party attacked the leadership of the UNC while appealing to its members as the true defender of veteran interests. In an article entitled "Anciens combattants tous à 20 heures Rond-points Champs Élysées," the ARAC declared that the UNC veterans would march side-by-side with those of ARAC and stand together for their rights. The slogans put forth for the march included both the updating of veteran pensions, as well as "down with fascism" and "down with the government." In a separate piece on the front page, the party extended the call to all communist organizations, canceling all party activities for the day since "the place of all the communists is at the head of the masses in the battle, according to the line fixed by the central committee."

The official report published after the February 6 events for the Chambre des Députées confirmed the communists had been infiltrating right-wing marches since late January. Further, several testimonies included in the report confirmed the ARAC had marched together with both the UNC and Croix de Feu, had chanted pro-soviet slogans and had provoked violence throughout.[93] On several occasions, groups of communists of around one thousand, which were being tracked by the police within the larger UNC group, threw projectiles at the police and were "vigorously charged."[94] In his account of his organization's march, UNC president Georges Lebecq testified that the ministry of the interior had informed them, in the afternoon of February 6, that armed communists were expected to march with their group, along the tree-lined sides of the boulevard. When the UNC reached the Pont de la Concorde, Lebecq noted certain troublemakers (éléments perturvateurs) had slipped into their column and were chanting "a la Chambre"![95] Several eye-witness accounts cited in the report mention the ARAC and other communists fighting the police, lighting fires, and shooting.[96]

In the words of Taffa at the meeting of the PCF's Political Bureau on February 15,[97] the communists had joined the veterans march on the 6th in order to transform it. The role of the party on the 6th and on the days which followed had been "énorme" and, Cadet concluded, a huge layer of people previously untouched by the party was now shaken up and turned into a powerful current for the united front. Further, Coquelin noted that the significant growth in *L'Humanité* readership included many socialists who "viennent à nous," as well as several radical party members. The public perception that the communists had been in some sense "associated" with the fascists during the marches was a small price to pay and could certainly be compensated, suggested Seres, by training the party to speak in the defense of the republic. Contrary to its public agit-prop and that of the Popular Front beginning in the spring and summer, the communists understood the "fascists" who marched on the 6th of February had *not* intended to seize power. When the party studied the text of a *L'Humanité* editorial at the Political Bureau meeting on March 1, Cadet noted that "we cannot say that on the 6th the fascists had the intention of seizing power." Taffa concurred and suggested instead the phrase "on their way to seizing power." As was the case in Spain and elsewhere "fascism" was a label masterfully used by the communists to objectify a dreaded enemy and unite all "proletarian" and "petit bourgeoisie" forces against it under communist leadership. Its successful involvement in and utilization of the February 6 protests enabled the PCF to build a political platform that would lead to the general strike and historic marches with the socialists on the 12th, and to the formation of the Popular Front shortly thereafter. Contrary to Jenkins, authoritarian options were present in *both* right and left in France as they were throughout the continent in the inter war period. However, only the French far left was explicit in its pursuit of violent regime change leading to a dictatorial, soviet-style system. Thanks to the "fascist scare" of February 1934, "antifascism became the dominant political fact in France, a thousand times more important than fascism."[98]

5

Schools of Communism

Revolutionary Opposition Groups in the Socialist Union UGT, 1932–6

Introduction

During the Comintern's Third Period, few tactics represented a clearer embodiment of the United Front from below approach than revolutionary opposition groups in "reformist" trade unions.[1] The debate over the correctness of creating new red unions in Western nations raged for years, but Bolshevik pragmatism dictated that opting for communist work *within* socialist unions or for the creation of new ones should depend on local circumstances. The path taken in several Western countries, Spain included, involved both options in parallel.[2] In this brief chapter, we will examine communist work within the socialist union Unión General de Trabajadores (UGT) in Spain, a topic briefly introduced in Chapter 1. To tell our story, as we have done and will continue to do throughout this book, Comintern and other archival material will be complemented by abundant references to period press. In our analysis, the official press organs of various UGT-affiliated unions in Spain will be seen to yield valuable insights into the extent and influence of Oposición Sindical Revolucionaria (OSR) groups as experienced within key unions such as that of metal workers in the 1932–4 period. The membership of the official PCE union the Confederación General del Trabajo Unitaria (CGTU) remained low throughout the period of our study. However, the numbers of socialist union members under OSR control, and their ability to infiltrate and effectively direct strike and other leadership committees was a substantial success rarely recognized in the literature. Tim Rees, in line with his hypothesis of a marginal communist influence in Spain in our period, affirmed:

> [T]he party did not make any real headway in its efforts to win over ... Socialists while attacking the leaders of their organisations ... it was simply not possible in

Spain, as elsewhere, to woo workers away from organizations to which they were deeply attached culturally and politically.[3]

As we will show in this chapter, this statement betrays a misunderstanding of the standard operating procedure of communists *within* the socialist trade union, as well as an overestimation of the internal coherence of UGT in our period. Antonio Elorza and Marta Bizcarrondo share Rees's low estimate of the power of the OSR organization within UGT, though they correctly interpret the shift to the "united front from above" tactic as a ploy in the continuing communist efforts to bring socialist union members under the control of the Third International.[4] Helen Graham has argued there was continued and "increasing pressure" from the OSR operatives on their socialist counterparts in the unions during the war years, but did not pursue a detailed analysis of this influence over time.[5] Our analysis of the continued and successful communist infiltration of UGT from 1932 to 1935 thus fills a missing link in the historiography of communist "work in the unions" in Spain leading up to and helping to explain the full merger that occurred in late 1935. The effective collaboration of OSR groups within as well as outside UGT, Red Aid, anti-fascist committees, and other communist-run organizations is yet another potent example of the network effect of Comintern resources in Spain that we develop throughout the book.

Work in the Unions: The Comintern Tactic of Revolutionary Opposition Groups from Design to Implementation

In early 1920, a meeting of active Russian Communist Party (b) and trade union members was held at the Labour Palace in Petrograd. Grigory Zinoviev addressed the 800-person crowd and produced the final report, which began with a definition of a trade union.[6] After rejecting explicitly the reformist character of trade unions as understood by the II International, the report reaffirmed the 1913 Bolshevik definition, produced in the context of debates with the Mensheviks:

> [A] permanent amalgamation of the workers of a given industry (by no means only of a given trade) which directs the economic struggle of the workers, and participates in permanent collaboration with the political party of the proletariat, in the struggle of the workers for freedom, for the abolition of wage slavery, and for the victory of socialism.

The report denounced the "theory of equal rights," by which trade unions and party are considered equal partners. True to revolutionary Marxism, continued the document, the party is the highest synthesis of all forms of proletarian struggle, and its overall leadership cannot be in doubt. The report affirmed that, while contemporary trade unions may not be formally subjected to the communist party, communists in those trade unions were obliged to create communist fractions and openly propagate communism. The communist party, continued the report, achieves its influence over trade unions only by means of the "daily, self-sacrificing work of communists INSIDE the unions, by promoting the most steadfast and faithful members to responsible posts in the unions [emphasis original]." Each communist cell within a trade union was to be seen as nothing else than the nucleus of the party and was under the leadership of the local committee of the party. Thus, shortly before the transition from war communism to the New Economic Policy, the party was asserting its overall control over trade unions, without making them a mere cog in the apparatus of the soviet state. As Carr noted, Lenin gave trade unions the role of non-party mass organizations which had to be won over by persuasion or by compulsion, as the situation required.[7]

In May 1929, the ECCI's Trade Union Commission met under the leadership of Gusev to prepare a set of theses for Comintern-wide implementation. The working document was entitled, "[T]he fight for the conquest of the working masses is found within the trade unions."[8] The document detailed the critical importance of infiltrating reformist trade unions through revolutionary opposition groups, an integral part of a larger network of party-controlled organizations. Revolutionary opposition groups, communist-led cells made up of revolutionary workers who were unhappy with the reformist tactics of the leadership, were to operate under the leadership of the communist fraction in the union, that is, the group of union members who were also card-carrying communists. The theses called upon fractions and opposition groups to take full advantage of the resources and personnel of communist "auxiliary organizations" such as International Red Aid and women's organizations. This template was to be applied everywhere, and the story of the German metal workers union in Berlin is presented as a model. The revolutionary opposition there succeeded in fighting expulsion by portraying the leadership as schismatic and undemocratic, and presenting itself to the members of the larger union as the defenders of internal democracy and the rights of minorities.

As early as January 1932, ECCI secretary Dmitry Manuilsky instructed the Spanish party to create revolutionary opposition groups within the UGT to turn the members against their reformist leaders. We find a detailed description of OSR operations in Spain in a 1932 report of the ECCI's Roman Secretariat.[9] In the current environment, instructed the report, as the members of these unions become radicalized and seek to stand against their reformist leaders, the OSR groups will be able to become the guide of these struggling workers. The statement is followed by an "analytical report" of strikes led by communists in which OSR groups managed to secure majorities in strike committees and other union leadership organs. Further practical instructions for OSR work in Spain were provided in the booklet published in Madrid by the communist youth organization and entitled "El Trabajo en las Células de Empresa."[10] Young communists, instructed this manual, should be permanently alert and able to discern the sentiments and desires of fellow workers. Every young communist was obligated to join an existing OSR group or create one, under the strictest conspiratorial rule of illegal work. Since the highest form of economic struggle in an enterprise is the strike, the manual affirmed, members should be instructed on how to secure decision-making roles in the strike committees by ensuring that their demands truly reflect the immediate concerns of the masses of workers. In support for their efforts, the young communists were instructed to leverage the local branches of Comintern mass organizations such as Red Aid, sports organizations, intellectuals, etc. The wider audience of communist sympathizers in Spain learned about the crucial work of the OSR groups around the world on the pages of the Comintern organ, *La Internacional Comunista*, which referred to the OSR cells as "escuelas de comunismo" and provided examples of their work, for instance, among the post and telegraph union of Shanghai.[11]

Central to the Comintern's playbook for work in the trade unions was the full utilization of the networked resources of communist front organizations in each country. The activities of Pablo de la Fuente Martín and Rafael Ochoa Alcázar from 1932 to 1934 illustrate this point rather well. Both men held executive leadership roles in Socorro Obrero Español (SOE), the Spanish branch of Willi Münzenberg's Internationale Arbeiterhilfe (IAH), an organization that gained less traction in Spain than its sister group, Socorro Rojo Internacional. De la Fuente,[12] Secretary General of SOE, was also OSR boss in UGT's rail workers union, the Sindicato Nacional Ferroviario, with a significant number of its operatives placed in the workers' council in the northern Madrid region. His expulsion from the union did not stop his subversive work in the OSR, and he was later indicted for inciting union members to participate in the 1934 illegal general strike. In their joint report to the IAH global leadership,[13] de la Fuente Martín and Ochoa Alcázar discussed the role played by the SOE in the penetration and subversion of the Madrid-based metal workers union. While an OSR group took control of the strike committee, the SOE led the agit-prop campaign on the streets which included parading the children of striking metal workers, support from the socialist Margarita Nelken and the communist writer Rafael Alberti, the Sportintern-affiliated FCDO (see on this our final chapter), and an event at a major Madrid theater with music and other performances. The outcome of all this activity was the control and radicalization of the workers, the extension of the strike, and the popularization of the communist approach to labor disputes among the socialist masses. These coordinated efforts led by de la Fuente and Ochoa provide a very revealing snapshot of the network effect of Comintern operations at work in Spain in our period.

From June 30 through July 2, 1932, the "Conferencia de Unidad Sindical" was held in Madrid under the auspices of a "Comité Nacional de Unidad Sindical." Few of the participants ignored this was a gathering of nationwide OSR groups and communist-affiliated unions to celebrate what had been achieved to date and plan further infiltration into and control of UGT, CNT, and autonomous unions. The street address of the publisher of the conference booklet was a give-away to any careful external observer. The provisional address of "Ediciones Unidad Sindical" was Calle Madera 45 in Madrid, the location of OSR gatherings as advertised in the press throughout 1932. The proceedings were published in the communist organ "Frente Rojo," of which a copy is held at the AHPCE. The Comintern archive holds the same conference proceedings, as well as valuable complementary material, most of which we will discuss here. In relation to this conference, two details are worth noting. First, the surprisingly high number of workers represented at the event. The conference booklet,[14] as well as the reports held by the Comintern mention there were 221 delegates present representing 104 OSR groups and factory committees, 322 affiliated unions, and a total of 267,000 workers nationwide. In his discussion of the topic, however, Rafael Cruz mentions only 175,000 as the total, including OSR members as well as unions affiliated with the Red International of Labor Unions (RILU).[15] A vast majority of these individuals were based in Madrid and Sevilla and would form the nucleus of the soon to be launched communist trade union, the CGTU Regardless of the exact figure, and the far larger numbers of UGT and CNT members in 1932, these numbers are significant, especially for Madrid and for the Andalusian regional capital. In addition, the frantic activism of the OSR operatives, in stark contrast with the passivity and lack of commitment of large numbers of UGT members (more on this below), allowed the OSR groups to punch well above their weight.[16]

Secondly, the multiple references to the "autonomous" Federation of Tobacco Workers, the Federación Tabaquera Española (FTE) and its president, communist party member Severino Chacon are worth commenting on. Fernando del Rey wrote a very helpful survey of the history of the FTE, with a focus on the republican period and its progressive radicalization which, del Rey argues, began in the run-up to the February 1936 elections.[17] In the conference proceedings we have just mentioned, the references to Chacón begin with the account of the opening session, in which the bureau proposes Chacón as president. Although initially rejecting the role, Chacón ends up accepting it after the intervention of Milla, a delegate from the printers in Alicante. During the second session, Chacón proposed that unions such as the one he represented should have the overall leadership in the unity movement and suggested that personal attacks against UGT and CNT leaders were likely to render the OSR groups' revolutionary propaganda fruitless. The leading role of Chacón in the conference is not surprising considering the significant part the FTE played in Comintern strategy in Spain, a fact largely ignored in the historiography. In August 1934, a report of the Spanish section to the ECCI addressed communist work in the reformist and autonomous unions.[18] The situation, affirmed the report, required the party to be extremely audacious in the application of its tactics. First, continued the report, a document should be published calling all proletarian organizations to unite. "This document should come from the Tobacco Federation. Later, the [communist] C.G.T.U. will join that campaign." This is one of the clearest instances of the Lenin and Stalin-prescribed conveyor belt tactic in operation in Spain in our period. In January 1935, as we detailed in previous chapters, the FTE was in the very first list of organizations whose support was obtained for the popular front by Comintern representative "Albert."[19] In June 1935, Henry Barbusse likewise secured FTE endorsement of the Concentración Popular, along with leading socialists and republicans.[20] It appears, therefore, that before it joined UGT in 1936, the FTE was autonomous in name only, and became, between 1932 and 1935, a potent tool of the Comintern's strategy for the infiltration and control of Spain's unions.

A Veritable Invasion: OSR Groups as Experienced by UGT Leaders

All the above notwithstanding, one may still ask to what extent this subversive communist work in the socialist and other trade unions was wishful thinking, made much of only by right-wing conspiracy theorists past and present. How were OSR activities perceived by UGT union leaders in Madrid, Sevilla, or Oviedo in 1932 to 1935? How successful were these subversive efforts in driving division and radicalization among socialist tram, metal, or printing unions? For a UGT leadership who, unsure of its support for what they saw as a bourgeois republic, struggled to manage hundreds of thousands of new members, the proof of the pudding was in the eating.

UGT experienced dramatic growth after the arrival of the II Republic, with 2,000 new members joining daily since its proclamation on April 14. From 500,000 members in July 1931 the astounding figure of 1,000,000 was reached a year later, thus becoming the largest union in the country.[21] When UGT leader Largo Caballero joined the republican government as labor minister in 1931, he immediately expressed his intentions to exploit his position to grow UGT membership. Greeting the workers who had come to welcome him to the ministry, he walked under their red flags and addressed them from the steps of the ministry building:

> In order to serve the republic with efficiency and independence ... you should join the U.G.T. and thus defend the common interest on which you depend ... And one final warning: The U.G.T. will organize the civil servants with itself and against those who oppose it.[22]

While Madrid was the region with the largest UGT membership, amounting to one third of the total, there was a UGT-affiliated union in every single province by 1932. Explosive growth, however, came at a price. As of 1933, only 40 percent of the members were paying their union fees, and the educational level, degree of commitment, and political motivations of the large masses of new joiners were perceived to be a mixed bag.[23] Further, as of 1932, 25 percent of UGT members were unemployed. In addition, the leadership of the union evidenced deep divisions as early as 1932, with heated debates over the correctness of socialist collaboration with a parliamentary regime threatening to break up the organization. Lastly, as Manuel Redero has shown,[24] the organizational changes the UGT leadership attempted to implement to increase the cohesion of the ranks were openly resisted by many of the unions nationwide. These issues were not to be easily resolved and rendered the union vulnerable in several ways. A review of the various UGT press organs in 1932–3 is an open window into the successful utilization of these vulnerabilities by the OSR groups.

In January 1932, writing in the organ of the UGT metal workers union, *El Metalúrgico*, a writer laments that union members are allowing themselves to be seduced by the proponents of the united front. It is Moscow, argues the author, who stands behind this ongoing effort to divide the socialist unions.

Communist-controlled factory committees do not seek the unification of existing unions, but their break-up and the creation of a new, communist union.[25] The press reported on the Metal Workers Union OSR's activities shortly after in connection with its leader Enrique Castro. Expressing its support for the striking food workers, Castro attacked the joint arbitration committees (mixed juries) created by the socialist minister Largo Caballero, as tools of the bosses, and affirmed that the government was regularly working to suppress worker rights. He asserted that the opposition group he represented would always stand side by side with the workers and ended his speech with a "¡viva la huelga!" (long live the strike!).[26]

One month later, José Gonzalo Aceña, leader of the UGT-affiliated Madrid tram workers union, addressed the members in an editorial published on *Transporte*. Gonzalo Aceña urged the members, in light of the important gains achieved by workers in the first few months of the republican regime, to keep working hard and increasing production, even if the socialist republic they looked forward to had not yet arrived. Above all, he concluded, "nada de tácticas y doctrinas utópicas."[27] We might be revolutionaries, he added, but always hand in hand with reality. Ángel Peña, whose article shares the front page of *Transporte* with Gonzalo Aceña's, zeroes in on the issue of "extremists" infiltrated in the tram workers union. By claiming a far-left radical vision, writes Peña, these individuals gain the confidence of careless tram workers. Once they are in, they begin to speak against the leadership and propose the most radical measures, which only benefit the bosses. Peña asks his readers to exercise caution going forward and investigate carefully the identity of those working to lead the membership away from the single path set by the leaders of UGT and the socialist party.

In April 1932, the leading editorial of *Fuerza*, the monthly publication of the National Federation of Transport in Spain, mentioned the enemy by name and demanded its members work to eliminate the threat it represents. In its inaugural issue, the leaders of *Fuerza* affirmed their identification with the Russian revolution and their belief that capitalism is being defeated. However, continues the editorial, while in the fight with the bosses the cry will always be "proletarians unite!," when it comes to the "fracciones de oposición" that seek to divide by means of demagoguery, "we will work to exterminate them."[28]

In June 1932, internal battles between OSR groups and the majority took place in the UGT-affiliated publishing workers union ("artes blancas" or "arte de imprimir"). The proposals from the OSR members to support the communist-led single front, and to block socialist government ministers from participating in the executive of UGT, were defeated after a debate. The vote was followed by a heated exchange in which the OSR attacked the leadership for refusing to participate in a march in support of the USSR. The leadership, including Ramón Lamoneda, responded that such a march was merely using the Soviet Union as a ploy to attack the republic, and that the OSR should not, on one hand, attack the socialist ministers, and request their support on the other.[29] A month later, the popular daily *La Libertad* published a summons of the Artes Blancas OSR to its youth organization calling them to a meeting at their headquarters on La Madera 45 in Madrid's popular Malasaña district.[30] In his 1935 volume, former interior minister (Ministro de Gobernación) Rafael Salazar Alonso highlighted the printers union as one of the UGT labor organizations in which "reformists" had been replaced by philo-communists under the leadership of Agapito García Atadell and Alejandro Pizarro.[31]

In October 1932, the official organ of the UGT-affiliated national union of postal workers detailed the manner in which its OSR group was using its assets and capabilities in the union to sow division and shape the messages delivered to the membership. On the occasion of the II congress of urban postal workers, a member of the OSR had been invited to serve as stenographer and editor of the record of proceedings. Instead of producing an accurate record of the discussions and speeches, this individual had eliminated from the record the details the OSR had no interest in, while including detailed accounts of heated debates that led to "unfortunate scenes." The result was a report that highlighted division and the role of the OSR as the truly revolutionary elite in the union. Antonio Segura responds, representing the majority, that the communist comrades are but a cog in the "Bolshevik machine" whose aim is merely to "divide and conquer."[32] Yet, the damage was done and was substantial, especially in terms of the nationwide reach of the falsified stenograph. That an OSR operative had been elected to manage the minutes of the meeting was, perhaps, the most revealing detail in this story.

In late 1932, the leadership of the tram workers union editorialized again on the challenges posed by the OSR groups in its midst, in a manner that reveals the magnitude of the problem. On the front page, Francisco Rebollo laments that the damaging effect of the "ultra-revolutionary opposition" in the union has been demonstrated time and time again. The OSR creates cells and reproduces among the membership, using all the means at their disposal to sow division, always backing the critical or discontented members in their attacks against the leadership. Rebollo issues an all-too-familiar call to be alert and protect the ranks against the communist threat from within. The cartoon published on the cover tells the story in an engaging and humorous manner: on one side, a tram worker appears to be stumbling. On the other, facing him, two OSR members holding a hammer and sickle stand in a threatening pose. The text in popular Madrid dialect reads: "[w]ow guys, if I don't watch out you would have gotten me. Thankfully I have a potent sense of smell and knew you were coming. By the way, don't play with these weapons you got there, 'cause you could hurt yourselves darlings."[33]

The width and depth of the influence of the OSR infiltration in UGT was acknowledged in *El Socialista*, the official organ of the socialist party in January 1933. In preparation for an extraordinary meeting of the Grupos Sindicales Socialistas, an organization re-launched by the UGT leadership in 1931 as a protection force again infiltration, the socialist party wanted to issue its own assessment and advice. The union opposition groups, affirmed the article, follow the tactics of the "Russian international" [*sic*], which never enjoyed a more opportune moment to pursue their aims. An honest and objective assessment of the workers organizations associated with UGT, continued *El Socialista*, reveals that the OSR agitation "reached *all* of them" [my emphasis].[34] The piece went on to label the work of the OSR groups in the "weaker unions" as an invasion, with the shoemakers' union as a paradigm. That union, affirmed *El Socialista* in January 1933, was in the hands of a board of directors made up of infiltrators whose primary aim had been a "senseless" shoemakers' strike, a conflict that remained open at the time of writing.

Strike action, especially violent, picket-driven general strikes and "solidarity strikes" of one industrial sector with an action initiated by another, was one of the constant objectives pursued by OSR leadership within UGT This was in line with the reports sent to the Comintern by the Spanish section in 1931–4, in which the number of strikes was mentioned as a key performance indicator and the growing trend of strikes was detailed province by province. Thus, while in 1929 the number of strikes was below 100 in the country, in the "years of the revolution" the numbers increased dramatically, with 710 in 1931, 830 in 1932, and 1499 in 1933.[35] General strikes, as opposed to pragmatic ones aimed at the attainment of concrete improvements in labor conditions, were seen as an essential means of bringing the "growing contradictions" of the capitalist system to a boil. It was a potent demonstration of the old Leninist principle, "chem khuzhe, chem luchshe, [the worse it is, the better it is]." Such a prioritization of general strikes was a faithful implementation of the guidelines of the Trade Union Commission of the ECCI in 1929, which stipulated that, as an instrument of class warfare, communist parties should ensure that strikes took on an increasingly revolutionary and political character.[36] In early 1934, the ECCI wrote to the Central Committee of its Spanish section, requiring them to send additional students to the International Lenin School, especially those who were members of UGT and CNT. Participation in violent strikes and street battles was a prerequisite for acceptance.[37] By 1934, the leadership of UGT realized they had lost control of many of their unions, as the leadership often learned about new strikes only after they were launched, and a request was made for "solidarity." In the words of Bizcarrondo:

> The executives [of UGT] only learn of the existence of many of the strikes launched in 1934 after they had already started ... this is the case of the general strike declared on the 8th of September 1934 in Madrid, "without the UGT – stated a National Committee publication in 1936—having the slightest advance notice of its planning."[38]

Such an assessment would not have surprised the Comintern leadership or its Spanish section. In the September 1934 report to the ECCI we have already mentioned, the party refers to the "recent successes" of its work within UGT With a majority among key sections of the metal workers union, the opposition managed to secure the reelection of the strike committee, in which seven out of sixteen members, including the chairman, were infiltrated communists.[39] In his retrospective report on the October 1934 armed insurrection, Victorio Codovilla commented that experience had already shown that when communists join the reformist unions they are able to find the support of the revolutionary workers, and soon get elected into the leadership. Further, Codovilla explained, an *entente* exists in many UGT unions between their left wing and the infiltrated communists. A case in point, he continued, is the Madrid-based metal workers union, where a common list made up of socialists and communists "are about to take over the leadership."[40] A set of directives issued by the Comintern to Spain two months later affirmed the time had come to begin merging the small CGTU unions with UGT and to initiate a final push for full merger under communist control.[41]

Starting in early 1934, references to OSR groups[42] in both the UGT press and the general press become far less frequent, with a few references to OSR groups in the socialist student union, the FUE, and one reference in the run-up to the October 1934 insurrection. In late summer, OSR groups within UGT were at the forefront of the provocation of general strikes,[43] many of which, as we have seen, were launched without the knowledge of the top UGT leadership. A September 1934 ECCI report provides additional insights into the success of OSR operations within key UGT unions at that time.

> The revolutionary opposition in the unions (revprofoppozitsiya) has had a particularly successful experience in the Madrid subway. The revolutionary

opposition won the leadership of the union and closed a collective agreement that satisfied the workers. We also have influence in the most important U.G.T. unions including printers, metal workers and transport ... we have two persons in the leadership of the builder's union. In the autonomous union of street vendors and in the day laborers of the garment section we have all the leadership in our hands.[44]

Once the Comintern approved the communist participation in the socialist-led Alianzas Obreras and their armed insurrection of October 1934, the communists saw the alianzas, "the embryo of soviets in Spain,"[45] as their best opportunity to consolidate and grow their conquest of both socialist youth and UGT. Indeed, in January 1935 Codovilla informed the ECCI in Moscow that, as a result of their role in the insurrection, especially among Asturian miners, the communists were no longer seen as the late-coming "poor relative" in the Alianzas and their position in them and among the socialists nationwide had been significantly strengthened.[46] A number of fighters in Oviedo had been card-carrying OSR members, and the coordinated, networked effort of all party organizations, especially the OSR groups, was critical in the process toward a full merger of the unions after the insurrection.[47] As of mid-1935, once the communists had secured the leadership of the alianzas liaison committees, they controlled 75 percent of local alianzas and five of the sixteen provincial ones, according to their report to the VII Congress of the Comintern in July.[48] The path to CGTU—U-GT fusion was all but clear of obstacles.

In October 1935, Leoncio Pérez, writing for *Transporte* from the Madrid Modelo jail, reflected on the imminent merger of socialist and communist unions in the context of the theses of the Comintern's VII Congress, held three months earlier with a socialist delegation present. Pérez acknowledged the urgency of trade union consolidation, a lesson drawn from the October insurrection. He believed the communists had been wrong to create the minuscule CGTU and quoted approvingly Wilhelm Pieck's statement, "It has been a mistake to transform the OSR groups into separate unions." With the changes he believed the VII Comintern Congress had implemented in its policy toward socialist unions, Pérez saw few if any real obstacles in the path to full merger of UGT and CGTU. As Caballero affirmed repeatedly, the socialist party had by 1935 reached all but full ideological alignment with Soviet communism.[49] In the crucible of the preparation and launch of armed insurrection, the OSR organization had been instrumental in moving violent revolution from the margins to the heart of UGT's agenda. The final merger of UGT and CGTU, achieved in late 1935, was largely the result of a multifaceted Comintern effort, with Socorro Rojo Internacional (International Red Aid) in 1935 having a leading role (see Chapter 2 on this), and direct involvement of Comintern agents Codovilla and Ercoli in negotiations with del Vayo, Caballero, and other socialist leaders. However, the tenacious work of the OSR groups within UGT for over three years, exploiting existing divisions and exacerbating revolutionary sentiment and action, was a crucial piece of this preparatory communist work not sufficiently acknowledged in the historiography.

Conclusion—Communist Trade Union Work in Europe in the Interwar Period: A Blind Spot in the Literature

As Helen Graham noted, the conspiratorial work of OSR groups did not end with the merger of the unions in late 1935, to the dismay of many in UGT, and drove a wedge between socialists and communists once the Civil War started. The more moderate socialists in UGT, however, had by April 1936 to resort to the language of humble begging in their appeals for the communist "brethren" to cease their operations as an active opposition within the union, and pursue instead the common good.[50]

In the larger European context, the pioneering work of Holger Weiss,[51] published in 2021 with a focus on Scandinavia, and that of Campbell and McIlroy for the UK (2018)[52] reveal a gap in the scholarly discussion of communist revolutionary opposition groups across the continent in our period. Weiss details the two-part Comintern strategy for the infiltration and control of socialist harbor and maritime worker unions. First, communist fractions within the target union were to create cells that would form the core of the revolutionary opposition groups. These groups were tasked with applying the united front from below tactic, that is, to win over the workers by turning them away from their reformist leaders. Secondly, Moscow would enable and support the groups in their deployment of agitation and propaganda as the means of controlling and growing the groups within the unions. Given the global reach of this effort and its substantial success in unions in Germany, Britain, Greece, and the United States, it is surprising that, until now, research in this topic was, in Weiss's words, "very rudimentary." Campbell and McIlroy's study of the communist party of Great Britain's infiltration into both the Labour Party and its trade unions from 1934 through 1937 also leverages Comintern archival documentation to correct a long-standing sanitization and downplaying, if not downright omission of communist subversion of the Labour party and its unions.[53]

All the above, therefore, confirms the existence of a time-honored blind side in the historiography of labor movements in the interwar period. As Haslam has shown, cold war polemics have often resulted in the neglect of the memory of Soviet communism as a persistent threat to the West before the outbreak of the Second World War, a neglect Haslam's latest tome is intended to correct.[54] Yet, in his chapter on Spain, Haslam fails to take full account of subversive Comintern activity in Spain, especially since 1931, which achieved substantial penetration of cultural and sports organizations, of the armed forces, and of the socialist trade union UGT. Our research has shown that the Comintern-designed and -supported deployment of revolutionary opposition groups within UGT unions is an essential step in the process of bolshevization of the Spanish socialist union in 1932–5 that deserves far more attention that it has hereto received.

6

They Paid for Our Olympiad

The July 1936 Popular Olympiad in Barcelona as a Case Study in Comintern Mass Organizational Operations

Introduction

In his brief discussion of the Barcelona Popular Olympiad of July 1936, Gregorio Luri[1] refers to the contemporary romantic and idealized interpretations of that event, often dressed in various shades of Catalan nationalism. Thus, anti-fascist groups, progressive Catalan sports organizations, and the regional Generalitat government would have joined together to defend equality, fraternity, and peace from the attack on those values the Berlin Olympics represented. The crucial question, however, suggests Luri, is to differentiate the individuals and groups displayed in the shop window from those effectively running the show.

The work of André Gounot in the Sportintern (the Comintern-run international sports organization) archives,[2] published in journal articles and monographs over two decades, has been a monumental milestone in the scholarly conversation about the Sportintern and its 1936 Barcelona event. Gounot has established that the Sportintern instructed the Communist-controlled (as of 1934) Federación Cultural Deportiva Obrera (FCDO) in April 1936 to organize the Popular Olympiad. In the same month, Gounot has shown the Barcelona-based Comitè Català pro Esport Popular (CCEP) was writing to the Sportintern[3] to inform its leaders the event was being planned and to request additional assistance. Further, Gounot has shown that a reference to the "Olimpiada Popular" appeared already in the Sportintern organ Internationale Sportsrundschau with date April 20, 1936, that is, before the CCEP announced the event publicly. Lastly, Gounot showed that the Sportintern appointed Fritz Lesch to manage the international dimension of the Popular Olympiad and Spanish communist youth member Andrés Martín to lead the project locally in Spain.

Curiously, Carles Santacana and Xavier Pujadas, publishing a second edition of their volume in 2006,[4] still argue that the Popular Olympiad was fundamentally a grassroots, progressive Catalan event, with the Comintern merely supporting what was initiated by a moderate left-wing Catalan sporting movement. Heavily dependent on Santacana and Pujadas and writing in 2020, James Stout argues that "nowhere in the documentary record is there any evidence of [the Popular Olympics being a creature of Communist sporting bodies]."[5] Stout shows no evidence of having engaged with archival sources, therefore, it is difficult to imagine what might be the referent of "documentary record" in his statement. Further, Stout's volume is plagued by a number of fatal errors that suggest his understanding of the larger context is flawed.[6]

In this chapter, I will build on Gounot's findings on the basis of substantial additional material from the Gottwald and Ercoli secretariat sections of the RGASPI files, documentation from Spanish and British archives, and regular cross-references to period Spanish and French press. I am grateful to Professor Gounot for our dialogue during the writing of this chapter, which has enabled me to add to and strengthen his theses, as well as extend the discussion in the larger context of Comintern mass organizations in Spain. The documentation reveals a clear timeline of careful Comintern planning and instruction to a significantly greater degree than was shown by Gounot. The archives and period press further show that Comintern instructions were implemented, often within days of their reception, by local communist officials working within the sports organizations FCDO and CCEP in Madrid and Barcelona, respectively. Full 1936 reports written a year later reveal with surprising transparency what the Sportintern saw as the successes of the year, as well as the names and organizations of those who were, official labels notwithstanding, working for Moscow. The material we will discuss demonstrates the CCEP can no longer be seen as anything other than a Comintern/Sportintern front, exploiting, as per the Comintern playbook for mass organization work, preexisting local organizations of various types, but utilizing them successfully to serve a larger Comintern objective. That final objective, the archival material confirms time and time again, was not, fundamentally, to boycott the Berlin Olympics. The true strategic objective of this effort was to use, once more, the compelling slogans of anti-fascism in order to bring the ripe-for-revolution million-person Spanish sports movement under communist control. Lastly, the original vision of the Sportintern as a classic Comintern mass organization whose aim it was to build a reserve of military-age fighters will be shown to have been realized in the days following the military insurgency in Barcelona, starting on July 19, 1936. The archival material reveals why, in the final analysis, hundreds, perhaps over one thousand "athletes," were able to become armed guerrillas from one day to the next. In the words of FCDO president Álvaro Menendez, they had been trained, both physically and politically, to make that transition.

Sportintern in the Context of Comintern Mass Organizations in Spain 1931–6

In an October 1935 report, the Executive Committee of the Communist International (ECCI) detailed the critical importance of mass organizations for Comintern strategy in every country in which it operated. Under the leadership of Czech communist Klement Gottwald, the Propaganda and Mass Organizations Secretariat's fundamental objective was to support the communist parties in their ideological fight and in their revolutionary activity within mass organizations, so as to ensure full compliance with ECCI policies.[7] Mass organizations[8] were designed to appear innocuous, non-partisan, and welcomed all proletarian and petit bourgeois men, women and youth of good will. Many of these, often referred to by outsiders as "front organizations," were created and managed from the start by the Comintern: International Red Aid, Friends of the Soviet Union, and the myriad of "anti-fascist" committees run by the "Münzenberg Trust" in Paris. In other cases, communists were instructed to identify, infiltrate, and control non-communist mass organizations in domains such as sports, peace, and national independence or separatist movements. In countries such as France and Spain, several Comintern-run mass organizations boasted memberships in the tens of thousands and became by 1935 the main body of a Comintern iceberg, its true size and impact underestimated to this day.

As we have shown in Chapter 1, as of 1933 the Comintern and its Spanish section were running in Spain Red Aid (Socorro Rojo Internacional), Friends of the Soviet Union (FSU, in Spanish, Amigos de la Unión Soviética), and multiple versions of anti-fascist committees that rivaled those of any other European country. According to a July 1935 report[9] produced by FSU leader, the British communist Albert Inkpin, Spain was second only to France in FSU membership with 20,100 individual members to France's 25,000. Holland was a distant third at 12,500, with England at 8,000. Inkpin was satisfied that, thanks to its nonpartisan approach, FSU had become a true mass organization. We have also discussed the millions of pesetas that Red Aid poured into Spain to support a massive campaign in favor of the October 1934 insurrectionists as well as to fund the

Popular Front electoral campaign, becoming indispensable to the leadership of the socialist party, PSOE. The Anti-Fascist Committee was launched in Spain in the summer of 1933 with direct involvement of Comintern emissaries Henri Barbusse and Ellen Wilkinson, and Willi Münzenberg would report a few months later on the positive return on investment this trip had brought to the Comintern.[10] Comintern front organizations in Spain, combined with the effective penetration of socialist and independent trade unions, extended communist power and influence in the country well beyond the apparently insignificant numbers of PCE members.[11]

Part and parcel of the Comintern mass organization strategy in Spain, as it was elsewhere, is what Spaniards refer to in the popular dictum "throw the stone and hide the hand that threw it." This is a reference to the "front" in front organizations, the flower and smiling children—laden façade in the Potemkin village. Thus, as we discussed in Chapter 2, when International Red Aid wanted to begin a process of exploiting victimhood and anti-fascist narratives to bring all prisoner aid organizations under its control, they launched the initiative and quickly moved away from the visible leading role. Further, as internal PCE documents from the period reveal, Red Aid made a significant effort to ensure its leadership included socialist party members throughout Spain, and members of the nationalist Esquerra Republicana in the Catalan region.[12] An initial launch of "Women against War and Fascism" with Red Aid visibly involved and the republican Dolores Merás as coordinator, was turned, two days later, into "Asociación Pro Infancia Obrera" headed by Dolores Merás and with no reference to Red Aid or the Word Committee. In an internal document providing instructions to the Spanish section, Red Aid was explicit: where our operations are not possible because of police or judicial problems, "it is necessary to organize under a different form and name, including sowing clubs to repair clothes for the children, patronage groups for specific Asturian villages, etc."[13]

Since its creation during the III Congress of the Comintern in 1921, the Red Sport International or Sportintern[14] was conceived as a mass organization whose aim was to infiltrate and control reformist, worker, and bourgeois sports organizations to bring them under communist control. The Sportintern existed from the start in the "interest of world revolution"[15] and was driven by the realization that the sport movement "in the hands of the bourgeoisie, is a wide reserve for bourgeois armies"[16] and must, therefore, become a high-priority target for communist mass organization work. Success in this effort would mean that European workers would become well-trained fighters in future revolutionary armies.[17] As we will show below, the revolutionary raison d'être and aims of the Sportintern remained unchanged in the early years of the Popular Front period, the focus of our study. As a true Comintern mass organization, it always presented itself to prospective members as independent, but this nonpartisanship was merely a façade, as internal documents openly stated.[18] While the lower-level members were allowed to focus on the technicalities and practice of sports, all of the middle- and higher-level leadership were communist party members reporting regularly to Moscow. In a May 1936 report detailing ongoing negotiations with their socialist sports counterpart, the Sportintern listed its own personnel involved in the work, including the Spaniard Andrés Martín, adding in relation to the entire list, "all Communist party members."[19] It fell upon these leaders to ensure local Sportintern sections achieved the strategic objectives of the Sportintern and its parent organization, the Communist International.

Sports as "a Weapon in the Fight against Reaction": The October 1935–April 1936 Sportintern Resolutions regarding the Tasks for Spain

André Gounot and Francisco de Luis[20] have traced the process of communist infiltration and control of the Spanish Federación Cultural Deportiva y Obrera (FCDO), which culminated in it joining the Sportintern in 1934. This is a process we will not retrace here. The significance of the merger of socialist and communist sports organizations under communist control, however, cannot be overstated. As of June 1933, the FCDO boasted 10,000 members,[21] that is, roughly equivalent to the total number of PCE members just a year earlier.[22] According to a 1937 Sportintern report we shall discuss below, FCDO membership had grown to 50,000 nationwide by the spring of 1936.[23] Gounot also introduced us to the April 1936 Sportintern resolution which communicated a number of tasks to the FCDO, including the organization of "Spanish popular games" (spanischer Volkspiele) to coincide with the Berlin games. The resolution document, however, together with a prior one issued in October 1935, provides many other insights into the vision, strategy, and level of control the Sportintern had over the FCDO in early 1935 that are worth detailing.

The October 1935 "Decision of the Secretariat of the ECCI on the matter of sport activity"[24] contains the first instance we have seen in the documents of an explicit instruction to the sections, including the Spanish party, to begin a campaign against the Berlin Olympiad. The communist parties of the United States, Great Britain, France, Sweden, Czechoslovakia, Finland, Poland,

and Spain are requested to provide suggestions as to how they will link their campaign against Berlin with the struggle to free Ernst Thälmann, the German communist leader imprisoned by the Nazi regime. Additionally, continues the instruction, local sections should explain how they will connect the campaign with the strengthening of the influence of communist parties and communist youth organizations in the leading sports movements in their countries. The French party is also tasked with the organization of a committee and congress, to be held in Paris in early 1936, to gather leading international sports people, both bourgeois and proletarian, "without distinction of political opinions." The participants must all be against the celebration of the Olympic Games in Berlin, and a Paris-based Committee, with the United States, British, and other nationalities in its board, will steer the event under the leadership of the French Communist Party leader Duclos. This is, in all likelihood, a first reference to the "Comité International pour la Défense de l'idée Olympique" which was created in Paris in December 1936, and to an associated congress that was held in the French capital in June 1936. Gounot already pointed out this committee and event were a Sportintern creation, with a Spanish version of the committee being announced shortly after by communist organ *Mundo Obrero* in Spain.[25] We now have full visibility into the Soviet design and management of both. In addition to the forward-looking instruction we have just mentioned, a retrospective 1937 Sportintern report never mentioned by Gounot was explicit in this regard:

> To better develop the work among the progressive sports people and join all forces against the Hitler Olympics the international committee "Fair Play—For the Defense of the Olympic Idea" was created. The Sportintern applies in this case for the first time a new method of work ... the committee acts as an independent association.[26]

Thus, far from being part of a global, grassroots "boycott movement" as Santacana and Pujadas and Stout argue,[27] the committee and associated congress were Comintern mass organizational agit-prop at its best. Consequently with its role as creator and sustainer of the committee, the Comintern issued several instructions to its sections throughout late 1935 and early 1936 to grow, strengthen or leverage their local versions of it.[28] The list of the Spanish delegation in the Paris congress should clear any doubts as to the overall Comintern management of the event: Ramón Mercader (of the youth organization of the Spanish Communist Party) representing CCEP, Andrés Martín (like Mercader, youth of the PCE), representing the FCDO, and Jaume Miravitlles (Esquerra Republicana de Catalunya, ERC, but also head of Red Aid in Catalonia, the

Thälmann Committee, and later also vice president of Friends of the Soviet Union, Catalonia branch), representing the regional Catalan government, the Generalitat.[29] ERC's connections with various communist organizations grew steadily throughout our period. As we shall see in our final section, the Esquerra Republicana youth organization had, by the spring of 1936, been integrated into the unified socialist and communist militias. As they followed these developments, some of the Labour leaders in the UK smelled a rat, as they had done with the "British parliamentary delegation" to Spain in late 1934 (see Chapter 2 on this). The British Trade Unions Congress, while not aware of all the details, expressed its suspicions that this was, in fact, a communist-run organization in which its members should not participate.[30] The requirement to connect the anti-Berlin campaigns with the already existing Thälmann Committee, chaired by Willi Münzenberg from Paris, was soon implemented in Spain. The Comitè Català pro Esport Popular (more on the CCEP below) began promoting the "Copa Thälmann," also referred to as "Pro-Thälmann Festival" in early April 1936, and the event was held in Barcelona on April 12.[31]

The April 1936 Sportinten resolution regarding tasks for Spain, part of a larger document detailing instructions for several of its country sections, is transparently clear about Moscow's vision and goals for the FCDO after the victory of the Popular Front in February. The document begins with a retrospective analysis of what it calls "the period of reaction," that is, the two-year period of conservative-republican government in Spain from November 1933 through February 1936. During this period, the FCDO did not pay enough attention, argues the report, to the "development of the worker sports movement as a weapon in the fight against reaction." Even after the reception of the October 1935 instruction to launch an anti-Berlin Olympics campaign, the FCDO neglected to link that effort with the struggle against rection and thus failed at its most critical task: to isolate the reactionary elements and drive them out of Spanish sport. With the victory of the Popular Front, however, new opportunities existed to win over about a million athletes scattered in many associations and clubs in Spain. Among these, the lowest hanging fruit is perceived to be the socialist "Salud y Cultura" organization. The sporting youth of Spain, argues the report, are in a revolutionary mood, and the opportunity to win them over and merge them into the FCDO must now be seized. This "most important task" is fully aligned with the original vision of the Sportintern and its parent organization, the Communist International, and is meant to run in parallel with ongoing efforts to assimilate the socialist union UGT, the socialist youth, and the socialist and republican prisoner aid organizations. Existing anti-fascist sentiment, stirred up in large measure in Spain by Comintern-led and -funded activity,[32] had since 1933 been a potent means to achieve these aims. The 1936 Berlin Olympiad, a truly global event, presented an unprecedented opportunity to deploy the Comintern's anti-fascist toolset in the context of the new Popular Front tactic. The 1937 retrospective Sportintern report reveals that this effort in Spain was deemed a great success, with the faithful implementation of Moscow's instructions resulting in further consolidation of sports organizations under communist control.

Specifically, the socialist "Salud y Cultura" organization operated in early 1936 in full unity of vision and action with the FCDO, fully focused on promoting the Popular Olympiad, even without an official merger of the two. As de Luis Martín has shown, already in 1934 Salud y Cultura's 5,000 members were under the influence of the revolutionary majority within the socialist youth who were pushing for unity with the communists.[33] With full control of a 55,000+ strong sporting movement in Spain under the banner of anti-fascism, the Sportintern was soon able to count Spain among the countries in which "unity of organization" had been achieved. On this basis, as the Sportintern prepared for the International Workers Olympiad in Antwerp in 1937, it was able to treat the Soviet and Spanish teams as a group fully under its control. Thus, as the Sportintern negotiated with the Czech members of the socialist sports international, opposed to unity with its communist counterparts, the Sportintern noted in its report that the Czech do not object to the Soviet and Spanish sports teams being in Antwerp. The report adds that, at the request of the Sportintern, the Spanish comrades are utilizing their membership in large international organizations in the manner requested. As for the Catalan section, the CCEP reported back to Moscow that, after a successful 1936, "the whole Catalan youth" were behind them, and, consequently, all the sporting federations of Catalonia have made a choice to support the Worker Olympics in Antwerp.[34]

The leadership of the Sportintern then proceeded, within the April 1936 report, to communicate the most urgent tasks that the FCDO was obliged to carry out. The Spanish section was to demand of the Spanish Popular Front government that the 400,000 pts. that had been allocated to Spain's participation in the Berlin Olympic Games be withdrawn and used instead "for the development of Spanish sports" as understood by Sportintern. Further, the FCDO was to demand the dissolution of the Spanish Olympic Committee and to fight against the "reactionary leadership" of Spanish sports federations until its complete elimination from these. Finally, the directives document mentioned that the Spanish popular games should be held in the summer, coinciding with the Berlin Olympics. All progressive athletes from Spain, Catalonia, and other nations were to be invited, as well as, possibly, sports teams from the USSR. Everything should be done, concluded the document, to strengthen the overall leadership of the FCDO in Spain, and the Sportintern would assist in this as needed.

The correct dating of this document is a matter of some importance. Gounot had noted that the document has no date and provided his own estimate of March 1936.[35] However, once we read through the entire document, including the similar set of instructions sent to other countries, we note that the very first page, instructions, and tasks to the Swiss section, does bear a date of April 22, which clearly applies to the entire document. The first page of the instructions to Spain does show a stamped date, April 23, 1936. This, however, is the date of the entry of the document into the Comintern archival system, following standard procedure on Comintern paperwork. The usual scenario in the production of these texts is a team effort over several days, with drafts being produced in several languages and editors making handwritten corrections and notes until the final draft was ready for distribution, in this case, on April 22. As was usually the case, it appears the implementation of the Sportintern tasks for Spain began immediately after issuance. On April 23, the Esquerra Republicana de Catalunya organ, *La Humanitat*, published a letter it had received from the CCEP.[36] The letter was addressed to Manuel Azaña, President of the Council of Ministers, and requested that the 400,000 pts. ear-marked by the previous government for participation in the Berlin Olympics now be assigned to the "popular sport movement." Specifically, the letter requested that at least some of the funds be allocated to the Popular Olympiad to be held in Barcelona, "the first international manifestation of the popular sport movement." This timeline seems to indicate CCEP was, from its organization in April 1936 of the "Thälmann Cup," through its participation in the Paris event and the request for the government funds, following closely Sportintern instructions. The letter from the CCEP to the Sportintern dated also April 22 leaves little doubt about this (see note 3 in this chapter on this). Nevertheless, Santacana and Pujadas and Stout argue that the CCEP was essentially a popular Catalan sports organization representative of a nationalist and progressive civil society seeking to use popular sports to build a new Catalan nation. In the following section, we will bring additional archival material to bear on this matter that should, it is hoped, settle the issue.

An Endearing Catalan Façade: Comitè Català pro Esport Popular

In a discussion held at a Comintern ECCI meeting in May 1936, with PCE leader Jesús Hernandez presenting, and the panel made up of "Ercoli" (Togliatti), Dimitrov, Kuusinen, and other leaders, Ercoli was transparent in regard to the origin of the Popular Olympiad. Ercoli refers to Raymond Guyot, leader of the Communist Youth International (KIM) and says:

> The last question, which will be very interesting for Raymond is as follows. The [Spanish] Minister of Public Instruction, *following the request of our unified youth* (in reference to the merged socialist and communist youth, the JSU), has decided not to give a cent to the fascist Olympiad and to give the money for *our Olympiad* instead (400,000 pesetas), a national Olympiad which *will be sponsored* (patronnée)*by our youth*. This opens the possibility of forming a large mass organization with the backing of the Government [emphasis mine].[37]

As we have already seen, the communist youth leadership of the CCEP became apparent with the participation in the Paris event of both Ramon Mercader and Andrés Garcia representing CCEP and FCDO, respectively. In Ercoli's words, the request to the Spanish government to reassign the funding came from the unified youth. This is a reference to the Juvetudes Socialistas Unificadas (JSU), the merged communist and socialist youth under communist control that joined the Comintern's youth organization (KIM) in early 1936, after negotiations in Madrid and Moscow. The sponsorship, Ercoli adds, the patronage and assistance in the organization of the Olympiad, would also come from the JSU.

In the course of our research, we came across a reference to an interesting document[38] that was held by the Centro Documental de la Memoria Histórica in Salamanca until its transfer to the Arxiu Nacional de Catalunya in 2014. The document was captured in Barcelona by the insurgent forces after the fall of the city in January 1939, and delivered to the Political and Social section of the archives under the "Servicio de Recuperación de Documentos." The two-page document is entitled "Comitè Català pro Esport Popular" and is part of a larger file category of documents belonging to the Catalan section of the Juventud Socialista Unificada's executive committee in Barcelona. It appears to be an early, foundational document, written in Catalan and detailing the nature and aims of the Committee, with a list of programmatic tasks. The CCEP, affirms the text, aspires to pursue its objectives in close collaboration with the existing sports organizations and any others which are free from commercial interests and stand against fascism and war. Further, the authors continue, the CCEP will educate the sporting masses of Catalonia in the "political and cultural sport sense" to build a wall against the reactionary forces. The themes in this document are well-aligned with those penned by Andrés Martín and other JSU writers in the spring of 1936: anti-fascism, anti-capitalism, anti-war, equality and fraternity among all nations but belligerence against the reactionaries and fascists, etc. The provenance of this foundational CCEP document within JSU files thus confirms Ercoli's assertion that both the request for government funds and the "sponsorship" of the games came from the JSU, thus making this event, in his words, "our Olympiad."

The August 1937 retrospective Sportintern report on its activities in several countries in 1936 provides fascinating details on the CCEP officials who were reporting to Moscow as "comrades with the mandate of the party."[39] The report is based on a meeting held in Moscow during August 9–11, 1937. The meeting was attended in person by the Sportintern-associated organizations from several European countries, including delegates from both Valencia, the seat of the Republican government in 1937, and Barcelona. The two delegates from France, Delaune and Deschamps, were leaders of the Sportintern-led FSGT, though Deschamps remained a committed socialist party member. The delegate from Valencia was Álvaro Menendez, president of the FCDO, and the delegates from Barcelona were Francesc Parramon Cortina and Josep Verdera Casayas, both in the executive committee of the CCEP. Parramon and Verdera were not the men we may have considered the obvious CCEP choices to attend a Comintern meeting in Moscow, such as were Ramón Mercader, "Jordi" Martin (Hungarian Comintern agent Gyorgy Martin Hajdu) or Lluis Otin. Rather, these were two Catalan sports leaders associated officially with nationalist civil society organizations such as the Ateneu Popular and Athletic de Catalunya. Yet, they were considered by Moscow "comrades" coming to the headquarters of the Comintern, with the mandate of the communist party and the Sportintern, to report to the management on their activities in 1936. Parramon and Verdera delivered their report immediately after Menendez spoke for Spain and began by listing among the successes of the previous year the forming of the committee and the organization of the Popular Olympics "with the collaboration of the RSI (Red Sport International or Sportintern)." Later, the Catalan leaders mention the creation of the Commissariat for Physical Culture and Sport in Catalonia, which was in 1937, they add "under the exclusive control of the Communists." Led by Commissar "Dr. Seler Damiens" (in reference to Joan Soler i Damians), the commissariat had a number of parties and organizations represented in its board, including: two members from the regional Catalonian Government, the Generalitat; one member from the school council; five members from the sports associations; one member from the anarchist CNT; and one from the socialist union UGT Parramon and Verdera conclude, however, "therefore, there are eight communists who have complete control." Based on the organizations mentioned, the likely candidates for communist "control" are the two members from the Generalitat, the five members from the "sports organizations" and the member from UGT, the socialist union that had merged with its much smaller communist counterpart in 1936.

Interestingly, while ignoring all the Comintern archival material we have discussed, Santacana and Pujadas argue correctly that there was a clear continuity between the July 1936 CCEP and the later Catalan Commissariat for Physical Culture and Sport. Indeed, Santacana and Pujadas provide the names that were missing in the Sportintern report we have just referred to and help us complete the puzzle: Joan Soler and Jaume Miravitlles represented the Generalitat, Josep Verdera represented the UGT, and Francesc Parramon and five others represented the CCEP. Santacana and Pujades conclude that the strong presence of the CCEP was indicative of the "strong activity of the leaders of popular Catalonian sport and of the institutional recognition of this fact."[40] This assumption is consistent with the authors' belief that the strong presence in Catalonia of sport organizations linked with the Communist International was "null."[41] Yet, once the campaign to secure participants for the Barcelona games got under way, it was Hungarian Comintern agent Gyorgy "Jordi" Martin Hajdu who was signing the invitation letters as head of the Organizing Committee of the Popular Olympics (COOP).[42] After his death in the Extremadura front in August 1936, both Spanish and Soviet communist media referred to Andrés Martín as "the organizer of the Popular Olympiad."[43]

It is worth commenting briefly on two of the other well-known members of the CCEP executive who were not officially communists, at least in some of their public roles. The first, Jaume Miravitlles, represented the Generalitat and his party, ERC, but had also led, as mentioned above, multiple Comintern front organizations in Cataluña, including Red Aid and the Thälmann Committee. In a private letter to POUM leader Jordi Arquer after the war, Miravitlles admitted that "efectivamente, la olimpiada estaba *noyautee* por los comunistas ... el presidente Companys me designó a mi para evitar que la infiltración fuera demasiado acentuada."[44] This postwar letter written to a POUM leader needs to be taken with caution, but it should not be merely dismissed. Miravitlles offers

Arquer a curious explanation for his appointment, to say the least, given his involvement in at least two Comintern organizations in early 1936. The second CCEP executive member who was often identified with roles that were not explicitly communist in early 1936 was the leader of the Catalan commercial workers union, CADCI, Pere Aznar. However, Aznar was also a leader of the Partit Català Proletari, which joined the Comintern in 1936. Aznar, as leader of CADCI in 1934, used the union's office in Barcelona to host the communist-initiated gathering of all workers' parties[45] and shortly after as insurrectional headquarters until the insurgency was defeated by the government forces. Both Aznar and the CADCI had become living symbols of the October insurrectional movement.[46] For the Comintern, especially during the Popular Front period, exploiting individuals with multiple sociopolitical identities was part and parcel of its mass organizational strategy. Miravitlles and Aznar fit the bill to perfection.

It seems fair to propose at this point, based on the documentary evidence, that the CCEP was created by the merged Spanish socialist and communist youth organization, the JSU, with guidance from the Sportintern and the Comintern ECCI in March 1936. The JSU created the CCEP as a front organization to bring under communist control the masses of Catalan sports organizations, many of which already had communists of various backgrounds in their leadership teams. While the strategy of the Sportintern nationwide in Spain was to strengthen the leadership and enlarge the scope of the FCDO, Moscow fully understood the importance of Catalan separatism for its overall strategy. Since at least 1932, the Comintern had been instructing its Spanish section to agitate constantly so as to "widen the gap between the central Government and the oppressed nationalities,"[47] and to rally around itself the separatist forces, explaining to them that only soviet power would lead to independence. In the context of sports, the April 1936 instruction to Spain we have discussed above included a final paragraph requiring the creation of (underlined in the text) sports federations for every major sport, independent from the Spanish federation. The creation of the CCEP was fully aligned with this larger Comintern strategy for the Catalan region, and was perceived to be a requirement, given the need to enlist ERC, Estat Català, and other nationalist groups for the Popular Olympiad project. This approach also matched what the Comintern was pushing in Alsace-Lorraine and other European regions with some degree of separatist sentiment. With all the major elements in place, the process of securing the attendance to the Popular Olympiad of Sportintern sections from the United States to the Soviet Union could begin.

Athletes to Fighters in a Day: Participant Profiles and the Raison d'être of the Sportintern

In a June 1933 letter from the Spanish Communist Party to "la casa," that is, Comintern headquarters in Moscow, a Spanish party leader begins by writing that he hopes Andrés is still there, so he can provide additional details on the topics the writer is addressing in the letter. Andrés is a reference to Andrés Martín del Llano, the communist youth leader who would later head the FCDO and Popular Olympiad project. Martín traveled to Moscow in 1933 where he studied, worked, fell in love, and in 1935 attended the International Lenin School, where he was trained on communist mass organizations, Leninist-Stalinist doctrine, and in the practice of subversion and armed struggle.[48] If not before, Martín would have been back in Spain in March 1936, as the Comintern instructed all Spanish immigrants to return to Spain after the Popular Front victory, including those attending school in Moscow. Martín was an ideal candidate to hold executive roles in both Sportintern and the FCDO in Spain. His unimpeachable proletarian background, leadership in the youth organization, and advanced training in Moscow enabled the Comintern to place upon him a level of responsibility not often entrusted to a twenty-four-year-old.[49]

The FCDO joined the Sportintern in January 1934. At about the same time, its socialist members began planning, acquiring weapons, and training their members for armed insurrection, the uprising that would break out in Asturias, Catalonia, and elsewhere in October 1934. In his 1937 retrospective report to the Sportintern, FCDO president Álvaro Menendez admitted openly that before 1934 his organization had been weak, small in numbers and plagued by sectarianism. The mentions of the October insurrection in speeches and writings of both FCDO and the socialist sports organization "Salud y Cultura" as a key reference and milestone of the proletarian sports movement in Spain were numerous. Grupo Alpino, for example, held an "October Cup" to remember the insurrection and to express its adherence to the Soviet 1917 revolution.[50] The Popular Oympiad "Manifest" would include a reference to the "heroic fight" of the Catalan people for their freedom, and CCEP executive member Pere Aznar was a veteran of the fighting on the streets of Barcelona. As de Luis Martín has shown, the October fighting gave the leadership and members of FCDO a clear bellicose outlook that would only grow in intensity after the Popular Front came to power.

The 150,000-strong JSU organization,[51] to which Andres Martín belonged, became the source of a vast majority of Spanish participants in the Popular

Olympiad, with its organ, *Juventud*, publishing front-page appeals and moving its operation to Barcelona for the event.[52] Some of the young participants achieved fame in the days before the event, and José Palma Leon provides an interesting example. A young blacksmith from near Sevilla, José Palma had never practiced any sports. The announcement of the Popular Olympiad, however, inspired him to take a large iron wheel, use it as a sort of unicycle without pedals and travel to Barcelona via Madrid, to the delight of local newspapers. On July 19, once fighting broke out in Barcelona, Palma took up arms and joined the first militias battling the military insurgency in the city. A year later Palma would be killed in action in the Madrid front, with *La Voz* running a story on his iron wheel and participation in the Barcelona Olympiad.[53] There are many well-known accounts of young participants in the Popular Olympiad who, when fighting broke out, left shorts or track suites behind and picked up rifles and machine guns. Testimonies indicating numbers of popular Olympians who became fighters range, however, from single individuals[54] to reports of large groups forming full infantry companies[55] to "many" of the athletes present in Barcelona.[56]

In light of the documentary evidence we have already discussed, this smooth transition made sense. The Sportintern's foundational vision was to capture for Communism the legions of young men in military age who were being lured by bourgeois organizations and turn them instead into a reserve force awaiting the ripening of revolution. In the first ever joint rally of the unified socialist and communist youth, the JSU, some 6,000 young men, roughly half an infantry division size, marched in uniform and tight military formation. In a fascinating article held at the Spanish Communist Party Archives entitled "What the popular army owes the Spanish youth," that event is discussed at some length. The article mocks the centrist socialist Indalecio Prieto, who, in early 1936 ridiculed the military training and parades such as the one mentioned. It further attacks those who believed the JSU was becoming reformist and losing its revolutionary zeal, when they witnessed the formation of sports clubs for the youth. We gave the critics a definitive answer, concludes the article, when those clubs were emptied on July 18, 1936, and "the totality of the members" picked up rifles to fight fascism.[57] The leader of the MAOC militias, most of whose members were also in the JSU, wrote to its cadres in April 1936 that they should "ingresar en las entidades o clubs deportivos con fines de instrucción y preparación."[58] In Catalonia, the nationalist youth organization Joventuts d'Esquerra Republicana Estat Català was, by the spring of 1936, fully integrated into the MAOC.[59]

According to internal Sportintern reports,[60] over 2,000 foreign athletes reached Barcelona in time for the scheduled start of the Olympiad on July 19.

Many testimonies are known of individuals and groups of these foreigners who made a similar smooth transition from the track to the barricade. Women such as the young Dutch communist Fanny Schoonheyt, or her British comrade Felicia Browne, former IRA member Bill Scott, a significant number of German communists such as Gerhard Wohlrat, Golda Weid, and Max Friedemann, all took up arms on July 19 or shortly thereafter. It was the French contingent, however, which made up the vast majority of the foreign participants in the Popular Olympiad, and it is worth taking a closer look at that large group. On June 11, 1936, the leaders of the French Communist Youth sent a communication to all its regions regarding the "Popular Olympic Games in Barcelona."[61] The bureau of the central committee, began the letter, is giving you the first instructions for you to organize a delegation to Barcelona in each of our regions, and we urge you to start working on that task. The letter added a transport and meals schedule and details of the border crossing as already organized by the party, although reflecting the dates that were later changed, in order to bring the event forward for a July 19 start. Do not hesitate, concludes the letter, to ask for our help to ensure the success of this event.

The French press followed closely the return of at least part of the French contingent just under a week after the beginning of hostilities. The French government sent two ships to Barcelona to collect its citizens, one of which, the Djenne, reached Marseille on July 24. The Djenne was carrying 1,095 French citizens, including 600 athletes. Fists raised and to the tune of L'Internationale, the passengers disembarked and Louis Eudlitz, the "people's commissar" spoke to the press about the courage of the athletes in Barcelona.[62] The *Le Courrier de Saône-et-Loire* reported on August 8 additional testimonies on the French athletes returning home on the Djenne. "One of the most revolting deeds, confirmed by multiple passengers on the Djenne, was the parody of a Catholic mass carried out by participants in the Popular Olympiad." The reporter wonders how the athletes obtained the props for their play. According to *La France de Bordeaux et du Sud Ouest* of September 7, 1936, a French woman who had come to the Popular Olympiad with a French sporting club was, two months later, leading an assault group, made up largely of men, in the Zaragoza front.

A brief word is also in order regarding the Soviet athletes who had been included in the program for the Popular Olympiad, though they dropped out in the last moment. Ercoli had been in touch with Comintern general secretary Georgy Dimitrov to inquire about the correct approach in regard to these Soviet teams. The letter[63] is interesting because it reveals, first, that the request to deploy the Soviet *Mannschaft* came from the Sportintern and, secondly, because it opens a window into the ongoing tensions in the sports domain between the Sportintern and the Soviet High Council of Physical Culture. The request to send the Soviet athletes to *both* Barcelona and Prague games, bore the signature of Alexander Kosarev, Communist Youth leader, but was "stuck" at the High Council of Physical Culture where its leader, Angarov, would not give the OK without a letter of support from the Comintern leadership. Ercoli suggests that a call from Dimitrov to Angarov may be sufficient to resolve the problem. As Barbara Keys has argued (see note 14), the Supreme Council had little interest in supporting Sportintern's global revolutionary outreach, and the ongoing tensions between the two organizations shed light on Ercoli's request. Ercoli's letter strongly suggests that both he and Dimitrov believed the Sportintern request was justified and warranted high-level support. Soviet athletes, in the end, were withdrawn in the last moment without any explanation,[64] most likely in an effort to reduce the Comintern's public profile in this event. This interpretation is consistent with the archival evidence of the careful way the Comintern managed the visibility of Soviet personnel in Spain in early 1936. For example, in April 1936, a Comintern representative in Spain, probably "Victor" (Vittorio Vidali, aka "Contreras"), had requested from Moscow the participation of Soviet Red Aid Personnel in a "Solidarity Congress" that was to be held in the country. After careful observation of media coverage, however, Moscow replied that, since "a major campaign is being waged by the whole bourgeois press against the alleged interference of the Soviet Union in the Spanish events ... I do not consider it absolutely necessary that a delegation of the MOPR of the Soviet Union take part in the Spanish Solidarity Congress (Red Aid)."[65] As we have seen above, Sportintern and Communist Youth sections from other countries were fully capable of carrying out the tasks set for the Barcelona games.

That Comintern leaders intended for their global sports mass organizational work to remain devoted to conspiratorial and revolutionary work is suggested by the outcome of the reorganization of the Propaganda and Mass Organizations department. A July 8, 1936, ECCI directive[66] announced that Moskvin, that is, Mikhail Trilisser, former NKVD functionary, was taking over responsibilities over sports organizations after the reshuffle of the Propaganda and Mass Organizations secretariat. In August 1935, after the VII Congress of the Comintern, Trilisser joined the ECCI replacing Osip Pyatnitsky and with the pseudonym Moskvin, because he was too well known as an NKVD operative. In the Comintern, Moskvin would manage the secretive International Liaison Department, OMS in the Russian acronym, the files of which remain classified to this day.[67] Thanks to the UK's MASK program, however, we have a record of

"Medina," that is, Comintern agent in Spain Victorio Codovila, asking Moskvin on February 6, 1936, to accelerate the sending of promised funds, urgently needed to support the Popular Front electoral campaign.[68] CCEP executive, NKVD officer, and later Trotsky assassin Ramon Mercader was, in all likelihood, in contact with Moskvin as early as mid-1936. The Comintern's VII Congress and its inauguration of the Popular Front tactic did not change the fundamentally revolutionary and insurrectional aims of the Communist International. Speeches and summaries of the sessions appealing to socialists and petit bourgeoisie were published and distributed publicly, while "secret military tasks" regarding army infiltration and insurrection were given privately to the participants.[69]

Perhaps the clearest statement on what enabled Sportintern "athletes" to turn so quickly and smoothly into fighters comes from Álvaro Menendez, President of FCDO in his retrospective report to the Sportintern in 1937.[70] As mentioned above, this multi-country report covers the activities carried out by the sections in 1936 and was produced on the basis of in-person discussions in Moscow. Located in the Gottwald Secretariat section of the Comintern files, this document is a valuable source in our investigation of the Barcelona Popular Olympiad. Menendez explains that the Popular Olympiad contributed significantly to the growth in members the FCDO experienced in the first half of 1936. After the military uprising, continues Menendez, "most of our members went to the front and took up arms" together with the other athletes who did not belong to any organization. The explanation of this transition Menendez offers is crystal clear: "da sie Physich und Politisch geschult waren," because they were physically and politically trained. Further, Menendez adds, "almost all of our members had a very strong anti-fascist upbringing, because our federations were led by the communists." There can be little doubt, therefore, that the Barcelona Popular Olympiad was, fundamentally, a faithful application and success story of Comintern operations in the sport domain.

Conclusion

The stirring anthem of the Popular Olympics, composed fittingly by Hanns Eisler, the composer of the Comintern's anthem, was never played for enraptured spectators and athletes in Barcelona in July 1936. Yet, in various retrospective reports looking back on 1936, Sportintern officials concluded its sections had performed according to plan and the project had been a success. The response of a vast majority of "athletes" when the bullets started flying was a key aspect of that success, and the FCDO president, Menendez, took pride in explaining this. Further, in fulfillment of the tasks set out for Spain in April 1936, a significant portion of the "ripe for revolution" proletarian sports masses in Spain, in excess of 55,000 men and women, had been brought under Comintern control. Additionally, the Sportintern's main event in 1936 had been organized and marketed with the cooperation and financing of the Spanish and French Popular Front governments, as Ercoli had noted with delight. The CCEP, as we have seen, fully managed by the unified socialist and communist youth, the JSU, had done its part in Catalonia and was expanding its power and influence through 1936. The commitment of ERC and other Catalan nationalists to this project was sealed, for example, in the July 5, 1936, communist "pep rally" ahead of the Barcelona event, held in Paris. On that stage, French, Belgian, as well as Catalan and Soviet flags stood behind the speakers, as CCEP representatives, together with Red Aid and French communist leader Duclos sang the Internationale.[71] While ignoring the primary sources we have detailed, Santacana and Pujadas have gone to great lengths to argue that communist infiltration and influence in other regions notwithstanding, the CCEP in Catalonia was managed, not by Moscow, but by progressive, nationalist Catalan civil society organizations. In this chapter, we have shown that there are, in fact, no grounds for a Catalan exceptionalism in this matter. While, according to the Comintern mass organizational playbook, various apparently non-partisan entities were delighting wide audiences on stage, committed communists were actively managing the show, as was the case with the FCDO.

Conclusion

In a March 2022 online discussion with New York University's Jordan Center,[1] Jonathan Haslam recalled the difficulties faced by historians of the Soviet Union in the 1980s, when Soviet archives remained closed and relevant Western archives were only open in part. More recently, as the holdings of Moscow-based archives became widely available, Haslam rightly lamented the chaotic organization of the material, as, for example, Comintern documents are often found under the most unexpected headings in the various repositories. Naturally, Haslam's views on Soviet foreign policy and other topics have evolved over four decades, as primary sources became progressively accessible, especially online, and he was able to spend substantial amounts of time combing through the material. His 2021 tome, *The Spectre of War*, represents the apex of that evolution and is deeply disruptive, dare I say, *revisionist*, of long-held assumptions in the historiography of the interwar period.

In the summer of 2003, the George W. Bush administration was desperate to find new arguments to discredit the critics of the Second Gulf War. Probably following the advice of Condoleezza Rice, the president affirmed that historians who were critical of his administration's justification of the conflict were engaging in historical revisionism. That is, the Bush administration was asserting that those who argued that the Iraq War of 2003 was fundamentally unjustified were intentionally manipulating history in the service of political aims. James McPherson, the president of the American Historical Association, responded to the Bush administration in a staunch and memorable defense of his guild, and of the legitimacy of revision:

> The 14,000 members of this Association … know that revision is the lifeblood of historical scholarship. History is a continuing dialogue between the present and the past. Interpretations of the past are subject to change in response to new evidence, new questions asked of the evidence, new perspectives gained by the passage of time. There is no single, eternal, and immutable "truth" about past events and their meaning.[2]

It seems clear that the abundant and multi-source archival documentation we have discussed in the present volume calls for a substantial revision of long-held opinions about the depth and width of Soviet communist influence in Spain before the outbreak of the Civil War. The fog of the Cold War, together with various shades and flavors of presentism, has kept a number of historians from grasping the real and present danger posed by Bolshevism in Europe in the interwar period. Spain, especially in the years 1931–6, is a case in point. We will not repeat again here the discussion of the state of historiographical play we undertook in the Introduction and in Chapter 1. The concerns US ambassador William Bullitt expressed to his superiors in 1935 about the threat posed to the United States by the presence of the Communist Party USA at the Comintern's VII Congress are well known. Similarly, our discussion of communist "army work" in France explains, at least partially, why socialists and radical republicans in the Popular Front government did not pursue the strengthening of the Franco-Soviet Pact with a military alliance. The words of Spanish republican prime minister Alejandro Lerroux to his cabinet in September 1935 are not as well known. Reflecting on the recently concluded Comintern VII Congress, attended by a number of Spanish communists and socialists, Lerroux noted that the III International continued to plan and execute various forms of intervention in the internal affairs of other nations. Specifically, he added, "[this holds true] very particularly in Spain, where we are painfully aware that communist activities ... constitute a real danger."[3] The pages of this book will enable the reader to gauge the gravity of that danger.

In Chapter 1, we introduced the fundamentally subversive and insurrectional aims of the Comintern in Spain, especially since the establishment of the Second Republic in 1931. In line with its assessment of the revolutionary maturity of the country, an assessment increasingly shared by many on the left, the Comintern deployed its standard agit-prop and insurrectional methods and tools which included training for armed revolt. Further, we showed that the Comintern's revolutionary efforts in Spain did not change after the celebration of the VII Comintern Congress, the Popular Front tactic notwithstanding. The secret military tasks distributed to each Comintern section at the end of the VII Congress, though never published, leave little doubt about the continuation of what was standard Marxist-Leninist theory and practice after the summer of 1935.

In Chapter 2, we explored in detail the Comintern's efforts to craft and deploy a victimization narrative after the October 1934 insurrection that became the cornerstone of the Popular Front platform. The narrative of proletarian victims and fascist aggressors, supported by the abundant funding of International Red

Aid, the thought leadership of the World Committee and other Comintern mass organizations, became deeply embedded in left-wing consciousness throughout 1935. The chapter reveals the level of control the Comintern exercised over message and tactics, and how these were carried out and experienced, especially among socialist party members. By 1935, the socialist party leadership, especially those directly involved in the insurrection, had become heavily dependent on Red Aid funding, and the process of unification of socialist youth and trade union with the communists had their full blessing. The socialist party's Bolshevik turn was complete.

In Chapter 3, we detailed the work of the Comintern publishing organization in Spain, from the arrival of Ediciones Europa América in Barcelona in late 1931 to the early summer of 1936. The active role of leading Spanish publishers and intellectuals in that organization, together with the successful deployment of large distribution networks based on "bourgeois" bookstores and kiosks enabled Redizdat Spain to achieve significant results by 1933. It was the October 1934 insurrection, however, which enabled Klavego and team to dramatically increase its partnerships across the political left and, contrary to expectation, grow its operation throughout Spain "as if nothing had happened." In his 1935 report, Klavego explained in no uncertain terms that, similarly to other Comintern organizations, Redizdat had a friendly "scientific" face, but its raison d'être was its illegal and subversive operation. After the February 1936 elections, we detailed how unprecedented financing, together with a reorganization of the management in Madrid, enabled Redizdat Spain to print and distribute 5 million pieces of communist revolutionary material throughout the country. According to the assessment of the opportunities in Spain made by Krebs in the spring of 1936, the sky was, indeed, the limit.

Chapter 4, our longest chapter, is a transnational study of Comintern "army work" in France and Spain as an objective threat to the national security of both countries. Contrary to what is a majority opinion among historians, the systematic infiltration of the armed forces on both sides of the Pyrenees continued unabated well into 1936. While in 1933 the Spanish party was applying French communist best practices in its army work, its successful involvement in the socialist-led October 1934 insurrection enabled the PCE to inspire and lead the communists north of the border in this critical aspect of Comintern work. The objective of work in the armed forces was identical in both countries: communist cells were to grow and multiply within regiments and ships and actively pursue class warfare-based disaffection, insubordination, and decomposition. In Leninist terms, this had to result in revolutionary defeatism, that is, communist-infiltrated military units were to prepare for the inevitable "imperialist war," at which time soldiers and sailors would turn their weapons on their officers and join the proletarian forces. North of the border, radical socialist leaders such as Édouard Daladier and the socialist Leon Blum always remained alert to the communist infiltration of the *Armée*, and regularly deployed surveillance and other countermeasures to curtail it. In Spain, however, government countermeasures were only partially successful during the republican-conservative biennium of 1934–5 and removed altogether by the Popular Front government after February 1936. In stark contrast with his socialist counterpart in France, Largo Caballero was the primary defender of the "republicanization" and "de-fascistization" of the armed forces in Spain 1935 and 1936, both terms, as we have seen, part of a larger revolutionary narrative which called for the extension of class war to every institution in the country.

Chapter 5 is our relatively brief treatment of the communist infiltration of the socialist union UGT through revolutionary opposition groups (Oposición Sindical Revolucionaria, OSR), barely touched upon in Chapter 1. The archival material helps us to quantify the phenomenon and to understand the tactics employed from 1932 to 1934. Our survey of key socialist trade union press organs yields fascinating insights into how this systematic infiltration was experienced by socialist union leaders in that period, and into the actions taken, with very limited success, to curtail that communist effort. The fundamental aim of OSR groups in Spain, as in France, Britain, and across Europe, was to drive a wedge between union members and their "reformist" leaders in a "united front from below" approach. The success of OSR groups within UGT was evidenced by the communist control of the strike committees of leading UGT unions such as metal workers or printers. The acknowledgment by the national UGT leadership of the fact that, contrary to their constant instructions to their local organizations, strikes were often carried out without the slightest advance consultation with the national committee is illustrative of the effectiveness of OSR groups within UGT in this period.

Lastly, Chapter 6 is a discussion of the July 1936 *Olimpiada Popular* in Barcelona as a case study in Comintern mass organizational work in Spain in our period. Building on the work of André Gounot, our research expands well beyond the Sportintern RGASPI files, and relies on material from the Gottwald Secretariat, the French Communist Party, the Juventudes Socialistas Unificadas (JSU) and other material not covered by Gounot. The documentation leaves little doubt that the Comitè Català pro Esport Popular (CCEP) was a creation of the communist-controlled JSU and fulfilled its role as the Catalan-friendly front of the Sportintern, with the same reporting structure into Moscow the FCDO had by 1934. The chapter details the fundamental paramilitary orientation of Sportintern and its Spanish affiliates FCDO and CCEP, whose members were, in most cases, affiliated with both the JSU and the communist and socialist unified militia. The almost immediate transformation of many of the Olimpiada athletes into fighters on July 19 is not surprising, since, in the words of the FCDO leader in 1937, they were physically and politically prepared to make that transition. The primary aim of the FCDO and CCEP was, contrary to its official propaganda, not the boycotting of the Berlin games, but the bringing of the entirety of the 55,000-strong military-age proletarian sports movement in Spain under communist control.

The brief discussion of the May 1936 dialogue between the PCE's Jesús Hernández, Dimitrov, and Moskvin in Moscow is, it seems to me, a fitting epilogue to the book. The title of Chapter 1 was taken from Ercoli's triumphalist speech in Moscow in mid-1936: the successful deployment of the Popular Front in Spain had required the "mobilization of all our forces." In a similar vein, Jesús Hernández addressed his managers at the Comintern in late May by going through the numbers of proletarians successfully brought under communist control. Those achievements had not, he insisted, fallen from heaven. Hernández's report and the dialogue that ensued were highly revealing of the status of the revolution in Spain in the "primavera trágica."

The key to all these achievements of the Comintern in Spain in our period is the potent network effect of all its organizations and resources working toward the same aims, while at the same time hiding the relationships among them behind a myriad of fronts, most bearing non-communist labels. Thus, Red Aid, together with Friends of the Soviet Union, the World Committee in Paris and Madrid, and countless republican and socialist fellow travelers, was able to unite all left-wing forces under the banner of anti-fascist and popular fronts. The large Europe-wide Redizdat organization was able to leverage its Spanish startups with the support of the party, Friends of the Soviet Union, and local printers and intellectuals to achieve and exceed the legal and illegal publishing quotas imposed on them by Moscow. The OSR groups, together with communist youth and Red Aid, were able to infiltrate and bring under communist control the strike committees of key socialist unions, including some of the jewels in the UGT crown such as metal workers. Communist cells in the army and navy, with active support from communist youth, OSR groups, Red Aid, and others, were able to grow their presence in key barracks in Madrid and elsewhere throughout the so-called black biennium. The Spanish worker sports organization FCDO and its branch in the Catalan region the CCEP were, by the summer of 1936, fully controlled by the JSU and Sportintern leadership and reported to Moscow on their true objectives which were not, first and foremost, to boycott the Berlin games.

The relationships among Comintern organizations were occasionally discussed in the conservative press on both sides of the Pyrenees, especially after the October 1934 insurrection in Spain and the Eberlein Affair in France. For the most part, such reports were quickly dismissed by republicans and left-wing parties as the work of obsessive conspiracy theorists. In a similar vein, leading historians of the Spanish Second Republic such as Southworth and Preston have insisted that the only substantial presence of Soviet communism in Spain materialized as a result of the military uprising of July 17, 1936. I wish to argue, on the basis of the present work, that such a view is no longer tenable.

Epilogue

One Foot in Soviet Power: Jesús Hernández reports to Dimitrov, Lozovsky, and Moskvin, Moscow, May 22, 1936

Jesús Hernández's report to his Comintern leaders in May 1936 exudes confidence and an excitement about the prospects for the party's work in Spain that the PCE leader can barely contain. The report, together with the dialogue that follows it, reminds me of many annual sales meetings in the high-tech industry, from the heart of Silicon Valley to London or Tel Aviv. When the sales quota has been achieved, star customer references have been won, and the immediate future looks bright, the regional manager stands confidently as he clicks through his presentation, all his content leading up to the climactic point: The numbers. The global sales management already knows what's coming, but they make an effort to challenge the successful sales leader, probing the assumptions and the mid and long-term strategy.

The documents containing the report and ensuing dialogue with Dimitrov, Lozovsky, and Moskvin at the meeting of the Presidium of the ECCI are the stenographic records of the French and Russian translations.[1] An accompanying document in Spanish is the annotated draft of an article that would be attributed to Jesús Hernández, was meant for a public readership, and was fully edited to ensure only the politically correct details were disclosed. The hand-written notes and edits reveal far more than the agit-prop piece itself, especially when taken together with the full text of the report and the dialogue in Moscow. Thus, the editor's pencil crosses out in the article the reference to the Presidium of the ECCI in the header, as well as an entire page depicting the breakdown of the rule of law in favor of the communists with the comment: "Esto no es publicable." In multiple instances, the severity of the violence detailed in the report is toned down in the article, and the reported number of "reactionaries" arrested by the Popular Front Government is halved. The report with internal discussion and accompanying article reminds us of the directives and carefully crafted letter of the Spanish immigrants we discussed in Chapter 2: the former was an internal document detailing the revolutionary and insurrectional aims of the Comintern in Spain, the latter was a Moscow-produced letter to be made public in Spain with stringent orders not to reveal its origins. The inability or unwillingness of a number of historians to differentiate between open and frank discussion among communist leaders and material crafted as propaganda for public consumption, between unchangeable aims and ever adaptable tactics, is the root cause of prevailing misunderstandings we have addressed throughout this book.

Hernández's open and confident detailing of the party's activities and the responses and questions from his managers make this document particularly valuable as a primary source. Other documents, such as the "decision on the Spanish question" written a month later, are statements of tactical alignment and of the careful management of the narrative, rather than frank, internal discussions of the actual actors and events. The few historians who have referred to this May 22, 1936, report appear not to have read both documents in any detail and draw conclusions that are not only not supported by the material but are fundamentally at odds with a careful reading of it in its entirety, handwritten notes included.[2] This is not surprising, given the majority opinion regarding the nature of Comintern aims in Spain in the spring of 1936. As we have shown in earlier chapters, much of II Republic historiography assumes that in the spring of 1936 the Comintern had put proletarian revolution on hold and was fully supportive of the "democratic bourgeois" Government of the Popular Front it saw itself as a part of. The French and Russian translations of the May 22, 1936, report and dialogue, fully in line with other archival documentation we have already discussed, reveal a rather different state of affairs.[3]

In his address to his superiors in Moscow, Jesús Hernández was celebrating full communist control of the socialist trade union UGT, youth organization, worker and peasant alliances, and militias. Further, as Caballero himself affirmed multiple times,[4] the Comintern believed a single revolutionary proletarian party was within reach in Spain, as a final step required to evolve the "democratic bourgeois" revolution to its final stage. Additionally, the dialogue confirms the unified MAOC militias, with socialist, Catalan ERC youth and communist membership, were armed and operational as a large extra-parliamentary force not in the service of the republican government, but of the Popular Front agenda. Lastly, the document reveals the Comintern leadership's complete readiness to implement in Spain Soviet power and the dictatorship of the proletariat, as and when the local circumstances enabled it. Neither the Comintern nor its Spanish section were committed to a timeline involving an acceptance of the government of the Spanish republic. As early as March 1936, the directives sent to the Spanish party left no doubt about the fact that the Azaña government was not a true government of the Popular Front.[5] The party's mission, in close partnership with the socialists, was to ensure the complete fulfillment by the government of the Popular Front program while at the same time growing its power through the extra-parliamentary and nation-wide Alianzas Obreras y Campesinas. The Alianzas, as deployed during the October 1934 insurrection, had been the "first implementation of Soviet power in the history of the Spanish proletariat," a theme repeated multiple times in the January 1935 Codovilla report.[6] Naturally, the May 22, 1936, documents placed significant emphasis on the growth and progressive communist control of the Alianzas, and of Caballero's agreement as to their continued relevance. For the Comintern the Alianzas, with membership extended beyond the socialists to all left-wing republicans, were the true center of gravity of socio-political power and key enablers of the transition to the proletarian revolution. A majority of the socialists agreed. The official organ of the socialist youth organization, *Avance*, provided its assessment immediately after the February elections:

> La victoria del Bloque Popular ha creado las condiciones para el desarrollo de la revolución democrática. Sólo las condiciones ... el resto ha de ponerlo el proletariado ... [esta es] la realización de los milagros de organización proletaria de que hablaba Lenin de febrero a octubre de 1917 ... la Alianza no puede ser un partido si quiere cubrir el papel que el Soviet tuvo en la Revolución Rusa ... Sucesivamente iremos especificando nuestro criterio sobre la Alianza Obrera y Campesina ... Por el momento, decimos a nuestros militantes que se preparen para una intensa cruzada con objeto de levantar con brío el doble Poder [sic] frente al cual saltará en pedazos el Estado de la burguesía.[7]

The dialogue between Jesús Hernández and Dimitrov as recorded in the May 22, 1936, report is illustrative of the Comintern's complete flexibility as to the timing of the widespread realization of Soviet power in Spain. Hernández details in his talk several examples of the breakdown of the rule of law in Spain under the Popular Front Government, all of them benefiting the communists. Strikes have become, Hernández argues, practical demonstrations of the "absolute united front," with the mere threat of a strike achieving the desired results, and the government unable to resist the pressure from the masses. Scabs ("esquiroles," "brisseurs de grève") have disappeared in Spain, affirms the communist leader, as strike breakers are promptly dealt with. In Asturias, provincial delegates of the republican government are communists, and being a law unto themselves, give new meaning, affirms Hernández, to the concept of people's justice. In many municipal governments across the country, recounts the communist leader, the unemployed peasants go straight to the communist councilmen who force the landowners to either hire the peasants or pay them their salaries without working.[8] To this Dimitrov replies: true democracy![9] In reply, Hernández explains that most of the country is in agreement with this modus operandi, and that he is only giving an example of many. Dimitrov concludes:

> If this is happening everywhere, we will be able to create the Soviet republic, because such things cannot reinforce the democratic republic.[10]

The seizure of factories or lands by workers' or peasant committees was also, in theory, associated with the seizure of power in the next phase of the revolution, explained Hernández, yet such seizures, like that of the Madrid trams, were already occurring and had the support of the party. As indicated by José "Pepe" Díaz a month later, the party would support such moves whenever and wherever local conditions allowed.[11] Local conditions in Spain had been very favorable indeed since the historic first implementation of soviets during the October 1934 insurrection. The merger of the socialist and communist unions and youth, and the new Popular Front Government opened unprecedented avenues for an accelerated move to the completion of the "democratic bourgeois" revolution.

The Comintern's merely instrumental view of the republican government in Spain was made abundantly clear in June and again days after the military uprising of July 1936. In the June 7 1936, report on the Spanish question, the party leadership made clear that if it became necessary for the left-wing parties to form "un gobierno del Frente Popular *en lugar del* Gobierno republicano actual (emphasis mine)," the party would seriously consider joining that cabinet.[12] Lastly, one week after the July 18 uprising of part of the military in Spain, Dimitrov left no doubt about the degree of commitment communists had to the republican government, now engulfed in civil war. Commenting on the fragmentation of the Spanish army as a result of the uprising in Morocco and elsewhere, the general secretary suggested that by seizing a garrison in the center, "we could launch a Bulgarian or Greek-style coup in 24 hours, overthrow the Azaña Government and announce a true, democratic republican Government."[13]

The events on the ground as detailed by Hernández in dialogue with his managers reveal that the assumed phases of the Spanish revolution were overlapping in Spain by May 1936 and the Comintern and its Spanish section believed the country had one foot in soviet power. The fundamental features of the "bourgeois-democratic" phase that was developing rapidly in the country, however, are not sufficiently spelled out in the literature. In the May 22, 1936, report, Jesús Hernández and the Comintern leadership make clear that the current "bourgeois democratic" revolutionary phase already involves the complete socio-political elimination and incarceration "en masse" of all parties to the right of Azaña's left-wing republicans. As already mentioned, the report estimates the number of "reactionaries" imprisoned at 11 to 12 thousand, an amount that is halved in the letter meant for public consumption.[14] As even a cursory perusal of the period press reveals, this was no communist fantasy, and arrests of supporters of parties on the right, priests, judges, as well as members of Falange were reported daily throughout Spain in April 1936.[15] Those numbers were considered insufficient, however, and Hernández affirmed the party was working with the socialists and others in the government to achieve the arrest of the entire political leadership of all parties outside of the Popular Front, from republican Lerroux to Calvo Sotelo and Gil Robles. The armed forces, law enforcement agencies, and the judiciary were also to be cleansed of fascists and reactionaries and were to be progressively replaced by the unified armed militias. This was the true nature of "republicanization" which, as we saw in Chapter 4, was promoted by the PCF in France and primarily by the socialists in Spain in early 1936.

Part and parcel of the socio-political elimination of "reactionaries" was the systematic burning of churches. In Hernández's words, very many (ochen' mnogo in the Russian translation, pas mal de … in the French rendering) churches are being burned in Spain. Contrary to what both the PCE and the Popular Front Government communicated in Spain in early May 1936, the communist leader informed his leaders in Moscow that the widespread arson had been fully justified. The shooting of workers from church towers, affirmed Hernández, and the storage or arms and ammunition by priests made the violent reaction of the masses fully justified and understandable. In the June 1936 report, the PCE leadership goes as far as affirming that the reactionaries were burning the churches themselves to be able to blame the communists. In his account before Dimitrov and the other leaders, Hernández highlighted the infamous story of the "fascist women" walking through the proletarian quarters of Madrid handing out candy to the children, and later spreading the rumor that the candy was poisoned. The indignation of the mothers was such, recounts the PCE leader, that the first responders sent to quell the violence were obliged to let them have their way with the churches, convents, and fascist homes. This account is at odds with the official communication of the PCE in Madrid in May 1936, in which, forced by government pressure, the party admitted that the rumor was a *patraña* and urged its supporters in the Cuatro Caminos district to ignore it and not resort to violence.[16] Multiple churches and other buildings had already been burned, as recounted by opposition leader José Calvo Sotelo in parliament and by the foreign press not subject to Spanish government censorship.[17]

Hernández's optimism in this report is, in the final analysis, backed up by the numbers of proletarians in Spain who had been brought under communist control, only a small minority of which were card-carrying PCE members. The merger of the socialist and communist trade unions, "following the counsel of the Comintern," is the jewel on the crown with 745,000 industrial workers and 253,000 peasants. As for the unified youth organization, the JSU boasted after the merger 140,000[18] members and was by the time of the report officially a member of the Comintern's youth organization, KIM Hernández continued detailing the numbers of pioneers (children and teens) at 22,000, various women organizations totaling "40–50,000," and the proletarian sports organization, the FCDO (see Chapter 6 for a detailed discussion) with 30,000. Lastly, Hernández addressed the unified militias, the MAOC the leadership of which was "more or less" in communist hands and had adopted the communist uniform of blue shirts and red ties. Though its origins were the "shock groups" in the socialist and communist youth, deployed in 1934 under the pretense of defensive action,[19] Hernandez explained to his audience the efforts being made to turn the militias into a mass organization open to all workers and peasants and having a legal status. In reply to Moskvin and Lozovsky's demand for concrete data, Hernández confirmed the militias were armed with pistols and with rifles and automatic weapons in Asturias, where "everyone knows they are armed." In line with the party's belief that police forces and military are full of reactionaries and fascists, Hernández described the growing role of the militias in the setting up of checkpoints outside Madrid, patrolling proletarian neighborhoods, arresting suspected fascists,[20] and searching their homes, all enjoying the cooperation of the "government forces."[21] In the final section of his report, the Spanish communist leader recounts his participation in the funeral of a murdered army officer which is very revealing of the complementary role of armed militias and communist army work in the barracks. An army officer had been shot by counter-revolutionary activists on a central Madrid street. Hernández came to the funeral and addressed a large crowd of military and party leaders, explaining "the problem of the army, why we are enemies of the army [and] how we understand the cleansing of the army." Immediately, he concluded, the merged socialist and communist militias marched in front of the coffin. Hernández informed Dimitrov and the rest of his audience in Moscow that communist cells were evolving from a closed, secretive organization into an "open" format of antifascist committees in the barracks following the popular front concept. As a result, the communists had reached "more officers than ever before." The murdered army man was Captain Carlos Faraudo, an engineering officer who had been working as a trainer of the by that time unified MAOC militias, and his funeral and burial was covered widely in the press on the May 9, 1936. According to the report in *El Sol*, in addition to Jesús Hernández and Pepe Diaz from the PCE, Nelken and de Francisco, the leading socialists who had returned from Moscow in April were in attendance, together with JSU leader Santiago Carrillo who urged the members of the military to "join their proletarian brothers in the fight."

Jesús Hernández was right. In his words in the report, all these achievements had not fallen from heaven. They were the result of the tenacious work of the Spanish party which effectively exploited the full network of Comintern assets in the country, especially after the leadership change in 1932. The documentation, as discussed throughout this book, deals a devastating blow to the myth of a marginal communist influence in Spain in 1934 to early 1936. The successful *grignotage*, the communist nibbling away of the socialist organizations left only the socialist party itself to be ingested, a step socialist leader Largo Caballero was committed to in May 1936. While that was, in theory, the final remaining task of the "democratic-bourgeois revolution" in Spain, the fires of proletarian revolution were already spreading far and wide in the tragic spring of 1936. In Jonathan Haslam's words, "there was a revolution going on in Spain before [Franco's] counter-revolution."[22]

Notes

Introduction

1. Jonathan Haslam, *The Soviet Union and the Struggle for Collective Security in Europe: 1933–1939* (New York: St. Martin's Press, 1984). This was volume II in a series on the subject. Arguing for the sincerity of Soviet collective security efforts in the period see also David Cattell, *Soviet Diplomacy and the Spanish Civil War* (Berkeley, CA: University of California Press, 1957); Barbara Jelavich, *Saint Petersburg and Moscow. Tsarist and Soviet Foreign Policy 1814–1974* (Bloomington, IN: Indiana University Press, 1974) 333–46.
2. Jiri Hochman, *The Soviet Union and the Failure of Collective Security, 1934–1938* (Ithaca, NY: Cornell University Press, 1984). Among the earliest rebuttals of the idea of a sincere soviet collective security policy in the period which would have brought about a turn away from the promotion of world revolution is Ivan Pfaff, "Stalins Strategie der Sowjetisierung Mitteleuropas 1935–1938. Das Beispiel Tschechoslowakei" in *Vierteljahrshefte für Zeitgeschichte*, Vol. 38 Jahrg., 4. H. (Oct., 1990) 543–87, especially his discussion of the true content and orientation of the VII Congress of the Comintern, pp. 547–8. For the skeptical perspective on Soviet collective security policy, see also Teddy J. Uldricks, "Soviet Security Policy in the 1930's" in Gabriel Gorodetsky (ed.) *Soviet Foreign Policy 1917–1991. A Retrospective* (Second ed.; New York: Routledge, 2013) 65–74; Stanley Payne, "Soviet Anti-Fascism, Theory and Practice, 1921–1945" *Totalitarian Movements and Political Religions*, Vol. 4, No. 2 (fall, 2003) 1–62; Alfred J. Rieber, *Stalin and the Struggle for Supremacy in Eurasia* (Cambridge: Cambridge University Press, 2015), especially his treatment of the constant conflict between Litvinov's push for collective action against fascism and Stalin's consistently doctrinaire and neutral stance in pp. 153–61.
3. Marilynn Giroux Hitchens's review of both volumes in *The American Historical Review*, Vol. 90, No. 4 (Oct., 1985) 985. Most recently, see Sean McMeekin, *Stalin's War. A New History of World War II* (New York: Basic Books, 2021).
4. Gabriel Gorodetsky (ed.), *Soviet Foreign Policy 1917–1991. A Retrospective* (Cummings Center Series; London: Routledge, 2013), Published originally in 1994.
5. Jonathan Haslam, "Litvinov, Stalin and the Road not Taken" in Gabriel Gorodetsky (ed.) *Soviet Foreign Policy*, 55–64.

6 Uldricks, "Soviet Security" in Gorodetsky (ed.) *Soviet Foreign Policy*, 71. Uldricks rightly affirms that the arguments of Haslam and others who posit a sincere Soviet defense of peace against Nazism in 1933–9 fit rather comfortably in officially sanctioned Soviet historiography.

7 Silvio Pons, *Stalin and the Inevitable War* (London: Frank Cass, 2002) x. But see Michael Jabara Carley's response in "Soviet Foreign Policy in the West. 1936–1941. A Review Article" in *Europe-Asia Studies*, Vol. 56, No. 7 (2004) 1081–100.

8 Stephen Kotkin, *Stalin Vol. I. Paradoxes of Power* (New York: Penguin, 2014); *Stalin. Vol. II. Waiting for Hitler* (New York: Penguin, 2017); James Harris, "Encircled by Enemies: Stalin's Perception of the Capitalist World, 1918–1941" in *Journal of Strategic Studies*, Vol. 30, No. 3 (2008) 513–45.

9 Harris, "Encircled," 533ff.

10 Haslam "Litvinov," 61. In the words of Michael Jabara Carley, "Litvinov did not 'speak Bolshevik' in his private communications." Carley, "Soviet Foreign Policy," 1082.

11 Kotkin, *Paradoxes of Power*, 558. Kotkin also shows that both Lenin and Trotsky had affirmed that, if revolution was delayed elsewhere, socialism had necessarily to proceed in Russia.

12 Joseph Stalin, "The October Revolution and the Tactics of the Russian Communists. Preface to On the Road to October" in *J. V. Stalin. Works* (Vol. 6; Moscow: Foreign Languages Publishing House, 1953) 419–20. The original "Socialism in one Country" article was written for *Pravda* and later published as part of Stalin's volume "On the Path to October."

13 Jonathan Haslam, *The Spectre of War. International Communism and the Origins of World War II* (Princeton: Princeton University Press, 2021), esp. "Introduction," 1–13.

14 The British Government's Code and Cypher School decrypted and processed Comintern communications to and from its European sections including Spain in our period. Comintern radio messages were classified most secret and were subsequently given the code name MASK. We shall refer to these files throughout this work; Likewise in France, Fonds de surveillance du Parti Communiste Français par la direction de la Sûreté nationale du ministère de l'intérieur sous la IIIe République (Série F/7 et "fonds de Moscou").

15 Haslam, *Soviet Union*, 231. Similarly, Cattell, before launching into his defense of Soviet collective security in the period admits that "the refusal of the Communists to abandon, even for the moment, their goal of subversion and world domination worked to undermine the Soviet goal of a popular front and collective security." Cattell, *Soviet Diplomacy*, v.

16 See Kotkin, *Waiting for Hitler*, and his discussion of this in his 1917 Centennial Series lecture entitled "War, Revolution, Socialism, War," given at Dartmouth University's Dickey Center in 2017, available online.

17 See on this, Kevin McDermott and Jeremy Agnew, *The Comintern. A History of International Communism from Lenin to Stalin* (London: Palgrave Macmillan, 1996) 126.
18 Dimitrov's speech on August 2, 1935, entitled "The Working Class against Fascism" in *VII World Congress of the Communist International* (London: Modern Books, 1935) 74–5.
19 Informations du CC des JC au CEICJ sur l'Unité d'Action avec les JS, September 1 through 30, 1935, RGASPI F. 533 Op. 10 D. 3327. Point one of the Chartre d'Unité affirmed the joint commitment to the dictatorship of the proletariat. The document also committed the socialists to the ongoing communist work in the French armed forces.
20 The majority of the drafts, final versions, and translations of the letter in RGASPI. F. 495. Op. 18 D. 1075a.
21 Secretariat Romain. Commission Espagnole. Janvier 17 1936, a presentation by PCE leader José Diaz and discussion involving Manuilsky, Codovilla, Diaz, and others. RGASPI. F. 495. Op. 20.D. 269.
22 McDermott and Agnew, *The Comintern*, 132–3.
23 Paul Preston, *The Spanish Civil War* (London: Harper Perennial, 2006) 146–7, a volume dedicated to the memory of the International Brigades.
24 Denis Smyth, "Reflex Reaction: Germany and the Onset of the Spanish Civil War" in Paul Preston (ed.) *Revolution and War in Spain 1931–1939* (London: Routledge, 2002) 249.
25 Gabriel Gorodetsky (ed.) *The Maisky Diaries. Red Ambassador to the Court of St. James 1932–1943* (New Haven, CT: Yale University Press, 2015). Viñas discusses what he considers to be significant contribution of this material to our understanding of Soviet collective security in a three-part internet blog article.
26 Rieber shows that Stalin's commercial emissary to Nazi Germany, David Kandelaki, was reporting to the dictator via Molotov, thus bypassing and working at cross purposes with Litvinov. *Stalin and the Struggle*, 159; Kotkin, *Waiting*, 271–2; 275; 279–80.
27 See, for example, Angel Viñas, *El Oro de Moscú* (Barcelona: Grijalbo, 1979); Hugo García, "Historia de un Mito Político: El Peligro Comunista en el Discurso de las Derechas Españolas (1918–1936)" in *Historia Social,* No. 51 (2005) 3–20; Svetlana Pozharskaya, who argues that "it was only after the revolt began that 'the Russian aspect' was a myth no longer but became real," "Comintern and the Spanish Civil War in Spain" in *Ebre*, Vol. 38, No. 1 (2003) 47–56; Eduardo González Calleja, "Los Discursos Catastrofistas de los Líderes de la Derecha y la Difusión del Mito del 'Golpe de Estado Comunista'" en *El Argonauta Español* [online], 13, (2016). Unfortunately, Stephen Kotkin also followed Preston at this point when he affirmed that the July 18, 1936 military uprising "galvanized the very leftist threat [it] had wanted to pre-empt." Kotkin, *Waiting for Hitler,* 615. In private correspondence with Kotkin, however, he has acknowledged to me he had not, at the time of

writing, examined the archival material we discuss in the present work, and he would no longer affirm what he did at the time of writing.

28 "Die Komintern und der Antifaschismus in Spanien 1931–1939" in Stefan Vogt, et al. (eds.) *Ideengeschichte als politische Aufklärung. Festschrift für Wolfgang Wippermann zum 65 Geburtstag* (Berlin: Metropol, 2010) 108–28; "Soviet Anti-Fascism Theory and Practice, 1921–1945" in *Totalitarian Movements and Political Religions*, Vol. 4, No. 2 (Fall 2003) 1–62; *The Spanish Civil War, the Soviet Union and Communism* (New Haven, CT: Yale University Press, 2004).

29 Antonio Elorza and Marta Bizcarrondo, "Una Explicación Previa" instead of the standard scholarly introduction that a volume of this type is expected to have, in *Queridos Camaradas. La Internacional Comunista y España* (Barcelona: Planeta, 1999) 15.

30 Throughout this book, I use the term "illegal" in the way the Comintern and its sections used the term, that is, as a qualifier of its subversive, below the surface work that placed it fully outside the law in the countries in which they operated.

31 Elorza, *Queridos*, 280.

32 For a discussion of this and other military and commercial agreements between the USSR and Germany in the period, the mutual most favored nation status and Moscow's "wooing" of Berlin see Hochman, *The Soviet Union*, 95–124; Kotkin, *Waiting*, 289; 291–2, etc.

33 See on this Roberto Villa, *1917. Estado Catalán y Soviet Español* (Barcelona: Planeta, 2021).

34 José Bullejos, *La Comintern en España* (Mexico DF: Impresiones Modernas, 1972) 11.

35 Leaflet reproduced in Victor Alba, *El Partido Comunista en España* (Barcelona: Planeta, 1979) 110.

36 "Il ne faut pas oblier qu'après les élections municipals du mois d'avril de 1931, fut proclamée la République en Espagne, les réactionaires et les fascistes veulent se servir des élections municipales de 1935 pour clôturer la période révolutionnaire qui dure depuis 5 ans en Espagne." Secretariat Romaine, orateur Codovilla, January 29, 1935, Question Espagnole. RGASPI F. 495. Op. 32. D. 165. The document includes questions and answers in dialogue with Ercoli and others during the presentation.

37 *El Socialista*, April 15, 1931.

38 Caballero explained how hard and frustrating it had been for him to support the republican government and that, once the party left that government, the socialist seizure of power would come by either legal or revolutionary means. Caballero was explicit on the validity of the Bolshevik model: Lenin was forced to face the circumstances by which, in order to avoid being neutralized, the Bolsheviks had to neutralize their enemies. "It's not that I believe we should imitate the Russians—argued Caballero—but the circumstances keep leading us to a very

similar situation." Caballero finished by urging the socialist youth to be prepared. *El Socialista*, August 13, 1933.

39 Cited respectively in Georges Vidal, "L'Armée Française Face au Problème de la Subversion Communiste au Début des Années 1930" in *Guerres Mondiales et Conflits Contemporains*, Vol. 4, No. 204 (2001) 43; Jean-Jacques Becker and Serge Berstein, "L'Anticommunisme en France" in *Vingtième Siècle. Revue d'Histoire*, Vol. 15 (Jul–Sep., 1987) 17–28. Leading generals in the French armed forces agreed with this view and produced various security assessments of the communist insurrectional threat starting in 1932, as we shall see in Chapter 4.

40 Cited in McDermott and Agnew, *The Comintern,* 137. In this section the authors discuss the substantial gains made by the PCF in French labor unions which resulted in their radicalization, and the ongoing suspicions of some of the socialist leaders as to the sincerity of communist claims to be a national party which supported democratic freedoms.

41 "From the [communists] all that separates us is a question of name, since we both have our doctrinal roots in Marx's Capital and in the Communist Manifesto …" Caballero also defended, in that speech, the violent seizure of power, which, he argued, even moderate socialists had accepted. As reported on *Ahora* January 2, 1934.

42 The Russian Historical Society's collection of documents classified under the heading of "Comintern and the Spanish Civil War" contains numerous materials dated from 1923 to July 1936, as well as wartime documents. The collection entitled "Comintern and the Idea of World Revolution" includes 1,029 files. A total of 2,850 documents, most of them containing multiple pages, are classified as Comintern documents, most of them with originals held at RGASPI. http://docs.historyrussia.org/ru/indexes/values/16835.

43 Federal Archival Agency of the Russian Federation, Documents of the Soviet Era, http://sovdoc.rusarchives.ru/.

44 The user-friendly interface, for example, allows the user to keep her desired zoom level from one page to the next. http://komintern.dlibrary.org/ru/nodes/3680-opis-1-ispolkom-kominterna.

45 Fonds de la Section Française de l'Internationale Communiste; Fonds français de l'Internationale Communiste; Fonds de la direction du Parti Communiste Français (1922–1939), in Le Portail Archives Numériques et Données de la Recherche (PANDOR).

46 https://www.nationalarchives.gov.uk/.

47 Burnett Bolloten, *The Spanish Civil War. Revolution and Counter-Revolution* (Chapel Hill, NC: University of North Carolina Press, 1991) xvii.

Chapter 1

1. This is the "center-periphery" debate and that over the process of Stalinization of the various national CPs. See Norman LaPorte, Kevin Morgan, and Matthew Worley, "Introduction: Stalinization and Communist Historiography" in Morgan LaPorte and Worley (eds.) *Bolshevism, Stalinism and the Comintern. Perspectives on Stalinization, 1917–53* (Basingstoke: Palgrave Mcmillan, 2008) 1–21; see also Tim Rees and Andrew Thorpe, "Introduction" in their edited volume *International Communism and the Communist International* (Manchester: Manchester University Press, 1998) who argue, writing a few years after the opening of the Soviet archives, that "the availability of the material does not necessarily lead to the closure of the debate … "10; also Kevin McDermott and Jeremy Agnew, "Introduction" in McDermott and Agnew *The Comintern. A History of International Communist from Lenin to Stalin* (London: Macmillan, 1996) xxiii–iv, presenting Carr and Claudin as best representatives of the "relative autonomy" and total subordination poles respectively. Transnational approaches have attempted to steer the debate into a new direction and force us to take account of the international leadership of the ECCI. See Oleksa Drachewych, "The Communist Transnational? Transnational studies and the history of the Comintern" in *History Compass*, Vol. 17 (2019) 1–12.
2. See, for example, McDermott and Agnew, *Comintern*, 134; Tim Rees, "The Good Bolsheviks: The Spanish Communist Party and the Third Period" in Matthew Worley (ed.) *In Search for Revolution: International Communist Parties in the Third Period* (London: I. B. Tauris, 2004) 175, 177. Togliatti: "… en ningún otro país han tenido tan amplia y profunda repercusión como en España las decisiones del VII Congreso ….también los socialistas han leído y comentado …" Palmiro Togliatti *Escritos Sobre la Guerra de España* (Barcelona: Crítica, 1980) 47; Alba: "En España las repercusiones del VII Congreso fueron inmediatas y considerables." Victor Alba *El Partido Comunista en España* (Barcelona: Planeta, 1979) 160. See also Hermann Weber's helpful Stalinization model, according to which the Spanish party would appear to have been highly Stalinized after the elimination of the Bullejos leadership. See the helpful discussion in LaPorte, Morgan and Worley, "Introduction," 4–7.
3. Antonio Elorza and Marta Bizcarrondo, *Queridos Camaradas. La internacional Comunista y España 1919–1939* (Barcelona: Planeta, 1999).
4. Paul Preston, "The Creation of the Popular Front in Spain" in Helen Graham and Paul Preston (eds.) *The Popular Front in Europe* (London: Macmillan, 1987) 84. In the same volume Helen Graham argues that the PCE was "numerically so slight as to be politically negligible," Graham, "The Spanish Popular Front and the Civil War," 107.

5   Santos Juliá, "The Origin and Nature of the Spanish Popular Front" in Martin Alexander and Helen Graham, *The French and Spanish Popular Fronts. Comparative Perspectives* (Cambridge: Cambridge University Press, 1989) 26.
6   Hugo García, "Historia de un mito político: el peligro comunista en el discurso de las derechas españolas (1918 1936)" in *Historia Social,* No. 51 (2005) 19.
7   Herbert R. Southworth, *Conspiracy and the Spanish Civil War* (London: Routledge, 2002). Southworth was open about his ideological commitment to the Popular Front in Spain, less so about his salaried work for Juan Negrín during and after the Civil War. The book comes with a Paul Preston prologue. Among Spanish historians the influence of Southworth has been significant, especially Angel Viñas, see Viñas http://www.angelvinas.es/?tag=fascismo&paged=3, Hugo García who quotes Southworth repeatedly, see above; Eduardo González Calleja, "Los discursos catastrofistas de los líderes de la derecha y la difusión del mito del « golpe de Estado comunista »." El Argonauta español [online], 13 | 2016. See also Boris Volodarsky, *El Caso Orlov* (Barcelona: Crítica, 2013), openly indebted to both Viñas and Preston for his understanding of the Second Republic, lapsing often into the language of class war.
8   Russian Centre for the Preservation and Study of the Documents of Newest History (RCKHIDNI) later reconstituted as Russian State Archive of Socio-Political History, RGASPI, F. 495, Op. 4, D.10, l. 28–32. http://docs.historyrussia.org/ru/nodes/101357#mode/inspect/page/6/zoom/4. Such a skill was considered essential to the role of the communist agitator. Thus a *Pravda* editorial from April 7, 1935: "[y]ou must know and study people, what worries them, what they are interested in ... to find paths to their emotions ... and convince them ...," "Agitatsya—Bolshoe Iskutssvo," http://docs.historyrussia.org/ru/nodes/91034.
9   RCKHIDNI, F. 495, op. 3, D.360, l. 8–10, 34–5. http://docs.historyrussia.org/ru/nodes/101374#mode/inspect/page/3/zoom/4.
10   RGASPI. F. 495. Op. 19. D. 97. L. 1. http://docs.historyrussia.org/ru/nodes/101991.
11   The OMS, Otdel Mezhdunarodnoĭ Svyazi, International Relations Department, was headed by Pyatnitsky from 1921 to 1924, who was later promoted to head of the ECCI Organizational Bureau, of which the OMS was a part. Few ECCI departments achieved more for international communism, and none suffered more in the 1936 purges. See especially Vladimir Pyatnitsky (Osip Pyatnitsky's son*), Osip Pjatnickiĭ i Komintern na Vesakh Istorii* (Minsk: Charbest, 2004) 173–208 who used his father's RCKHIDNI file as well as an abundance of materials from his father's papers and interviews with some of his colleagues. The OMS in Germany and Western Europe was headed by Alexander ("Jacob") Mirov-Abramov, from 1921 to 1930, and Huber affirms Abramov was actually overall OMS head from 1926 to 1935, remaining as deputy one more year. See W. G. Krivitsky, *In Stalin's Secret Service* (New York: Harper, 1939) who knew Abramov personally, 54–5; see also the Abramov

file at The National Archives TNA, KV-2-2957-1, with many details of OMS operations in Spain 1934–6, see below. The most complete and accurate treatment probably in Peter Huber, "The Cadre Department, the OMS and the Dimitrov and Manuil'sky Secretariats During the Phase of the Terror" in Mikhail Narinsky and Jürgen Rojhan (eds.) *Centre and Periphery. The History of the Comintern in the Light of New Documents* (Amsterdam: International Institute of Social history, 1996) 122–52, esp. p. 149 with a valuable appendix detailing the OMS leaders and deputies; Milorad M. Drachkovitch (ed.) *A Biographical Dictionary of the Comintern* (Stanford, CA: Hoover Press, 1986); Barton Whaley, *Soviet Clandestine Communication Nets* (Cambridge, MA: MIT, 1969); Rees and Thorpe, *International Communism*, 55; McDermott and Agnew, *The Comintern*, 22. The OMS was operative in Spain throughout the period of our study, its representative in early 1936 being "Raul"/Raoul, that is, Carlo Codevilla, who transported funds to Spain as a courier and dealt with coded communications, among other tasks, reporting to Abramov. See TNA KV-2-2957-1. See also Margaret Buber-Neumann's account of her January 1933 visit with Abramov in Moscow in which he commissioned her and Neumann to become active participants in "le jeu occulte du communisme international" in Berlin and Spain. Buber Neumann, *La Révolution Mondiale* (Fr. edition; Paris: Casterman, 1971) 314–31. The archival material of the OMS is located in RGASPI, F. 495, Op. 23, and remains classified to this day.

12 Izdatel'stvo can also be rendered publishing house. The PCE organ, *La Antorcha*, was already being published since 1922.

13 José Bullejos, *La Comintern en España* (Mexico: Impresiones Modernas, 1972) 44–7. The works of communist dissidents need to be treated with skepticism, naturally, though never merely dismissed. In the present work, Bullejos merely confirms what we are establishing from the archival documentation, period press, and other sources. See also Alba, *El Partido*, 86–7, who cites further documentation on the dissatisfaction the Comintern felt in relation to this congress, taken from Colomer's extensive original documents collection. See Eduardo Comín Colomer, *Historia del Partido Comunista de España* (Madrid: Editora Nacional, 1965) 137–8.

14 RGASPI. F. 17. Op. 162. D. 2. L. http://docs.historyrussia.org/ru/nodes/100282.

15 RGASPI. F. 495. Op. 19.D. 97. L. 74. http://docs.historyrussia.org/ru/nodes/101996.

16 This was the understanding shared by much of the socialist union UGT, the youth branch FJS and even among the leadership of PSOE. See, for example, *El Socialista*, April 15, 1931, referring repeatedly in the leading editorial to the events of April 14 as "el triunfo de la revolución," "el hecho histórico de la revolución," etc. This is a theme we will develop throughout the book.

17 RGASPI. F. 534. Op. 8.D. 199. L. 12. http://docs.historyrussia.org/ru/nodes/102007.

18 On Tina Modotti, see Brigitte Studer, *The Transnational World of the Cominternians* (Tr. Dafydd Rees; Basingstoke: Palgrave Macmillan, 2015) 2, 77; Letizia Argenteri,

Tina Modotti: between Art and Revolution (New Haven, CT: Yale University Press, 2003) 158–9, though the author confuses Comintern names and aliases at various points.

19 RGASPI. F. 534. Op. 8. D. 199. L. 28–9. http://docs.historyrussia.org/ru/nodes/102008 and RGASPI. F. 534. Op. 8.D. 199. L. 102. http://docs.historyrussia.org/ru/nodes/102009.

20 Average daily salary (jornal) for agriculture in 1931 was about 3.50 pesetas or 105 pesetas monthly, and for metal workers 7 pesetas for a second-year apprentice, or 210 pesetas monthly, and between 5 and 6 pesetas for cable car workers in Madrid. See *Estadística de las Huelgas*, Memoria Correspondiente a los Años 1930 y 1931 (Ministerio de Trabajo y Previsión Social, Madrid, 1934). (Transporte, Año 6, Número 61, January 1931).

21 On the Unión Local de Sindicatos, its association with PCE and SRI (Spanish delegation of the Cominters's International Red Aid [MOPR]), see Manuel Angel Calvo Calvo, "Crímenes Sociales y Pistolerismo en la Sevilla de 1932" Universidad de Sevilla, available online. On Manuel Roldán, see a well-researched Andalucian blog with multiple stories from the local press in the 1920s and 1930s. http://donamencia.blogspot.com/2010/10/manuel-roldan-jimenez-el-agitador.html.

22 See Antonio Plaza Plaza, "El Sindicalismo Ferroviario Anarquista en España hasta la Guerra Civil. De los Sindicatos únicos a la Federación Nacional de la Industria Ferroviaria (1919–1936)," Vitoria-Gasteiz: VI Congreso de Historia Ferroviaria, 2012, available online, 12.

23 See Bullejos's report to the ECCI in which he mentions increasing numbers of strikes as a success metric. RGASPI. F. 495. Op. 32.D. 144. L. 230–47. This is a classic example of how communist influence in Spain was not merely a matter of PCE membership. Similarly, discussing the French Popular Front and the PCF's key role in it, Levy writes: "[PCF-inspired intense strike activities] had produced very little in the way of formal trade union or party membership but they did help to create a mood of militancy with an explosive potential." David Levy, "The French Popular Front 1936–1937" in Graham and Preston, *Popular Front*, 69.

24 RGASPI. F. 495. Op. 32. D. 144.L. 230–47. http://docs.historyrussia.org/ru/nodes/102017 Bullejos also wrote openly about the PCE programs for infiltrating the UGT and CNT unions: "Se fundaron los grupos sindicales *dentro de* los sindicatos de la Unión General de Trabajadores" (emphasis mine), Bullejos, *Comintern*, 158.

25 Data taken from the *Communist International* periodical of November 20, 1934, cited in Jonathan Haslam, "The Comintern and the Origins of the Popular Front 1934–35" in *The Historical Journal*, Vol. 22, No. 3 (September 1979) 685.

26 Stepanov was the pseudonym of Stoyán Miniéevich Mínev, known in Spain as Moreno. RGASPI. F. 495. Op. 32.D. 214.L. 21–5. http://docs.historyrussia.org/ru/nodes/102014.

27 Indicative of the progressive penetration of Socorro Rojo Internacional (International Red Aid) throughout Spain is the growing number of references to it in the press from 1931 to mid-1936, with the first half of 1936 having the greatest number of references. References to "Socorro Rojo" in the press in 1933 were 98, 101 in 1934, 192 in 1935, and 169 from January 1 to July 17, 1936. Many of its activities were costly events involving dances, concerts, transport, and, especially, travel to the Soviet Union for selected members of UGT, PSOE, and fellow traveling intellectuals who spread far and wide their praises of the Soviet Union in highly popular series of articles such as Nelken's or Sender's. SRI funding in Spain exploded in late 1934 with outstanding results for the Comintern and its Spanish section, see below.

28 Amigos de la Unión Soviética (AuS) was founded by leading cultural influencers in Spain with Comintern funding and masterful management, with outstanding results. AuS achieved seven thousand members nationally in a few months, most of them non-PCE members, and by mid-1936 it had chapters in over thirty cities. See Daniel Kowalsky, *Stalin and the Spanish Civil War*, chapter 6 "Soviet-Spanish Cultural Relations Prior to the Civil War," available online http://www.gutenberg-e.org/kod01/frames/fkod09.html.

29 See detailed report in RGASPI F. 495 Op. 20 D. 898.

30 Alba, *Partido*, 161. See also Alba's description of the PCE's infiltration of the socialist youth, which in the run-up to the creation of the joint JSU, counted on the active support of Margarita Nelken, who helped the Valencian communists "penetrar en las Juventudes Socialistas," a scheme denounced by Gorkin; Alba, *Partido*, 171.

31 Bullejos, *Comintern*, 157–8, also 155–6. A number of historians of the Second Republic assume mistakenly that PCE/Comintern influence in our period was directly proportionate to the numbers of PCE members ("afiliados"). See Juliá, "The Origins and Nature of the Spanish Popular Front," 26.

32 Elorza and Bizcarrondo, *Queridos*, 230.

33 RGASPI. F. 495. Op. 32. D. 215. L. 132–3 http://docs.historyrussia.org/ru/nodes/102015.

34 Neumann, *Révolution*, 318. Elorza and Bizcarrondo mistakenly identify "Octavio" as Purmann, *Queridos*, 171.

35 Bullejos, *Comintern*, 111.

36 RCKHIDNI, f. 495, op. 3, d.262, l. 8–9, 13–15. http://docs.historyrussia.org/ru/nodes/101366. See also Bullejos, *Comintern*, 130–5.

37 RCKHIDNI, F. 495, Op. 170, D. 5, l. 53–7. http://docs.historyrussia.org/ru/nodes/101371.

38 RCKHIDNI, F. 495, Op. 3, D.360, l. 8–10, 34–5. http://docs.historyrussia.org/ru/nodes/101374.

39 Thus, for example González Calleja, "Los Discursos," following Southworth and Viñas, who takes some Comintern public documents at face value and argues that the Comintern after the VII Congress "could not be further away" from promoting insurrectional actions. He also argues the socialist Jiménez de Asúa could not have been supportive of soviet-inspired insurrection, since he was a part of the socialist centrist faction. See below on Jiménez de Asúa.

40 RCKHIDNI, f. 494, op. 1, d. 1, l. 5–14. http://docs.historyrussia.org/ru/nodes/101383 Kuusinen chaired this preparatory commission made up of seventeen members including Manuilsky, Ercoli (Togliatti), Pyatnitsky, Kun, etc.

41 RCKHIDNI, f. 494, op. 1, d. 3, l. 191–2. http://docs.historyrussia.org/ru/nodes/101386.

42 See, for example, the final section of Caballero's speech to the socialist summer school, published in *El Socialista* August 13, 1933. See also the many references in José Manuel Macarro Vera, "The Socialists and Revolution" in Manuel Álvarez Tardío and Fernando del Rey Reguillo, *The Spanish Second Republic Revisited* (Eastbourne: Sussex Academic Press, 2012) 40–57.

43 RGASPI. F. 495. Op. 20.D. 270.L. 13–51.

44 RCKHIDNI, f. 495, op. 25, d.1349, l. 1–6, 9–10. http://docs.historyrussia.org/ru/nodes/101376.

45 This last phrase is a mantra of Comintern communications to its sections, and we shall have more to say about it in the below discussion of the terminology used by the Comintern to refer to armed uprisings and seizures of power.

46 See the chapter entitled "Communist Activity to Subvert the Armed Forces of the Ruling Classes" in the textbook Walter refers to in this document: Neuberg, *Armed Insurrection* (London: NLB, 1970) 151–70. The objective was to agitate and create disaffection via the creation of cells made up of soldiers, NCOs, and officers. who would at the right time become the core of the proletarian army and result in the disintegration of the army.

47 In reference to Stefan Rovecki (1895–1944), a Polish army officer, whose book *Walki Uliczne* (street fighting) of 1928 is available online here https://polona.pl/item-view/c76029f5-b7bc-4119-80fd-20b181f733bc?page=6. I am grateful to Frederick Litten of the Bavarian State Library for this reference.

48 See two ads in *La Tierra* of April 9 and 11, 1932: "En este libro, recientemente escrito y ya perseguido en todo el mundo capitalista, se hace un detenido examen de las principales insurrecciones proletarias de Europa y Asia, señalándose la táctica del bolchevismo en la batalla definitiva contra el poder burgués. Su autor, A. Neuberg, activo revolucionario, ha luchado en varias insurrecciones, ha enseñado táctica militar revolucionaria en el Instituto Lenin de Moscú, y es hoy uno de los grandes valores del comunismo internacional. Pedidos a Editorial Roja, Calle Raimundo Fernández Villaverde 10, Madrid." New Left Books of

London published a helpful English edition in 1970, which included a very interesting introduction by someone who was involved directly in the project: Erich Wollenberg. In his introduction, Wollenberg mentions the book was commissioned by Pyatnitsky in 1928, that Ercoli had an editorial role, and that the writers were Pyatnitsky and a number of the leaders in the insurrections presented in the book as case studies for global learning. Wollenberg explains that the Armed Insurrection text was needed because the earlier insurrection guide, "The Path to Victory: A Theoretical Discussion on Marxism and Insurrection," by "Alfred Lange" (Tuure Lechen), was aimed at fighters versed in Marxism-Leninism. Pyatnitsky wanted a follow-up work aimed at wider audience including fellow travelers.

49 See *Renovación* February 10, 1934, p. 3: "Por considerarlo de transcendental interés en los momentos actuales, damos a continuación fragmentos del interesante libro de A. Neuberg ... Las Juventudes Socialistas deben leerlos, estudiarlos, comentarlos y adaptarlos," the fragment selected dealt with guerrilla warfare in cities; *Renovación* February 17, 1934, p. 2; also *Transporte*, the organ of UGT's transport union on February 15, 1934, with its leading headline reading: "Los tranviarios de Madrid se pronuncian por la insurrección armada." After the Popular Front was declared the winner of the February 1936 elections, the expectation of a new armed insurrection, this time benefiting from full unity among socialists and communists, was declared at a rally including Socorro Rojo, as well as both socialist and communist leaders. See *La Libertad*, March 19, 1936.

50 I have used for this survey the Hemeroteca Digital of the National Library of Spain, a collection of 143 historic newspapers and magazines from all sides of the political spectrum and most Spanish provinces. In 1991, there were three mentions of the phrase "insurrección armada"; four in 1932, of which two were ads for the book; three mentions in 1933; nineteen mentions in 1934, most in reference to the socialist-led armed insurrection of October, and several in open calls to armed insurrection in the socialist periodicals, others in the monarchical and Catholic press warning of the danger of armed insurrection, including references to the book; thirty-six mentions in 1935, all but two in connection with the October 1934 armed insurrection, but several in the moderate socialist newspaper *Democracia* arguing against armed insurrection; twenty-seven mentions from January 1 to July 17, 1936, either in reference to October 1934 or of future insurrections.

51 RGASPI. F. 495. Op. 32. D. 219. L. 34–5. http://docs.historyrussia.org/ru/nodes/102016.

52 "In October 1928, the Politburo of the Central Committee of the CPSU(b) authorized the Executive Committee of the Comintern to introduce into the MLS curriculum a number of new military disciplines." V. Pyatnitsky, *Osip Pjatnickij i Komintern*, 269. Vladimir Pyatnitsky cites RTSKHIDNI Fund 17.162, D. 7 as the source. Strictly military instructors like Wilhem Zaisser taught at both ILS and the military school at Bakovka station (see below). Nigel West writes that the military

training came at the end of the ILS regular program, see Nigel West, *Mask, MI5's Penetration of the Communist Party of Great Britain* (London: Routledge, 2005) 289; Kirchenbaum writes that street fighting and shooting were part of the curriculum in 1936 and "perhaps earlier," Lisa A. Kirschenbaum, *International Communism and the Spanish Civil War* (Cambridge: Cambridge University Press, 2015) 16; in May 1932, Finish graduates of the ILS were immediately deployed to armed insurrectional operations, see RGASPI. F. 495. Op. 25 D. 1399. L. 139–41. Details of the military ILS course material are known from the testimonies of Steve Nelson and other Americans who attended ILS in the same period (early 1930s) including weapons training, guerrilla tactics, etc. See *The Case of Steve Nelson from the Records, Appendix to Part I, Proposed Anti-Subversion Legislation* (Washington: US Government printing Office, 1959) 635–53.

53 RGASPI. F. 495. Op. 32. D. 224. Part 1. L. 4v. http://docs.historyrussia.org/ru/nodes/102018.

54 See E. V. Elpátievsky, *La Emigración Española en la URSS. Historiografía y Fuentes. Intento de Interpretación* (Tr. Encinas Moral (Madrid: Exterior XXI, 2008) 46–72, for a discussion of the forty-five socialists hosted by the Comintern in Russia with the approval of Ercoli and Diaz, correspondence between them and del Vayo, activities and discussion with Nelken, etc.

55 The communication exchange between del Vayo and MOPR leader Stasova is in the TNA Stasova file, KV2-3596.

56 Lehen is the "Alfred" of "The Path to Victory: A Theoretical Discussion on Marxism and Insurrection," and was a frequent lecturer at all the military schools. He had been deployed to Germany in 1929 to infiltrate the army there and was a veteran of insurrectional work in Austria in addition to his home country of Finland and would be sent to the Spanish Civil War in 1936.

57 RCKHIDNI, f. 495, op. 25, d.1335, l. 122–5. http://docs.historyrussia.org/ru/nodes/101405.

58 For the secret unpublished clauses of the VII Congress on mandatory military work by the sections see RCKHIDNI, f. 494, op. 1, d.437, l. 2. http://docs.historyrussia.org/ru/nodes/101403. The document was given to the sections with a cover letter signed by Walter.

59 Zaisser was later sent to Spain during the Spanish Civil War as "General Gomez." He later led the Stasi in East Germany. See his biography at Ministerium für Staatssicherheit, (aka Stassi) Lexicon. https://www.bstu.de/mfs-lexikon/detail/zaisser-wilhelm/.

60 RCKHIDNI, F. 495, Op. 4, D. 310, l. 15–21. http://docs.historyrussia.org/ru/nodes/101389.

61 Enrique Lister, *Memorias de un Luchador* (Madrid: G. del Toro, 1977) 57. Lister writes that at the military academy he was accompanied by other Spaniards, one of which had participated in the October 1936 insurrection.

62 Ibid. 59.
63 RGASPI. F. 495. Op. 20.D. 270.L. 13–51. http://docs.historyrussia.org/ru/nodes/102028. On July 18, 1936, the "Cuartel de Pacífico" or Cuartel de Daoiz y Velarde, was guarded by JSU and UGT elements, and several soldiers from the barracks collaborated in the supply of weapons to socialist militias. See Antonio Cordón García, *Trayectoria: Memorias de un Militar Republicano* (Madrid: Editorial Crítica, 1977).
64 Mr. Calvo Sotelo argued that the infiltration and undermining of the armed forces was one of several subversive activities being supported by both socialists and communists, working as a cohesive force within the Popular Front coalition. Thus Calvo Sotelo: "¿Es que no sabe S.S. que se desarrolla en los cuarteles una política enorme de indisciplina? (grandes y prolongados rumores) Aquí tengo un número del Soldado Rojo que ha llegado a mis manos, en el que se dan nombres y apellidos de jefes y oficiales, señalándolos a la brutalidad de las gentes comunistas." *ABC* April 16, 1936.
65 Manuel Espada, "Informe del Camarada Espada a los Camaradas de la Dirección," AHPCE, Manuscritos de Libros, Tesis, Memorias, 35/1. Espada's fascinating report confirms several details about the communist infiltration of the navy, the leading role of Jose Antonio Paz Martinez, and the communist control of the UMRA and others made by Fernando Moreno de Alborán and Salvador Moreno de Alborán, in *La Guerra Silenciosa y Silenciada* Vol. I (Madrid: Gráficas Lormo, 1998).
66 For the Comintern work in the British army see, for example, Christopher Andrews, *The Defence of the Realm. The Authorized History of MI5* (London: Penguin, 2009) 161–85; West, *MI5*, 271, 294–5. For the Comintern army work in France see George Vidal, "L'armée française face au communisme du début des années 1930 jusqu'à 'la débâcle" in *Historical Reflections/Réflexions Historiques*, Vol. 30, No. 2 (Summer 2004) 283–309. See also, for example, *Le Figaro* of April 10, 1936 warning of recent Comintern instructions for the French section to "intensifier le travail dans l'armée francaise."
67 See Douglas Little, "Red Scare, 1936: Anti-Bolshevism and the Origins of British Non-Intervention in the Spanish Civil War" in *Journal of Contemporary History*, Vol. 23, No. 2 Bolshevism and the Socialist Left (Apr., 1988) 291–311. The fact that the "Zinoniev letter" was a fake does not turn the Comintern operations in the UK, so carefully tracked by MI5, into mythology. See in The National Archives, the TNA KV2 series.
68 "M. Jean Fabry lut dans un silence impressionant les documents officiels du Komintern qui donnent les consignes por les temps a vénir." In an article entitled "Jean Fabry Évoque Les Dangers de L'Heure," in *L'Intransigeant*, April 26, 1936.
69 See Martin Conway and Peter Romijn, "Political Legitimacy in Mid Twentieth Century Europe" in Conway and Romijn (eds.) *The War for Legitimacy in Politics and Culture 1936–1946* (Oxford: Ber, 2008) 1–27.

70 A revolt, a coup. The noun is a cognate of revolyutsiya, revolution. The noun appears 4,233 times in all its inflected forms in the 109,000-document electronic library of historical documents of the Russian Historical Society. The search was carried out in January 2022, and later additions to the database may alter these numbers, though not likely the overall proportions. The noun is used in reference to the 1930 left-wing coup attempt by Spanish army officers at Jaca, of the July 17 uprising led by Mola, Franco, and other generals, of the 1939 Casado uprising against the communist-controlled Negrín government, and, interestingly, of an insurrection against Azaña Dimitrov told the ECCI was an option in late July 1936: "with the army divided, if we can take a garrison in the center we can do a coup (perevorot') and overthrow Azaña in 24 hours … then do a manifesto for a truly republican and democratic government" RGASPI. F. 495. Op. 18.D. 1101. L. 21–3.

71 Putch, appears 303 times in the electronic document database. It is used in reference to the December 1933 anarchist insurrection attempt, of the Comintern-alleged 1937 putsch attempt by the POUM "Trotskyists" in Spain, and also of the putsch-like tactics of the socialists in October 1934, essentially for not including the Communists sufficiently in the plan and execution.

72 Over 10,000 times, including references to insurrections supported by the Comintern in Greece, Bulgaria, Finland, and of the Spanish and Austrian insurrections of 1934, etc.

73 RCKHIDNI, f. 495, op. 2, d. 196, l. 82–94. http://docs.historyrussia.org/ru/nodes/101394.

74 RGASPI. F. 495. Op. 20.D. 262.L. 16–21. http://docs.historyrussia.org/ru/nodes/102020. In line with Togliatti: "La Victoria electoral de febrero 1936 abre una nueva fase de la revolución en España … una espléndida victoria táctica … impulsa a nuevas masas por el camino de la lucha revolucionaria contra los terratenientes, la gran burguesía y el capitalismo." *Escritos sobre la Guerra*, 42–3.

75 The instructions to pursue a merging of the unions came together with the permission to join the Alianzas Obreras in the run-up to the October 1934 armed uprising. The instruction was to exploit and grow existing penetration of UGT so as to control the management, and then move toward a congress for unification and to a merger based on class warfare, create armed worker-peasant militias, etc. See RCKHIDNI, f. 495, op. 4, d. 310, l. 15–21 already cited above.

76 RGASPI. F. 495. Op. 19. D. 99. L. 10. http://docs.historyrussia.org/ru/nodes/102004.

77 RGASPI. F. 495. Op. 32.D. 109.L. 14–52,151–7. http://docs.historyrussia.org/ru/nodes/102012.

78 Luis Araquistain, "The Struggle in Spain" in *Foreign Affairs* 12.3, April 1934, 470.

79 Araquistain brands Gil Robles a fascist, before whom "se ha acabado el socialismo reformista, democrático y pacifico … pronto no habrá más que un socialismo revolucionario, insurreccional en el mundo …" *Heraldo de Madrid* February 15, 1934.

80 I have used the digital archives of the Biblioteca Nacional de España. *La Nación*, March 10, 1933.
81 *Siglo Futuro* March 20, 1933, recounts anti-fascist attack on the Escuela de Obreros Catolicos; *La Libertad* March 23, 1933, recounts how communist and union youth went to obstruct an Accion Popular rally with Mr. Goicoechea speaking; *Ahora* March 28, 1933, "Comunistas sevillanos. mitin antifascista ... combatieron el fascismo y propugnaron la unión de los elementos revolucionarios para combatir *a las derechas*" (emphasis mine).
82 As reported on *Heraldo de Madrid*, March 27, 1933.
83 *Heraldo de Madrid*, July 6, 1933. The congress had moved to Paris, which enabled the participation and support of the significant Comintern and French Communist Party organization there.
84 Ellen Wilkinson, MP, was an intimate friend and collaborator of both Willi *Münzenberg* and Otto Katz, the creators and managers of the Comintern's anti-fascist agit-prop machine in Paris. See the substantial Otto Katz and Willi *Münzenberg* files detailing Ellen Wilkinson's regular communication and financial arrangements with the Paris-based Cominternians, *TNA KV-2-1383; KV-2-773*.
85 Barbusse would soon take over from *Münzenberg* as lead Comintern Anti-Fascism propagandist, with Comintern funding of around 100,000 francs per month, and 3,000 francs in personal expenses, as of September 1934. RGASPI.495-60-246a, 142–4, 150, cited in Sean McMeekin, *The Red Millionaire, a Political Biography of Willi Münzenberg* (New Haven: Yale University Press, 2003) 363. See also Helmut Gruber, "Willi Münzenberg: Propagandist for and against the Comintern" in *International Review of Social History*, Vol. 10, No. 2 (1965) 193–6. See also RGASPI 495.19.213, which includes documents from Henri Barbusse about the management of anti-fascist fellow travelers connected to the Comintern in Spain, including Ellen Wilkinson. Also, part of Münzenberg's team in Paris, KPD expatriates like them, were Heinz Neumann and Gustav Regler, like Otto, Spanish speakers who had resided in Spain at various points under Comintern assignments in the early 30s. Neumann's file at TNA is KV-2-1058, and Regler's KV-2-3506.
86 *Heraldo de Madrid*, July 13, 1933.
87 See, for example, the article on UGT's transport workers union, *Transporte* of June 15, 1933, reporting on the Paris Congress of the Anti-fascist front. The article, citing the French socialist reporter at the congress, attacks the communist organizers for pretending to be in favor of a united antifascist front while excluding some socialists and "Trotskyists."
88 See on this the study based on complete Soviet archival research on Barbusse and his close relationship with Stalin and the Comintern in Romain Ducoulomber, "Henri Barbusse, Stalin and the making of the Comintern's International Policy" in *French History*, Vol. 30, No. 4 (2016) 526–45, esp. 540. Ducoulomber shows the

growing influence of Barbusse with Stalin and the latter's approval of Barbusse's strategy that led to the creation of the Committee as a merger of the Amsterdam and Pleyel movements.

89 The German text followed by the version in a large set of documents related mainly to the October 1934 armed insurrection. An die Politkommission. Material Zur Frage: Gründung Einer "Volksfront" in Spanien. RGASPI. F. 495. Op. 32.D. 225. http://komintern.dlibrary.org/ru/nodes/3253-delo-225-obzor-pechati-romanskogo-lendersekretariata-ikki#mode/inspect/page/88/zoom/7.

90 See, for example, the editorial notes added to RGASPI. F. 488. Op. 1. D 15. L 23. http://docs.historyrussia.org/ru/nodes/101408. "Max Albert" is the pseudonym of Hugo Eberlein, who was also referred to simply as "Albert," for example, in the record of his speech at the first Comintern Congress. On Hugo Eberlein see Drachkovitch, *Biographical Dictionary*, for a career survey; see Vladimir Pyatnitsky who writes that Eberlein was his father's closest confidant, *Osip Pjatnickij i Komintern, 168, 214, 538;* Gustav Regler, *The Owl of Minerva* (New York: Farrar, 1960) 209, 228. Regler was Eberlein's KPD comrade and partner in multiple operations. Regler tells the fascinating story of Eberlein's arrival in Moscow fresh out of the German revolution in 1918. There was no sugar for his tea and Lenin proceeded to search the Kremlim until he came back with sugar for Eberlein, wrapped in a page out of *Pravda*. Eberlein and Regler were together in the Saar during the failed 1935 Comintern campaign there, during which Eberlein was keeping a tight rein on the Comintern funding. See also reference to Eberlein in the TNA Abramov file. See also Marie-Cécile Bouju, *Lire en Communiste: Les Maisons d'édition du Parti Communiste Français 1920–1968* (Rennes: Presses Universitaires de Rennes, 2010) 84.

91 See Frederick S. Litten, "The Noulens Affair" in *The China Quarterly*, Vol. 138 (1994) 501.

92 Jiménez de Asúa had also been an early member of the Comintern-funded Amigos de la Unión Soviética (Friends of the Soviet Union), and Frente Antifascista, participating in the rally addressed by Barbusse in July 1933 (see above). Southworth may not have known this and found his inclusion in an alleged Comintern candidate commissars list incredible, given that he was a "supporter of parliamentary Government." Southworth quoting Gabriel Jackson approvingly in Southworth, *Conspiracy*, 91.

93 Literally unbound (razvyazannye). RCKHIDNI. F. 494. Op. 1.D.423. http://docs.historyrussia.org/ru/nodes/91238.

94 Juliá, "The Origins and Nature of the Spanish Popular Front" in Alexander and Graham, *The French and Spanish*, 35. Helen Graham, "The Spanish Popular Front and the Civil War" in Graham and Preston, *Popular Front* 106.

95 Rees writes that "The PCE was even more fortunate in finding itself as part of the Spanish Popular Front, given that it played no active part in its creation." Tim Rees, "The Popular Fronts and Civil War in Spain" in Silvio Pons and Stephen Smith (eds.) *Cambridge History of Communism. Vol. I, World Revolution and Socialism in One Country 1917–1941* (Cambridge: Cambridge University Press, 2017) 262–3. Even if Rees sets aside the "Albert" document and the Comintern's larger popular front strategy emerging from the VII Congress, Rees cannot ignore the fact that the non-inclusion of the PCE was a deal breaker as per the socialists demands, and that Caballero and the PCE were in constant discussions while the PSOE considered Azaña's invitation to the electoral alliance.

96 Graham and Preston, "The Popular Front and the Struggle against Fascism," 16. In the same volume, David Levy explains the French Communist Party's leading role in the creation of the French Popular Front: "The [PCF] became the moving force behind the Popular Front, providing both the political initiatives and the slogans for the movement," even the very phrase Front Populaire, drafted by the Comintern representative Fried. Levy, "The French" in Graham and Preston, *Popular Front*, 58–83.

97 Preston, "The Creation of the Popular front in Spain" 85. Preston engages here, as he does elsewhere, in fairly obvious straw man building. He quotes a popular and rather colorful francoist account in order to discredit the thesis and establish guilt by association of anyone else holding such a view. Preston's own ideological commitments are fairly transparent in this discussion. A more balanced view is presented by McDermott and Agnew who see the origins of the Popular Front in a triple interaction of factors, but certainly including the Comintern's leading. McDermott and Agnew, *Comintern*, 121.

98 "El frente popular es hoy la orden de Moscú," *Democracia*, September 20, 1935, though *Democracia* appreciated the concept of the popular front as an electoral coalition. This identification of the popular front with Moscow and the Comintern was, of course shared in the Catholic and monarchist press in Spain and in the conservative press north of the Pyrenees. Thus, *Le Matin* of December 13, 1935: "Stalin, patron du front Populaire."

99 Preston "At the time of the formation of … the Popular Front, the Communist Party played merely a peripheral role," Preston, "The Creation of the Popular front in Spain" in Graham and Preston, 84. Likewise Graham: "… the PCE was numerically so slight as to be politically negligible," "The Spanish" 107.

100 The term used in the manifesto was not "Frente Popular" but "Coalición de Izquierdas." Interestingly, La Libertad of the same day claims to have led the initiative and refers to the pact using the Comintern nomenclature of "frente único" and had referred to it as "frente popular" on January 15. As we saw above, the *La Libertad* Subdirector Antonio de Lezama was among the names mentioned

by Eberlein in the Comintern report. Indalecio Prieto, on the other hand, had used "frente popular" and "coalición de izquierdas" interchangeably in *La Libertad* of January 10. See the text of the Manifiesto Electoral de las Izquierdas, for example, on *Heraldo de Madrid*, January 16, 1936. The socialists signed in their own name and in the name of ("en representación de") UGT, PCE, FNJS, Partido Sindicalista and POUM. However, Vicente Uribe of the PCE signed the document as well.

101 This could have happened the very same day, see Santos Juliá, "The Origins," 31.

102 Luis Araquistain, *El Comunismo y la Guerra de España* (San José: Costa Rica, 1939) 9. Balloten, *The Spanish*, 131–2.

103 Balloten, *The Spanish*, 130–1.

104 Prieto, however, favored giving priority to negotiations with Azaña and the republicans. See Juan Simeón Vidarte, *El Bienio Negro y la Insurrección de Asturias* (Barcelona: Grijalbo, 1978) 494. In the author's words, Caballero's thinking in those days was heavily influenced by his desire for the "bolshevization of the party."

105 RCKHIDNI. F. 495. Op. 2.D. 222.L. 129–38. http://docs.historyrussia.org/ru/nodes/91242.

106 Record of the conversation of the General Secretary of the Central Committee of the CPSU (b) I.V. Stalin with the German writer Leon Feuchtwanger. January 8, 1937. http://docs.historyrussia.org/ru/nodes/126138.

Chapter 2

1 Anthony Pemberton and Pauline G. M. Aarten, "Narrative in the Study of Victimological Processes in Terrorism and Political Violence: An Initial Exploration" in *Studies in Conflict and Terrorism*, Vol. 41, No. 7 (2018) 543.

2 George L. Mosse, *Fallen Soldiers. Reshaping the Memory of the World Wars* (New York: Oxford University Press, 1990).

3 Brian D. Bunk, "Your Comrades Will Not Forget. Revolutionary Memory and the Breakdown of the Spanish Second Republic" in *History and Memory*, Vol. 14, No. 1–2 (Spring-Winter 2002) 65–92, quote on p. 67.

4 MOPR is the Russian acronym of the International Organization for Aid to the Fighters of the Revolution, headed by Helena Stasova. Internationally the organization was known as International Red Aid, Rote Hilfe in the German-speaking world, and Socorro Rojo Internacional in Spain.

5 Juliá argued that there was no real popular front in Spain until the start of the Spanish Civil War, and that as late as November 1935 there was still no unity of action among communists, socialists, and others, the distribution of substantial Soviet aid notwithstanding. See Santos Juliá, "The Origins and Nature of the Spanish Popular Front" in Martin Alexander and Helen Graham (eds.) *The French and Spanish Popular Fronts* (Cambridge: Cambridge University Press) 27.

6   In order based on volume consulted for this chapter: The Russian State Archive of Socio-Political History (RGASPI); The National Archives of the UK (TNA), Labour History Archive and Study Centre (LHASC); and Archivo Histórico del PCE (AHPCE).
7   See, for example, Martin Alexander and Helen Graham, "Introduction" in *The French and Spanish Popular Fronts*, 2; Helen Graham and Paul Preston, "The Popular Front and the Struggle against Fascism" in Graham and Preston (eds.) *The Popular Front in Europe* (London: Macmillan, 1989) 4; Helen Graham, "The Spanish Popular Front and the Civil War" in *Popular Front in Europe*, 109. Graham identifies correctly the amnesty demand as the focus of popular fervor in the Popular Front campaign, but considers it grassroots driven.
8   For example Paul Preston, "The Creation of the Popular Front in Spain" in Helen Graham and Paul Preston (eds.) *Popular Front in Europe* (London: Macmillan, 1989) 85.
9   Avec M. Alexandre Lerroux, président du conseil. *L'Oest Eclair*, December 6, 1934, p. 2.
10 See the account Juan Simeón-Vidarte claimed to have heard directly from General Lopez Ochoa. Juan Simeón-Vidarte, *El Bienio Negro y la Insurrección de Asturias* (Barcelona: Grijalbo, 1978) 361. Simeón-Vidarte played a leading role in the preparation of the armed insurrection, as well as in the amnesty campaign that followed it and his memoirs should be read more critically than Preston seems to have done.
11 Cited in Luis Pericot Garcia, *Historia de España Vol VI* (Madrid: Instituto Gallach, 1967) 129.
12 Simeón-Vidarte, *Bienio Negro*, 341.
13 On the long and tense debates among the members of the cabinet see Ricardo de la Cierva, *Fracaso del Octubre Revolucionario: La Represión* (Madrid: Arc Editores, 1997) 85–94.
14 The number of red prisoners shot, often summarily, after the Finnish Civil War exceeded 10,000 and included many women. See Toumas Tepora and Aapo Roselius (eds.) *The Finnish Civil War 1918* (Leiden: Brill, 2014). For a brief discussion of the European context, including the Finnish repression, see Stanley G. Payne, *The Collapse of the Spanish Republic 1933–1936* (New Haven: Yale University Press, 2006) 101–3.
15 This is a correct technical term as per socialist and communist understanding of the events, see Caballero in *El Socialista* April 21, 1934: "Los momentos actuales no permiten otra salida que la insurrección armada de la clase trabajadora para adueñarse del poder político íntegramente, instaurando la dictadura del proletariado," and Graciano Antuña's own language cited below. See also a detailed discussion on Comintern training on armed insurrection and its application in Spain in Chapter 1. An account of the victims caused by the revolutionaries

hosted by the socialist Fundación Pablo Iglesias mentions a total of 1,377 killed, of which 326 were army and police forces, and nearly 3,000 wounded. http://archivo.fpabloiglesias.es/files/Unidades/AH/70/AH-70-42.pdf. The accounting carried out by Aurelio de Llano, which Ricardo de la Cierva considered the most accurate, added up to 1,196 killed and 2,068 wounded including both the loyal forces and loyal civilians. See de la Cierva, *Fracaso*, 39.

16 Antuña appears several times in the lists of socialist, communist, and anarchist émigrés kept in the Comintern archives. See A.V. Elpátievsky, *La Emigración Española en la URSS* (Madrid: Gráficas de Diego, 2008) 56–72.

17 "Una vez aceptado, como esta por el Partido Socialista Obrero Español la necesidad de la violencia para la revolución por medio de la insurrección armada a fin de establecer la Dictadura del Proletariado [sic], no sería fácil ... desplazarle de la posición actual." Handwritten and signed letter in Spanish and cover note in Russian requesting an urgent response in RGASPI 495. Op. 32.D. 225.

18 The full prisoner population in Spain as of October 13, 1934, was of 25,000. The government budget commission approved an increase of 4 million pesetas to cover the population increase in October, once the total reached 25,000. See, for example, "25000 presos en las cárceles de España" in *Heraldo Segoviano*, October 13, 1934. On October 26, the Madrid daily *La Voz* covered the minister of justice's trip to the prison in Oviedo and detailed that the prisoner increase attributable to the insurrection was of 743, that is, the number before the insurrection was 239 and 982 after. On November 2, *Ahora* reported the number of prisoners in Oviedo was up to 1,047. See also the Anuario Estadístico Español data for 1934 in Luis Gargallo Vaamonde, *El Sistema Penitenciario de la Segunda República* (Madrid: Ministerio del Interior, 2010) 201.

19 See on the correspondence between Antuña and the exiles with Caballero J. A. Sánchez, y Jimenez Saúco *La Revolución de 1934 en Asturias* (Madrid: Editora Nacional, 1974) 152.

20 Bruno Alonso, "Salvemos a la República," article published in *La Libertad* and reprinted in the socialist *Democracia*, July 27, 1935. In this piece, Alonso issues a passionate call for the formation of the left-wing block on the sole basis of promoting the rights of the prisoners from the October armed insurrection.

21 This is the first of several Comintern messages to its UK sections on the topic, all intercepted by UK intelligence as part of the MASK program. Nigel West, *MASK. MI5's Penetration of the Communist Party of Great Britain* (London: Routledge, 2005) 132.

22 On the long and tense debates between Alcalá Zamora and the centrist republicans and conservatives on the topic of the death sentences, a debate won by the president of the Republic without de support of the Supreme Court, see Stanley Payne, *The Collapse of the Spanish Republic* (New Haven, CT: Yale University

Press, 2006) 97–8. As Payne points out, the conservatives also failed to see the implementation of their motion for an investigation of the involvement of the unions in the insurrection.
23 July 1933 telegram from Roman Lander Sekretariat to ECCI. RGASPI Fond 495. Op. 4.D., 254. Heckert, Losowksi, and Piatnitsky were commissioned to study and reply on this matter.
24 January 18, 1934 World Committee report on cooperation with other organizations and committees. A handwritten note indicates this is for the information of Bela Kun. The report includes highlights from several individual countries. RGASPI 495. Op. 60. D. 248a. A July 1933 expense report held in the files of the correspondence of the Anti-War Commission details the cost of Lord Marley's travel from Madrid to Marseille at 1,000 French Francs. RGASPI. F. 495. Op. 60. D. 242a.
25 *Ahora*, November 15, 1934. The opinion expressed by José Calvo Sotelo that day made it to the pages of the monarchist daily ABC: "eso es realmente indigno," the columnist adding that several members of the Cortes would investigate the suspicious entities behind this visit. On the 17th *The Scotsman* published, upon the return of the British politicians, Ellen Wilkinson's assessment of the visit. She claimed that the hostile reception they had in Oviedo was "engineered" as an excuse to escort them to the border, and that their visit had been simply "a private party organized to satisfy our curiosity." Wilkinson's explanation notwithstanding, the Labour Party discussed in internal communications Wilkinson's lack of credentials for this activity and the fact that it was giving the Labour Party "a bad name." Labour History Archive, LP/WG/SPA 56–63. See also the colorful description of the visit in *Time Magazine* of November 26, 1934, in an article entitled "Spain. Priests into Pork." On Münzenberg's organization of the visit and his subsequent friendship with del Vayo and other "pro-Russia socialists" see also Babette Gross, *Willi Münzenberg: Una Biografía Política* (Tr. Ruth Gonzalo; Vitoria: Ikusager, 2007) 368.
26 Correspondence between Ernest Robinson and the Assistant Secretary of the Labour Party, LP WG SPA 56.
27 See on this Laura Beers, *Red Ellen. The Life of Ellen Wilkinson, Socialist, Feminist, Internationalist* (Cambridge, MA: Harvard University Press, 2016) 299.
28 E. Stasova letter to the Political Commission of the ECCI, November 14, 1934 RGASPI F. 495. Op. 4. D. 441.
29 November 19, 1934 telegram in West, *MI5*. 134–5.
30 See on this Neus Samblancat Miranda, "Clara Campoamor, Pionera de la Modernidad" in Clara Campoamor, *La Revolución Española Vista por una Republicana* (Barcelona: Universidad Autònoma de Barcelona, 2002) 37. See, for example, *Heraldo de Madrid* of November 18, 1934, for coverage of the launch of this government program. On the 19th, *La Voz* reported Campoamor was in

Santander visiting the Gobernador Civil to announce the building of orphanages for the children of the victims.
31. See article on the cover of *Heraldo de Madrid*, October 20, 1934.
32. See RGASPI F. 558 Op. 2 D. 115, mentioning the amount in pesetas and its equivalent of 350,000 gold rubles.
33. January 7, 1935. A la Commission Politique de l' I.C. Sur la Campagne Internationale Contre le Terreur en Espagne. RGASPI F. 495 Op. 204 D. 441.
34. Arthur Koestler, *The Invisible Writing* (Boston: The Beacon Press, 1954) 224.
35. In the summer of 1932, International Red Aid was at Villa de Don Fadrique after the shootout between communists and Guardia Civil agents, attempting to bring some of the children of the communist peasants killed and wounded to Madrid. Codovilla waited for the group at the train station in Madrid, but the government had forbidden the removal of the minors. Codovilla felt the campaign had been a great success, nonetheless. Undated letter from Medina to Moscow, probably from August 1932, RGASPI. F. 495. Op. 32. D. 213. In late February 1934, the Comintern instructed Codovilla to organize campaigns in favor of the orphans of the Austrian insurrection, including sponsorships. Moscow to Spain, February 28, 1934, TNA HW 17/26.
36. *El Dia de Palencia*, 31 de enero 1934. A similar report in *Diario de Almeria* of 10th of February 1935. Laura Branciforte, takes the Red Aid propaganda at face value and affirms that Socoro Rojo "se ocupó del socorro y de la evacuación de los niños." Her entire paper needs re-writing in light of the archival evidence. Laura Branciforte, "Legitimando la Solidaridad Femenina Internacional" in *Arenal*, Vol. 16, No. 1 (2009) 27–52.
37. *Secretariat Romaine, orateur Codovilla, January 29, 1935, Question Espagnole. RGASPI f. 495. Op. 32. D. 165.* The document includes questions and answers in dialogue with Ercoli and others during the presentation.
38. See the report in *Hoja Oficial del Lunes* of May 27, 1935.
39. See "Au C.C. du P.C. Espagnol," January 11, 1935, RGASPI F. 495 Op. 32 D. 224; Lista de Consignas para la Jornada Internacional Femenina, Ibid. The Comintern and its Spanish section struggled to reach Spanish women with their message, these efforts notwithstanding. In late May 1936, a draft resolution for work "among women" determined that the February 1936 elections had revealed that women were "perfectamente susceptibles" to be wrenched from the hands of fascism, provided the Communists could show they respected the "religious" feelings of women. It was decided, therefore, that Dolores (Pasionaria) should publicly announce that the PCE is not against the feelings of believers. Additionally, a brochure should be published "in very popular language" about several key problems women face, connecting these to the political situation. Protokoll (A) 47 May 29, 1936 and accompanying draft document Work Among Women RGASPI F. 494 Op. 18 D. 1092.

40 Begleitbrief zum Brief der PC. Betreffs MOPR Arbeit. An Das ZK der KP Spaniens. RGASPI. F. 495. Op. 32.D. 224. Letter is written in South American Spanish using "ustedes" instead of "vosotros," perhaps by Ercoli. This is a stylistic mistake corrected in other similar letters sent to the Spanish party from the center I have seen.
41 Thus *Diario de Palencia* January 31, 1935 report on the activities of Pasionaria and Asociación Pro-Infancia entitled "Captando niños para envenenarlos de odio revolucionario."
42 On August 18, 1933, UGT advised its members that Red Aid was a communist organization set up "against" the socialist Fondo Matteotti, and that UGT members should only contribute funds to the socialist fund. "El Fondo Matteotti," in *Justicia Social* of that date. In August 1933 UGT decided to reject an invitation to visit the USSR made to them by Red Aid and Friends of the Soviet Union in Spain, explaining that UGT only sends to foreign destinations the delegations selected by itself and for purposes aligned with its own objectives. See brief report "Unión General de Trabajadores. Reunión de la Ejecutiva," in *Luz*, August 11, 1933.
43 J. Martínez Amutio, *Chantaje a un Pueblo* (Madrid: G. del Toro, 1974) 269–70.
44 Protokoll die Pariser Hilfskonferenz *für die Opfer* der Faschismus in Spanien, fourth point in the discussion. RGASPI. F. 495. Op. 4.D. 471.
45 Protokoll (A) Nbr. 14 Der Sitzung der Sekretariats der EKKI vom November 16, 1935. RGASPI. F. 495. Op. 18. D. 1030.
46 The data on del Vayo's activities in the Comintern archives requires a heavy revision of the apologetic of del Vayo put forth, for example, by Cristina Rodriguez Gutierrez, "Julio Álvarez del Vayo y Olloqui. ¿Traidor o Víctima?" in *Espacio Tiempo y Forma*, Vol. 16 (2004) 291–308.
47 Correspondence and report in RGASPI F. 543. Op. 1. D. 25.
48 See two separate references to at least two separate visits of Willi Münzenberg to Spain in TNA HW 17/26 March 22, 1936, Moscow to Medina, and March 26, 1936, "Epoca" to Medina.
49 Sayagués is listed as speaker in the Concentración Popular rally, see *La Libertad*, August 9, 1935. Sayagués was also listed as a supporter of the Popular Front in the "Albert" report I have discussed in Chapter 1, see RGASPI. F. 495. Op. 32 D. 225 L. 95–100.
50 See on this Avilés Farré, *La Izquierda Burguesa y la Tragedia de la II República* (Madrid: Comunidad de Madrid, 2006) 380.
51 Regarding the issue of the death penalties, as we saw above, the Comintern was forced to suggest to its UK sections that the commutation of the death sentences in 1935 was a mere "fascist ploy." As we shall see below, Azaña informed his soviet intelligence interlocutor in September 1935 that any further executions were extremely unlikely. Of the twenty-three death sentences initially given, only

two were carried out, and this brought about the resignation of the three CEDA ministers in March 1935. See on this Félix Gordón Ordás, *Mi Política Fuera de España* (México: Victoria, 1961) 297. As to conditions faced by the leading insurrectionists in jails, PCE leader José Diaz and Ercoli discussed with Manuilsky and others in January 1936 the fact that when the Comintern representatives wanted to meet Caballero and the youth leaders in prison, the director of the jail gave them a room to hold their meetings because he was sympathetic to their cause. Elsewhere in the report Codovilla writes that "le directeur de la prison laisse faire …" See Transcript January 17, 1936 meeting of the ECCI's Roman Lander Secretariat—Spanish Commission. RGASPI F. 494 Op. 20 D. 269. As to the freedom to hold rallies and meetings, as we shall see below, the Comintern representatives in Spain were surprised at the fact that a Red Aid rally was able to be held legally, and that the government would ban a rally and then lift the ban the following day after limited street protests. Codovilla's amusement at Spanish police weakness in the face of the staged "aid the children" rallies has already been mentioned. Lastly, see our chapter on publishing for Klavego's optimism as to the Comintern's opportunities in Spain in 1935.

52 Kent and Sayagués together spoke at the Izquierda Republicana rally in Madrid on May 4, 1935. Sayagués spoke at the rally against war together with Claudín of the Communist Youth and others, on August 4, 1935, see *La Libertad* of August 2.
53 See Avilés Farré, *La Izquierda Burguesa*, 348.
54 See for a brief discussion of this trip Santos Juliá, *Vida y Tiempo de Manuel Azaña* (Madrid: Taurus, 2008).
55 Report addressed to Ercoli, Gottwald on meeting with Manuel Azaña, signed "Gilbert." September 26, 1935. RGASPI F. 495. Op. 12.D. 92.
56 Leopold Trepper, TNA KV2-2074-1 and KV2-2074-2. The literature on Trepper focuses almost exclusively on his leadership of the Red Orchestra spy ring during the Second World War, and not on his work in the early to mid-1930s. In his autobiography, Trepper reads his later disillusionment with Soviet communism into the account of his life in Moscow in 1934–5 and does not cover any of his work in Paris or Spain in 1935 which we know of from the archival material cited. Leopold Trepper, *Le Grand Jeu* (Paris, 1975).
57 A helpful explanation of the Russian archival classification system is provided by the University of Reading here https://research.reading.ac.uk/archives-guide/former-soviet-archives-structure/.
58 Letter from Gilbert to "dear friend," a superior in Moscow, dated September 17, 1933, in which Gilbert makes a request for the approval of travel for his wife and child. ECCI, Documents des comités antiguerres dans différents pays, RGASPI F. 543 Op. 1 D. 123.
59 With cover note from Bela Kun to Dimitrov, RGASPI. F. 495. Op. 60 D. 249.

60 In the course of the interview, Azaña mentioned he lost the 1933 elections because his land policy amounted to little beyond talk. As Malefakis argued, Azaña and many of the left-wing republicans shared a "sentimental attachment to a distant and imperfectly understood objective." In addition, Azaña had a "naively optimistic assumption that he held a semi-permanent mandate to power," which led him to think he would solve all the difficult land challenges eventually. Edward E. Malefakis, *Agrarian Reform and Peasant Revolution in Spain* (New Haven, CT: Yale University Press, 1970) 254–6.

61 In a January 1936 report on the situation in Spain presented in Moscow, Codovilla and Pepe Diaz explained that the socialists were campaigning for the nationalization of land, failing to understand, that, according to Comintern tactics, nationalization of land belonged only in the following phase of the revolution and not in the then current "democratic-bourgeois" phase, unless local conditions clearly allowed this move. Secrétariat Roman. Commission Espagnole, January 17, 1936, RGASPI F. 495 Op. 20 D. 269. In presenting collectivization as the correct measure for Spain in 1935–6, there was no discussion of the cost in human lives that collectivization had just had in the USSR. See on this Stephen Kotkin, *Stalin Volume II, Waiting for Hitler* (New York: Penguin, 2018) 34ff. on the liquidation of the "kulaks" as a class.

62 Wir versuchen schon ständig, die Concentracion Popular auf diese Aufgabe zu orientieren.

63 Azaña's letter to Prieto cited in Octavio Cabezas, *Indalecio Prieto, Socialista y Español* (Madrid: Algaba, 2005) 281.

64 See *El Adelanto de Salamanca*, October 6, 1935, "El señor Azaña rectifica una noticia," with Azaña denying he had signed a manifest against war as was published in a conservative daily. The Catholic daily, *El Siglo Futuro*, had suggested the day before there was a degree of hypocrisy in the communist, socialist and republican stance against war in Abyssinia and elsewhere, while at the same refusing to condemn the slaughter carried out by the insurrectionists in Spain exactly a year earlier. "¿Habrá llegado ya el Turquesa a Etiopía?." Azaña's support for the "World Committee against War" was, on this occasion, equally hypocritical, argued *Siglo Futuro*.

65 Santos Juliá attributes the massive crowd exclusively to Azaña's own charisma and the attractiveness of his vision to "redeem the republic," making no mention of the PCE and left-wing socialist support, and of the large far left contingent evident in the crowd, whose slogans and symbols were fundamentally at odds with much of his speech. Santos Juliá, "The origins of the Spanish Popular Front" in Martin Alexander and Helen Graham, *The French and Spanish Popular Fronts* (Cambridge: Cambridge University Press, 1989) 28–9. Likewise, Avilés Farré, *La Izquierda Burguesa*, 368.

66 Quotes taken from the full speech as reported by *La Libertad* October 21, 1935.
67 The declaration of April 11, 1935, a basis for unity among three leading republican parties including Azaña's, was a reformist, legalist defense of law and order within the constitution. It responded to the conservative government's plans of lifting the state of war by deeming them "insufficient," while at the same time demanding, not blanket amnesty, but a regime of strict legality for prisoners, including the punishment of crimes that were "debidamente probados." See the declaration in *Heraldo de Madrid*, April 12, 1935.
68 Preston also acknowledges this disconnect and refers to Azaña's surprise at the thousands of clenched fists and "proletarian passion." see Preston, "The Creation of the Popular Front in Spain," 100.
69 *La Libertad* October 15, 1935, five days before the rally in Comillas.
70 According to *La Región* of September 13.
71 Cover note with handwritten note by Ercoli and "Otto" report in RGASPI F. 495 Op. 12 D. 92.
72 There was a degree of confusion regarding these two events, given the communist and socialist presence in both. The Sevilla event was the "legal" national conference of Socorro Rojo Internacional, Red Aid in Spain, and was to be held in Sevilla on September 7 and 8. Its self-identification as a "legal" event notwithstanding, the government banned the event, but lifted the ban after protests ensued and the conference finally took place on 10 and 11. See the account in *La Region* September 15, 1935, section fittingly entitled "Lucha de Clases." The Valencia event was set up as a non-partisan "national plenum of aid committees," though communists and socialists were in a majority and the executive committee was made up of communists as "Otto" reveals in his report. The dates for that event were originally of September 14 and 15 and, according to "Otto" the event was delayed by one day. The fact that a government which was, according to Comintern doctrine and propaganda, a fascist tyranny, would lift bans on revolutionary events less than a year after an armed insurrection on account of limited popular protests does not provoke any commentary by "Otto," aside from expressing surprise and delight.
73 Rapport de la Camarade Stasova au Secretariat du C.E. de L'I.C. January 25, 1936. RGASPI F. 495. Op. 20. D. 905.
74 See Elorza and Bizcarrondo on this, *Queridos*, 249; Stasova file in TNA, KV2-3596 with a letter from Victor about receiving campaign cash etc. Comintern financing of the Popular Front campaign was widely discussed in the conservative press in Spain. Also, the organ of Socorro Rojo Internacional, *Ayuda* February 27, 1936, page 1, "La Victoria del Frente Popular," which highlights the fact that Red Aid had "mobilized millions of pesetas."
75 See *Ayuda* February 27, 1936, page two, "La propaganda electoral y la amnistía." "Nuestra foto representa algunos de los numerosos carteles que, con el grito de ¡amnistía!, llamaban a votar por el frente popular."

76 See Commission du MOPR, Séance du 19 Février 1936, Orateur, Lucia. RGASPI F 495. Op. 20 D. 907. Barón noted that the Spanish right-wing press had been correct in their reading of what a vote for the left-wing parties truly meant.
77 On February 21, *La Libertad*'s leading headline was "¡Todo el Poder Para el Pueblo!" The subheading read: "La ansiedad popular está pendiente de la acción rápida y justiciera del Gobierno." On a side piece the theme is picked up again. Fast justice is the first demand of popular anxiety.
78 Lengthy report on Caballero's words to the press in *Heraldo de Madrid* February 17, 1936.
79 Rafael Salazar Alonso, radical republican leader and Minister of Gobernación (interior) in 1934. In his January 1935 report cited above, Codovilla refers to him as "that bloody little dog" (un petit chien sanglant). In 1934, Salazar Alonso opposed the armed insurrection and defended constitutional legality. His 1935 book *Bajo el Signo de la Revolución* contains an abundance of documentation he gained access to from police files demonstrating the direct socialist and communist involvement. He was arrested by left-wing militias in August 1936 and shot. The sentence against him mentions his book explicitly and argues that the book contained statements "contrary to the constitution." See Juan M. Martínez Valdueza, "El Hombre y su Destino" in the 2007 reprint which includes the text of the August 1936 sentence (Astorga: Akrón, 2007).
80 Elpátievsky cites Comín Colomer's estimate of 150, but believes, based on his own research in RGASPI, the total figure exceeds 200 slightly. See Elpátievsky, *La Emigración*, 55.
81 The protokoll, as well as the various drafts, final versions and translations, and part of the drafts of the letter in RGASPI F. 495 Op. 20 D. 262. Most of the drafts, final versions and translations of the letter in RGASPI. F. 495. Op. 18 D. 1075a. The directives document, addressing the Central Committee of the PCE, bears a reference number #452 in the original Russian draft, as do all versions and translations. The letter bears the reference number #453, also in all versions and translations.
82 See the five conditions for unification in Dimitrov's speech on August 2, 1935, entitled "The Working Class against Fascism," in *VII World Congress of the Communist International* (London: Modern Books, 1935) 74–5.
83 José Díaz; "Nuestro Camino," series of articles in *Mundo Obrero*, June 6, 1936.
84 ECCI Sekretariat, protokoll (A) 37, March 22, 1936, RGASPI. F. 495. Op. 18.D. 1083.
85 See *Mundo Gráfico* of April 29, 1936; *Ahora* April 25, 1936; *Transporte U.G.T.* Año 1 No. 117, May 1936: *ABC* Sevilla April 25, 1936; *El Cantábrico* April 25, 1936.
86 See *La Tarde de Zamora* on March 16, 1936 on the "refugees" who had been exiled "hasta ayer mismo," including Nelken and Acuña.

87 For the multiple communications between Madrid and Moscow on the status of the journey, and Moscow's concern over visas and the legal status of six of the comrades accused of terrorism, see TNA HW 17/26, February 28, 1936, April 8 and 11.
88 *La Libertad* April 11, 1936 reporting on the rally on the evening of the 10th. Pepe Diaz spoke in identical terms. See "Sin el movimiento revolucionario de octubre no habría en febrero Frente Popular." Speech given in Oviedo on July 5, 1936, published as a pamphlet by PCE. AHPCE—Dirigentes-José Diaz.
89 Ibid.
90 *La Libertad*, March 26, 1936.
91 "Agitatsya, Bolshoe Iskutssvo," *Pravda* April 7, 1935, available online http://docs.historyrussia.org/ru/nodes/91034-agitatsiya-bolshoe-iskusstvo#mode/inspect/page/1/zoom/4.
92 The Spanish phrase refers to the recruitment office of a military unit.
93 Alexander and Graham "Introduction" 2. See my introduction above.
94 Contra Preston, for example: "The Creation of the Popular Front in Spain" 1.

Chapter 3

1 The literacy rates for girls aged 11 to 15 grew 18.5 percent in the 1920s, from 53.32 in 1920 to 71.88 in 1930. The growth rate decreased in the following decade for both sexes and increased dramatically again in the decade of the 1940s especially for women. See Narciso de Gabriel, "Alfabetización y Escolarización en España (1887–1950)" in *Revista de Educación*, No. 314 (1997) 217–43. See also Antonio Viñao Frago, "Los Destinatarios de la Educación Popular: Una segunda Oportunidad para Adolescentes, Jóvenes y Personas Adultas" in *CEE Participación Educativa*, número extraordinario (2010), 25–36: "Los mayores avances en alfabetización se habían producido, pues, en el primer tercio del siglo XX."
2 Hipólito Escobar extends the designation to the first thirty years of the twentieth century in Spain, though the figures he provides support the thesis of the 1920s as the most fruitful decade. Hipólito Escobar Sobrino, *Historia del Libro Español* (Madrid: Gredos, 1998) 258–63.
3 Martínez Martín seems to use a generic category of "sociedades anónimas de artes gráficas" including both printing and publishing companies. See his chart detailing number of companies from 1919 to 1935. Jesús A. Martínez Martín, "La Edición Moderna" in Martínez Martín (ed.) *Historia de la Edición en España 1836–1936* (Madrid: Marcial Pons, 2001) 183–4. These companies, writes Martínez Martín, "consolidaron a lo largo de la II República una situación anterior." As to "empresarios o editores de obras de todas clases" the growth between 1922 and 1930 is even higher at 51 percent, though he does not provide data for earlier or later years, p. 177.

4   José Carlos Rueda Laffond, "La Industrialización de la Imprenta" in *Historia de la Edición*, 210.
5   "… los resultados de la II República no concuerdan," as, for example, data on book exports indicates a decrease in the years 1931–4 in relation to 1930. As to the number of titles, the BNE catalogue shows a significant decrease as well for the II Republic years, while *Bibliografía Española* shows stagnation for the years 1930-2 and a dramatic increase in 1933. Guillermo Gil-Mugarza, "Las Letras y los Números. La Producción Española de Libros en el Siglo XX a Través de la Fuentes Estadísticas" in *Revista de Historia Industrial*, Vol. 56, Año XXIII (2014) 151–87.
6   See, for example, "Ediciones Oriente" in *La Gaceta Literaria*, November 15, 1929, detailing some of the "infinidad" of works in its pipeline, or "Historia Nueva" featuring an interview with its director, Cesar Falcón in *La Gaceta Literaria*, September 1, 1929.
7   See the coverage in all the major newspapers. Quote in *El Debate*, April 25, 1933. Ramón J. Sender wrote a piece critical of Kerensky and apologetic of Lenin and the Soviet Union, nation which had achieved, in his view, peace, land, and bread. "El Probre Kerenski" in *La Libertad* April 26, 1933.
8   For Comintern publications in France, see Marie-Cécile Bouju, *Lire en Communiste: Les Maisons d'Édition du Parti Communiste Français, 1920–1968* (Rennes: Presses universitaires de Rennes, 2010) esp. 29–64; "Les Maisons d'Édition du PCF, 1920–56" in *Nouvelles Fondations* 2007/3 n° 7–8, 260 à 265.
9   Antonio Elorza and Marta Bizcarrondo, *Queridos Camaradas. La Internacional Comunista y España 1919–1939* (Barcelona: Planeta, 1999) 85–6. These authors attribute a key role to André Marty in the Paris-based Bureau d'Editions without any awareness of the Redizdat organization in Paris, refer to "Krebs," believe only the material work of printing was carried out in Barcelona, not discussing Klavego's vast work, etc.
10 Rafael Cruz, "La Organización del PCE. 1920–1934" in *Estudios de Historia Social*, No. 31 (1984) 282. For example, Cruz believed Ediciones Europa América and Edeya were the same company.
11 See, for example, the brief articles on Ettore Quaglierini and Ediciones Europa-América in Gustavo Bueno Sánchez, www.filosofia.org. Bueno Sanchez affirms Clavego (Klavego, Ettore Quaglierini) only returned to Spain in early 1936, instead of March 1935, and leaves out of his brief treatment the voluminous archival documentation we discuss in this chapter.
12 Within the large body of RGASPI archival material covering organizations and institutions of the Comintern (Fond 495), Opis 78 contains all the Redizdat documentation, mainly reports and correspondence from 1924 through 1938. The files of the ECCI's Roman Secretariat (Opis 32), Political Commission (Opis 4) and that of Gottwald's secretariat (Opis 13) also contain material related to publishing that complements and shed additional light on Redizdat, as we will show in this chapter.

13 In many of the documents in its German translation, Verlagsabteilung. Very little has been published thus far on the Redizdat. On the Comintern and PCF's publishing operations in France see Bouju, *Lire en Communiste*, esp. 29–64; "Les Maisons." For her brief discussion of Kreps and his organization she relies on Peter Huber for the organizational details and Pierre Broué for his brief biography of Kreps in *Histoire de l'Internationale Communiste 1919–1943* (Paris: Fayard, 1997).

14 The departments within the central apparatus were functional, technical or regional in nature and lower ranking than the Comintern's governing bodies and secretariats. See on this Bernhard H. Bayerlein, "Das neue Babylon—Strukturen und Netzwerke der Kommunistischen Internationale und ihre Klassifizierung," in *Jahrbuch für Historische Kommunismusforschung* 2004, 181–270.

15 Full details in Rezoliutsia Sekretariata EKKI ot 2 Oktiabria 1935 o Strukture Apparata Sekretariata EKKI, Russian text followed by German, English etc. RGASPI. F. 495. Op. 18. D. 1051. On the reorganization of the ECCI see also Serge Wolikow, "The Comintern as a World Network" in Silvio Pons and Stephen A. Smith (eds.) *The Cambridge History of Communism, Vol. I World Revolution and Socialism in One Country 1917–1941* (Cambridge: Cambridge University Press, 2017) esp. 238ff.

16 "... ein organ der propagandischen Arbeit und des ideologischen Kampfes des EKKI," Ibid.

17 Referent is the term used in the Russian original as well as in German and French (référént). The referent is a senior political analyst, manager and link between Kreps and the local Redizdat apparatus in a country or group of countries. Land secretaries and local country leaders were obliged to keep their referent informed of all country developments. See a detailed job description in the Marty Secretariat material, "The referents' Work" in RGASPI F. 495. Op. 14 D. 4. Local referents also existed in the various secretariats of the ECCI.

18 See Shtaty Redizdata na 1935 for the management team and salaries, and an additional eight personnel working in the Western European sector, RGASPI F. 495 Op. 4 D. 353. A July 3, 1935, discussion at the ECCI's Political Secretariat further stated that outside of the eight managers, the remaining workers would be charged to the revenues of the publishing house. Protokoll (A) 460, Der Ditzgung der Poilitkommission des Pol. Sekret. Der EKKI July 3 1935, RGASPI f. 495 Op. 4 D. 353. See also the second paragraph of Kreps's letter to Pyatnitsky and Brokowski of June 3, 1935, in which he mentions the budget issue. Political Commission files, RGASPI F. 495 Op. 4 D. 353.

19 "The Redisdat must as far as possible TRANSFER ITS WORK TO THE COUNTRY SERVED." Resolution on the Report of the Redisdat [sic] at the Polit Secretariat, April 29, 1934. RGASPI F. 494 Op. 78 D. 119. Prior to EEA's arrival in Barcelona, the PCE had its own local Publishing House, Editorial Roja which used the Argis print shop and continued to operate in 1932.

20 "Sur le Contenu, le travail et la difusión des editions en France," a resolution of the Roman Secretariat in response to Cical's ("Sical") report dated December 29, 1933, RGASPI F. 495 Op. 32 D. 124.
21 Undated typewritten letter in official EEA Paris letterhead, announcing the move to Barcelona and addressed to its "clientes y amigos," RGASPI F. 495 Op. 78 D.116.
22 Detailed report covering the work carried out since the move to Barcelona in November 1931 to the time of writing dated November 22, 1932, with prior correspondence between Barcelona and Paris dated May to November 1932. RGASPI F. 495. Op. 78. D. 96.
23 December 18, 1933, Pierre to Ireneo, RGASPI F. 494. Op. 78 D. 104. See also Ettore Quaglierini's file at The National Archives, listing his aliases "Bono," "Clavego" (though not Klavego) and Pierre, but misspells his name "Quagliarini." TNA KV2/1782. Gustavo Sánchez Bueno correctly identifies "Clavego" and "Pierre" as Quaglierini relying on Julián Gorkin's account and summarized his findings in an online blog https://www.filosofia.org/ave/001/a437.htm. Cruz was less informed, depending only on the account written by the communist dissident Enrique Matorras, and affirming that EEA was the same as EDEYA and was led by an Italian named Bono. Cruz, "La Organización del PCE. 1920–1934," 282.
24 On Cical, his strong character and his battle with the leadership of the PCF, which led to his marginalization in 1935 as the party took over direct management of publishing operations, see Boujou, "Les Maisons" 261–2.
25 Bullejos's own account in José Bullejos, *La Comintern en España* (Mexico, D.F.: Impresiones Modernas, 1972) 201–9. The record of the tense conversations in Moscow in the Political Commission, Plenum of the ECCI on the Spanish Question September 10–13, 1932, RGASPI F. 495 Op. 170 D. 314.
26 From the Roman Secretariat files, Medina correspondence and reports, RGASPI F. 495. Op. 32. D. 213.
27 October 1, 1932, Medina to "Caros camaradas" on the internal situation of the party after the dismissal of the "A.B.V. group." RGASPI F. 494 Op. 32 D. 213.
28 "Enlaces de Cenit y Mundo Obrero" in *El Financiero*, December 7, 1934.
29 Enrique Matorras, *El Comunismo en España* (Burgos: Aldecoa, 1935) 72–3. The works of dissident and former communists cannot be taken at face value but are useful as additional perspectives on events and actors that can be cross-checked with other sources. In his account of Comintern publishing in Spain, Matorras seems to be largely correct in light of the archival material. Victor Alba also attributes the overall management of the operation to Ángel Pumarega, although he affirms the funds came from Cenit. Alba cites only Comín Colomer as his source. *El Partido Comunista en España* (Barcelona: Planeta, 1979) 141. Gonzalo Santonja, however, was intent on denying any official affiliation of Giménez Siles with the PCE, let alone the Comintern. Santonja, *La República*, 44.

30   Thus, the combined operations were not the result of moving the newly acquired printing machinery to the location of a friendly printer, as Medina had imagined, but the other way around. Before 1932, Cenit had used the Argis printing shop where Mundo Obrero was also printed. After 1932, we see Cenit printing at the Imp-Rot facility (e.g., Fedor Gladkow's Soviet realist novel *El Cemento* in 1933), as well as continuing to use Imprenta Helénica and others.
31   Letter from Medina to "Caro amigo," that is Klavego, the head of EEA in Barcelona dated September 15, 1932. RGASPI F. 495 Op. 78 D. 96. It was EEA who had invited Cenit to attend a book trade show in Moscow and then failed to follow-up as required by the importance of this prospect.
32   *La República*, 75. Santonja insists on denying any formal ties between Giménez Siles and the communist party.
33   Report detailing the situation of the Spanish Committee against War, probably addressed to Henri Barbusse (top of the page was torn off), dated August 10, 1932, and signed "La Fracción. Dirección: Rafael Giménez Siles … Ateneo de Madrid," in the International Antifascist Organizations files, RGASPI. F. 543. Op. 1. D. 17.
34   Letter from Klavego dated January 20, 1933. RGASPI F. 495. Op. 78. D. 104. Klavego suggests the sales price was high at eighty cents, since total costs, he believed, did not exceed eighteen cents per booklet. More of an economically driven publication than cadres' education, he concludes.
35   Brief von Klavego, March 8, 1935, RGASPI F. 495 Op. 78 D. 138.
36   French language letter from Klavego, probably to "Bruno," that is Mikhail Kreps, since Klavego is in Paris with Bertrand before returning to Barcelona. Ibid. Regarding the relationship between the Comintern and Cenit, Bullejos wrote that "Las Ediciones de Moscú concertaron directamente con Editorial Cenit de Madrid la edición española de las grandes obras del Instituto Marx y Engels, entre ellas, las obras completas de Lenin." Bullejos, *La Comintern*, 156. Bullejos reflects in his recollection the view so strongly opposed by Codovilla that Madrid printers did not want to print the communist materials and the PCE had to opt for acquiring their own infrastructure.
37   Santonja argues that the publication by Cenit of Trotsky's books is evidence of the fact that the publisher was not controlled by communists. See the Cenit catalogue in Santonja, *La República*, 77–95. However, Santonja does detail one clear example of communist control, see pp. 46–7 on the visit of the Malik Verlag representative Wieland Herzfelde.
38   On Wertheim, see the biographical summary in *Transdisziplinäre Konstellationen in der österreichischen Literatur, Kunst und Kultur der Zwischenkriegszeit*, available online https://litkult1920er.aau.at/litkult-lexikon/wertheim-johannes/ A direct identification of "Betrand" and Johannes Wertheim is made by Wertheim's son in Georges Wertheim, "Die Odyssee eines Verlegers" in Siegwald Ganglmair

(ed.) *Jahrbuch 1996*. Dokumentationsarchiv den *Österreichischen* Wiederstandes (Vienna: DOW, 1996) 209. Since 1933 the Rediztat documentation shows him as reporting to Kreps and managing publishing in several European nations. A 1929 document discussing publications in the United States mentions J. Wertheim as the person appointed by Kreps's organization to own 51 percent of the shares of the Comintern-run International Publishers. Untitled report dated June 15, 1929, on the US publishing plan after a meeting with Kreps and the Small Commission of the Presidium of the ECCI, RGASPI F. 494 Op. 78 D. 37.

39 For example, both Lipo /Litpol and Hoym delivered stocks of literature to the Heinrich Tejml firm of Prague as working capital, since these stocks did not need to be paid for initially. This arrangement is part of the contract which also details the Czech company's future work in distributing Comintern literature as well as books dealing with "special problems" in German and Czech. Bericht. Buchverlage und Vertriebsapparate der Tschechoslowakei, June 1932. RGASPI F. 495. Op. 78. D. 96. Similarly, the financial role of both LIPO and Hoym in the set-up of Arbeiderforlaget in Denmark is clear in the 1932 Bericht über den Arbeiderforlaget Dänemark, RGASPI F. 495. Op. 78. D. 96. Lastly, Interbook issued Comintern loans to various publishing enterprises within the Redizdat network, as was the case with Edeya. See letter from Buno (Kreps) to Bertrand (Wertheim) dated June 11, 1936, instructing him to send immediately to the editors in Copenhagen 3,000 crowns from Interbook. TNA HW 17/14/1.

40 Santonja, *La República,* 48. Ana Martínez Rus follows Santonja on the alleged Independence of Giménez Siles and Cenit in "Rafael Giménez Siles, editor comprometido y moderno: Impulsor de la Feria del Libro de Madrid" *Trama & Texturas*, Vol. 42 (2020) 79–91.

41 Listed in German in Franz's report.

42 See, for example, Anna Louise Strong, *La Conquista del Trigo por los Soviets* (Madrid: Cenit, 1932). The reality on the ground was, in fact, the exact opposite of the myth disseminated in Spain and elsewhere by the Comintern and its network of publishers. These booklets were being published shortly after the forced collectivization of the land by Stalin's orders, and the elimination of the "Kulaks" as a class, resulting in the deaths of millions in Ukraine, Kazakhstan, and elsewhere. Voluntary collectivization had only been embraced by 1 percent of the land-owning peasants as of 1928. A Land Commissariat internal report in early 1932 noted that peasants were quitting the collectives by the hundreds of thousands to roam industrial sites in search of food. See on this Stephen Kotkin, *Stalin Vol. II. Waiting for Hitler 1929–1941* (New York: Penguin, 2017). After the outbreak of the Spanish Civil War the theme of the happy and prosperous Soviet peasants continued to be developed by EEA, see, for example, *El Campesino Feliz en la Unión Soviética* (Así es la URSS series, Madrid: EEA, 1937).

43 "Los Madrileños se han Gastado en Literatura Más de Cuarenta Mil Duros." Including an interview with Giménez Siles, in *La Voz*, May 16, 1934, p. 4.

44 See graphic No. 1 in Marie-Cécile Boujou, "La production des maisons d'édition du P.C.F. 1921–1956" a 1999 thesis at Ecole Nationale Supérieure des sciences de l'Information et des Bibliothèques. Boujou mentions 65 as the number for 1934. Her graph is not detailed enough to give us a concrete figure for the previous year, but it appears to be roughly the same.

45 This is most likely a reference to Vicente Sánchez Ocaña, who also had a management role at *Heraldo de Madrid*. The June 10, 1933, issue of *La Estampa* included an illustrated six-page report on the Soviet Union written by Alexis Malwesky. The article described Soviet peasants attending a congress in Moscow, whose clothes were of a quality "one thousand times superior" to those worn by Muscovites.

46 Franz admits in his report that the Marxist Library volumes were read by intellectuals, petit bourgeoisie, and "a few" workers.

47 Before returning to Spain from France in 1932, he asked his friends to send him, in preparation for his librarian exam in Spain, material on the libraries in the USSR. He adds, "eso tendría un gran efecto, porque todo lo que tiene relación con la URSS está aquí muy de moda." Ramón Salaberria, "Las Bibliotecas Populares en la Correspondencia de Juan Vicéns a Lulu Jourdain y Hernando Viñes (1933–1936)" in *Anales de Documentación*, No. 5 (2002) 310. Full article 309–32. Beyond this pragmatic interest, the correspondence reveals Vicéns communication exchanges with VOKS, the Soviet Union's organization which handled Western intellectuals visiting Moscow, his PCE membership, etc. Among the materials Vicéns sent to VOKS in Moscow was the yearbook of the Misiones Pedagógicas. "Las Bibliotecas," 319.

48 Llopis authored in 1929 *Como se Forja un Pueblo: La Rusia que Yo He Visto* (Madrid: editorial España, 1929), "yet another book on Russia," as he put it. The book is the result of his stay in Russia, hosted by the regime during and after a pedagogy congress. He concluded that "the Soviet Union is but an immense school" in which the "opium of the people" is discarded, and children and women are liberated. See Bàrbara Molas, "Aprendiendo la Revolución: Rodolfo Llopis en el País de los Soviets," an analysis of Llopis's book in the context of his visit to the Soviet Union, available online https://www.academia.edu/39923882/Aprendiendo_la_Revoluci%C3%B3n_Rodolfo_Llopis_en_la_Uni%C3%B3n_Sovi%C3%A9tica_1928_ See also Rodolfo Llopis, *La Revolución en la Escuela. Dos Años en la Dirección General de Primera Enseñanza* (Madrid: M. Aguilar, 1933). In the words of Elorza and Bizcarrondo, "Llopis se encuentra predispuesto a sancionar todo aquello que sustente una impresión de novedad radical, suscitada por el espectáculo de la sociedad soviética." *Queridos Camaradas*, 88.

49 See for example the list of works sent by the Patronato de Misiones Pedagógicas to a Galician school in 1935 in Xosé Manuel Malheiro Gutiérrez, "Las Bibliotecas Escolares en la Primera Década del Franquismo" in *História da Educação*, Vol. 21, No. 53 (2017) 247. The Engels book was digitized by Google still bearing the stamp of the Patronato, available online. The volume was part of the Libros Proletarios collection printed in the Argis print shop together with Mundo Obrero until 1933. See below on Argis.
50 La Rambla is the street location given by Klavego to his management in his reports. Period advertising on the socialist youth newspaper gives the nearby address of Paseo de Colón 4 as the location of the EEA bookstore. *Renovación*, August 25, 1934.
51 See *El Día Gráfico*, December 16, 1934, which lists the detainees upon their release as "Pedro Bou, Ricardo Marín Consola, Rito Esteban y Juan Manido Gómez," adding that these men had been arrested with three others at the Europa-América bookstore.
52 See my chapter entitled "Save the Children …" for a brief discussion of the ways in which Comintern agents in Spain were surprised by the significant freedoms they enjoyed during the so-called "bienio negro."
53 The identification can be made after careful study of all the material, including the hand-written notes. For example, on a February 16, 1935 note from Bertrand to "Bruno," a handwritten note at the bottom reads "Gel. K.," which I interpret as "Gelesen Kreps," that is, read by Kreps. Kreps is also fully spelled out in the left margin. A May 1, 1935, unsigned letter Kreps bears a handwritten note in Russian at the bottom that reads T. Krepsu, that is [send to] comrade Kreps.
54 It is not clear if these numbers included the amounts published by the communist youth organization in Spain, which, as of December 5, 1935, had published 40,000 copies of a pamphlet with Dimitrov speeches, among others. Communication from "Evaristo," that is, communist youth organization leader Trifón Medrano, to the KIM leadership in Moscow, December 5, 1935, TNA HW 17/26.
55 See, for example, *El Socialista* of December 21, 1935, "Un Folleto Interesante. El VII Congreso de la Internacional Comunista y su Repercusión en España"; also "Dimitrov Habla a Todos los Partidarios de la Paz y la Libertad"; an ad from Redizdat Spain's latest brand El Monitor Bibliográfico, Aptdo. De Correos 890 Barcelona, for the main VII Congress booklets including the Dimitrov speeches. In August 1934 the socialist party's youth organ, *Renovación*, ran a story on EEA entitled "Una Acertada Iniciativa Editorial," recommending to their members EEA as the "finally available" source of revolutionary materials at reasonable prices. *Renovación* August 25, 1934.
56 The first number was dedicated to cover the Dimitrov speeches, together with those of "Pasionaria," Jesús Hernandez, José Diaz etc. *Internacional Comunista*, Año 1, número 1, Valencia, December 1, 1935.

57 *Democracia*, October 25, 1935 cover page.
58 "¿No queréis que sea vuestro jefe Dimitrof? Pues Votad a Acción Popular." Conservative slogan cited mockingly on Heraldo de Madrid on January 29, 1936; Similarly, "Todo ciudadano que vote la dramática farsa del frente popular, vota a Dimitroff y a la Komintern de Moscú." In *La Espiga*, Federación Católica-Agraria Salmantina: Year V No. 181–January 18, 1936.
59 Commission du MOPR, Séance du 17 Fev. 1936, Orateur: Lucia, RGASPI. F. 495. Op. 20.D. 907.
60 "Un Acto Socialista. El Mitin de Anoche en el Cine Europa." In *La Libertad*, March 26, 1936, p. 3.
61 See the favorable account in "La Gran Manifestación de Ayer en Madrid": "La Unión de Juventudes era portadora de tres gigantescos retratos de Lenin, Stalin y Dimitrof." In *Heraldo de Madrid*, March 2, 1936, p. 2.
62 Mikhail Kreps communicated directly with the PCE leadership in January 1934 requesting the biographies of Cesar and Irene. TNA HW 17/26 January 10, 1934. By November 30, 1934, César was working as correspondent for the Comintern's *International Correspondence* newspaper, among other roles. In December 1935, Codovilla approved his move to the Soviet news agency TASS. See Communication from "Luis" (Codovilla) to Moscow, November 20, 1935, December 7, 1935, both TNA HW 17/26.
63 P. Yuma, *El Escándalo de la Telefónica* (Ediciones Frente Popular; Hombres y hechos de Hoy series; Barcelona: El Monitor Bibliográfico / Madrid: FYL, Jan. 1936). Other titles in the series as advertised on the back cover: V. Riscos, *El Problema de los Alquileres*; Cicúendez, *La CEDA en el Campo* etc. Some of the authors used an alias, but not José Diaz, ¿Quiénes son los Patriotas?, Cicúendez (Luis Cicúendez) and perhaps Clemente Cimorra (C. Cimorra).
64 *La Literatura Antifascista en la Nueva Escuela* (Barcelona: Ediciones de la Cooperativa FETE, ¿1937?). See on this Alejandro Mayordomo and Juan M. Fernández Soria, *Vencer y Convencer. Educación y Política, España 1936–1945* (Valencia: Universitat de Valencia, 1993) 78–105. See also, establishing the ideological connections between republican education before and after the outbreak of war Juan M. Fernández Soria, "Revolución Versus Reforma Educativa en la Segunda República Española. Elementos de Ruptura" in *Historia de la Educación*, Vol. 4 (Jan. 1985) 337–53.
65 Bertrand to A. S. dated April 30, 1934. As we will show below, we have good reasons to believe A. S. is a reference to Stasova of International Red Aid in Moscow. RGASPI F. 495 Op. 78 D. 136.
66 On one hand, both Giménez Siles and Roces have been easy targets of libertarian critics of the communist party and its network of organizations, see on this Santonja, *La República*, 43. On the other, Santonja himself and a number of others

promote a sectarian and somewhat dualistic vision of the II Republic in which Roces, Gimenes Siles, and others are often described in hagiographic terms and their communist affiliation is denied at all costs.

67 See Julia Köstenberger, *Kaderschmiede des Stalinismus: Die Internationale Leninschule in Moskau (1926–1938)* (Wiener Studien zur Zeitgeschichte; Band 8; Vienna: Lit Verlag, 2016).

68 Klavego to Bruno, "Rapport sur La Mise en Practique des decisions Adoptées lors de l'Entrevue de B." Undated but lcertainly in the fourth quarter of 1935. RGASPI F. 494 Op. 78 D. 138. On the role of October insurrection on the electoral campaign of the Popular Front, see also my chapter "Save the Children …"

69 Kreps to Comrade Dimitrov, February 27, 1936, RGASPI F. 495 Op. 78 D. 141.

70 See for example communication from Moscow to "Medina" in Spain on February 8 and 13, 1936, mentioning 200,000 and 80,000 French Francs "for election expenses" and "for the elections" respectively as already sent, TNA HW 17/26. See also my chapter entitled "Save the Children" covering other financing through Red Aid etc.

71 Interestingly, José's brother, Pedro Laín, a member of Falange, became after the war the director of publications for the Franco regime.

72 Bruno to Klavego and "Medida" (Medina, Luis, that is, Victorio Codovilla), March 2, 1936, TNA HW 17/26.

73 TNA HW 17/26 which covers December 27, 1933, through end of June 1936, and 17/14/1 for July 1936. The numbers of the individual messages in the TNA archiving system are not always in sequence, so we have done a manual count for each of the periods mentioned.

74 This is not a government of the Popular Front because, argues the writer of this message, probably Dimitrov, it is a bourgeois government without representation from workers organizations and will "necessarily vacillate." February 26, 1936 message to Luis from Moscow, TNA HW 17/26.

75 "Pasionaria Habla para Crónica" in *Crónica*, March 1, 1936.

76 Medina to Bruno, April 28, 1936: "Bruno, we think it is essential that you use your influence with Klavigo [sic] so that he should come immediately [to Madrid] and work in conjunction with our department of agitation and propaganda … we will work in agreement with him and do what he thinks right." TNA HW 17/26.

77 *Kontrolle* and its cognates are repeated seven times in the first two pages of the report.

78 See Abramson's brief account of her work with Roces at Ediciones Europa América in Paulina and Adelina Abramson, *Mosaico Roto* (Madrid: Compañía Literaria, 1994) 47–9. Paulina (Comrade Abramson) is also mentioned in the brief progress report on publishing in Spain signed by Kreps and Spain referent Ozrin on May 7, 1936, as having already been sent to Spain, together with Roces. RGASPI F. 495 Op. 72 D. 141.

79 At the end of 1934, prestigious Spanish writer Pio Baroja was making a maximum of 6,000 pts. annually. Of course, Roces had other income besides this. See on the compensation of writers and intellectuals who contributed regular articles to newspapers in 1934–5, Manuel Tuñón de Lara, *Medio Siglo de Cultura Española (1885–1936)* (Madrid: Tecnos, 1984) 294.

80 See, for example, Spain to Moscow, May 25, 1936, TNA HW 17/26. The identification is possible thanks to a February 21 message from Medina to Moscow, in which he requests visas for the two PCE youth leaders who would soon travel to Moscow with the socialist youth's Santiago Carrillo and Federico Melchor to agree the unification of both youth organizations. The two others in need of Soviet visas mentioned are Trifón Medrano ("Evaristo" in most of the messages, Medrano in others) and Felipe Muñoz Arconada ("Ernesto" in many of the messages to KIM in Moscow on the unification negotiations, on the *Juventud* publication, etc.) Muñoz Arconada became secretary general of the merged Juventudes Socialistas Unificadas for Madrid.

81 The "Fiesta del Libro" was launched as an annual event coinciding with the birth of Cervantes on October 7 by royal decree in 1926. The book fair was to be held nationwide and involved the moving of books from the shelves of bookstores to the streets, often with festive displays, discounts, and other attractions. The government decree required the set-up of popular libraries, especially among the neediest, and the distribution of free books in schools, hospitals, and other locations. The fair was considered a great success, leading to significant increases in books sales, especially at popular prices. See, for example, "Se celebra la Fiesta del Libro con Extraordinaria Animación" in *El Sol*, October 8, 1929; "La Fiesta del Libro" in *La Libertad* of the same date, mentioning the purchase by the government of over 60,000 for school and itinerant libraries that year alone.

82 As late as 1935, Cenit continued publishing works that matched closely Redizdat's catalogue of "Classics" of Marxism-Leninism-Stalinism and popularization of the Soviet Union, along with the politically neutral popular medicine booklets. Among the works published in 1935 were: Marx, *El Capital* (1935); Marx, *El Manifiesto del Partido Comunista*; Franz Mehring, *Marx y los Primeros Tiempos de la Internacional*; Stalin, *Balance del Primer Plan Quinquenal*; Stalin, *La Situación del Capitalismo y de la Unión Soviética*; Henri Barbusse, *Stalin*.

83 TNA HW 17/26, March 22, 1936.

84 "En el Palacio de Comunicaciones, la policía se incauta de noventa y cinco paquetes de propaganda comunista enviada desde Moscú," in *Ahora* January 7, 1936.

85 Additionally, the centrist politician had requested the outlawing of armed militias, including those of socialists and communists which were already in the process of merging. "El Señor Sánchez Román expuso los motivos que le impulsaron a no firmar el Pacto del Frente Popular" in *El Sol*, March 10, 1936, p. 3.

Chapter 4

1 The theme appears at the beginning of the speech, throughout its sections and at the very end. The French edition of the speech is Georges Dimitrov, *L'Unité de la Classe Ouvrière dans la Lutte Contre le Fascisme* (Paris: Bureau d'Editions, 1935). The final phrase of the speech is "… l'unité de la classe ouvrière dans la lutte contre l'offensive du Capital, contre le fascisme et la menace d'une guerre impérialiste."

2 Dimitrov, *L'Unité, 17, 36*.

3 Georges Vidal, "Le PCF et la Défense Nationale à l'Époque du Front Populaire (1934–1939)" in *Guerres Mondiales et Conflits Contemporains*, Vol. 3, No. 215 (2004), 47–73, available online. Much more on Vidal's thesis below. Julian Jackson sees the shift away from army work to the support of national defense in France beginning in May 1935. *The Popular Front in France. Defending Democracy, 1934–1938* (Cambridge: Cambridge University Press, 1988) 34.

4 On transnational approaches to Comintern studies see Oleksa Drachewych, "The Communist Transnational? Transnational studies and the History of the Comintern" in *History Compass*. 2019; 17, 1–12; Brigitte Struder, *The Transnational World of the Cominternians* (Cambridge: Cambridge University Press, 2015).

5 *L'Humanité* in a November 2, 1934 article entitled "Guerre Civil en Espagne et le Prolétariat International," signed by Ercoli.

6 On the MMF and, more generally, the French military's reaction to the Bolshevik revolution see Paul-Marie de la Gorce, *La République et son Armée* (Paris: Fayard, 1963); Claude Delmas, "Une Mission Militaire Française à Petrograd après la Révolution d'Octobre (octobre 1917–mars 1918)" in *Revue*, No. 247 (Juin 1966) 1084–94; Général (C. R.) Jean Delmas, "L'État-Major Français et le Gouvernement Bolchevique (1917–1918) Stratégie et Idéologie" in *Relations Internationales* No. 35, (automne 1983) 291–303; Georges Vidal, *Une Alliance Improbable: L'Armée Française et la Russie Soviétique (1917–1939)* (Rennes: Presses universitaire de Rennes, 2015). For the French government and military reaction to soviet communism in the interwar and later periods see Georges Vidal, "Le PCF et la Défense"; especially his published doctoral thesis, *La Grande Illusion? Le Parti Communiste Français et la Défense Nationale à l'Époque du Front Populaire (1934–9)* (Lyon: Presses Universitaires de Lyon, 2006); *L'Armée Française et l'Ennemi Intérieur (1917–1939). Enjeux Stratégiques et Culture Politique* (Rennes: Presses Universitaires de Rennes, 2015); "Le(s) Communisme(s), la Guerre et le Facteur Militaire" in *Histoire Documentaire du Communisme*, Jean Vigreux and Romain Ducoulombier [dir.], Territoires contemporains—nouvelle série [on line], March 3, 2017, n° 7; Nicolas Texier, "L'Ennemi Intérieur: l'Armée et le Parti Communiste Français de la Libération aux Débuts de la Guerre Froide" in *Revue historique des armées*, Vol. 269 (2012) 46–62.

7   Cited in Georges Vidal, "The French army and the Bolshevik revolution (October 1917–November 1918)" in *Dissidences*, online.
8   See on this de la Gorce, *Armée*, 175.
9   Ibid. 266.
10 Cited in Frédéric Dessberg, "From Mistrust to Hostility: Perceptions of the Russian Revolutions Among French Political Circles (1917–1919)" in Valentine Lomellini (ed.) *The Rise of Bolshevism and Its Impact on the Interwar International Order* (Cham: Springer Nature, 2020) 126.
11 See on this George E. Brinkley, *The Volunteer Army and Allied Intervention in Southern Russia 1917–1921* (South Bend, IN: University of Notre Dame Press, 1966) 74–5, 107–8.
12 Theses on the conditions of admission to the Third International, *Minutes of the II Congress of the Communist International, 1920*. https://archive.org/details/2nd_congress_of_communist_international_proceedings Contrary to Georges Vidal's thesis, the Comintern's emphasis on "army work" remained unchanged after the VII Comintern Congress, as we shall see.
13 See Fonds de surveillance du Parti Communiste Français par la direction de la Sûreté nationale du ministère de l'intérieur sous la IIIe République, with material from 1920 the year the PCF was founded until 1940, a year after it was declared illegal. https://pandor.u-bourgogne.fr/archives-en-ligne/ead.html?id=FRAN_IR_050130&c=FRAN_IR_050130_e0000053&qid=.
14 Cited in Vidal *L'Armée Francaise*, 41.
15 Ibid. 43. On the moderate socialism of Léon Blum, the socialism of Jaurès, see Pierre Birnbaum, *Léon Blum. Prime Minister, Socialist, Zionist* (New Haven: Yale University Press, 2015) 56, 73, etc. See also Serge Berstein, *Léon Blum* (Paris: Fayard, 2006).
16 A summary of police surveillance of communist work in the French army, detailing propaganda material, lists of communist cell members, intercepted communications etc., is available online in the PANDOR portal: Signalements de propagande communiste dans l'armée, 1926-1939, https://pandor.u-bourgogne.fr/archives-en-ligne/ead.html?id=FRAN_IR_050130&c=FRAN_IR_050130_c-7s9vw6sb9-1gtguljb8djt4&qid=.
17 Service Historique de la Défense, Département de l'Armée de Terre, Vincennes, cote 9 N 366. Discussed in detail in Vidal, "L'Armée Française Face au Problème de la Subversion Communiste au Début des Années 1930" in *Guerres Mondiales et Conflits Contemporains: Revue d'Histoire*, Vol. 4, No. 204 (2001) 41–66. See also on the later "Plan Z" to deploy the army in reaction to a possible communist insurrection in Paris Andrew Orr, "Plan Z: The Popular Front, Civil-Military Relations and the French Army's Plan to Defeat a Second Paris Commune, 1934–1936" in *International Journal of Military History and Historiography*, Vol. 39 (2019) 63–87.

18 The standard Comintern manual and textbook used at the International Lenin School, *L'Insurrection Armée*, attributed pseudonymously to A. Neuberg, was published in France in 1931 by Bureau d'Éditions (see Chapter 1 for full details on the book and its authors). The continued commitment to armed insurrection as a means of seizing power was affirmed consistently by French communist leaders and official media from 1931 through 1936. In the context of its coverage of the socialist-led armed insurrection in Spain in October 1934, *L'Humanité* editorialized in a November 2 article entitled "Guerre Civil en Espagne et le Prolétariat International," signed by Ercoli: "L'Insurrection armée pour le pouvoir dans un des pays de l'Europe capitaliste! … les soviets victorieux …!"; in the 1935 edition of the PCF booklet *Que Veulent Les Communistes?*, the party affirmed its belief that in the current imperialist period, only armed insurrection would bring victory for the workers. (Troisième édition; Paris: Bureau d'Éditions, 1935) 44, 61; in January 1936, in an address to the VIII Congress of his party, Maurice Thorez affirmed that the PCF expected a future Popular Front government to allow the preparation for the total seizure of power by the working class, "in short, a government which is the preface to armed insurrection and the dictatorship of the proletariat." Maurice Thorez, *La Union de la Nation Française. Rapport Présenté au VIII Còngres National du Parti Communiste SFIC Villeurbane, 22–25 Javier 1936* (Paris: Publications Revolutionnaires, 1936) 79.
19 Articles in *La France Militaire* cited in Vidal, "L' Armée Francaise Face" 46.
20 Reunion Chez le Camarade Manouilsky le 2-5-34, Orateur: Vassart. RGASPI F. 495. Op. 18.D. 992ª.
21 Thus, *L'Humanité* of April 20, 1935, ran a story on a very successful "goodbye wine" event run by the party in the village of Villejuif, which involved 400 conscripts. The piece added that the local party leader had been present to express the communist rejection of the two-year military service and to demand the acquittal of party members imprisoned for their work in the barracks. The article adds that conscripts sang the International and chanted "Soviets everywhere."
22 Lenin et la Guerre. La Doctrine de Lenin sur la Guerre et les Tâches Actuelles du Prolétariat (Paris: Collection Syndicale Internationale, 1935) 40–1.
23 Of French and German soldiers on the left bank of the Rhein, and in 1924 as the communist youth instructed soldiers in Morocco to fraternize with Abd-El-Krim's forces they were sent to fight.
24 "… des jeunes, à comprendre l'importance de faire le travail anti-militariste, en utilisant différent moyens come par example les femmes, por puovoir influence les soldats." Vassart report cited.
25 Subtitled, "4–12 Février. Une Semaine de Lutte et de Fraternisation." A. Mortier (Paris: Les Publications Révolutionnaires, 1934), sold for 50 cents. "A. Mortier" authored military-related articles in *L'Humanité*, for example, a piece on the "political rights" of soldiers on the front page of the September 1, 1934 issue.

26 Conseils aux bureaux regionaux, a four-page letter signed by Leonce Granjon on August 5, 1936. RGASPI F. 533 Op. 10 D. 3338, available on the PANDOR portal.
27 Direction Centrale des Renseignements Généraux (DCRG). A brief summary of the history available at the French National Archives online http://www.archinoe.fr/console/ir_ead_visu.php?eadid=FRAD047_000001267&ir=24411#.Yg5ZAJYo-3A.
28 For example, Maurice Thorez's speech "Alsace Loraine sous le Joug," Alsace-Lorraine under the yoke, given at the Chambre des Députées on April 4, 1933.
29 Hugo Eberlein, Comintern agent expert in anti-military work and financing of subversive operations, had entered French territory from Germany bearing a Danish passport in the name of Daniel Nielsen. The arrest and investigation uncovered the substantial Comintern funding of separatist publications and groups in Alsace-Lorraine, as well as nationwide. For a small sampling of the very extensive press coverage of the arrest and the investigation, see "Le Danois Nielsen et l'Agent Secret Ugo[sic] Eberlein n's ont qu'un seul et Même Momme Véritable Entrepreneur de Guerre Civile" in *Le Journal*, September 29, 1935; "L'Activité en France de L'Allemand Hugo Eberlein Délégué du Komintern" in *Le Matin*, October 2, 1935; and the response on *L'Humanité*: "La Presse de Laval Multiplié les Infamies á Propos de l'Affaire de Strasbourg." See also Frédéric Charpier, *L'Agent Jacques Duclos. Histoire de l'Appareil Secret du Parti communiste français (1920–1975)* (Paris: Seuil, 2015).
30 Cited in Elisabeth Du Réau, *Edouard Daladier, 1884–1970* (Paris: Fayard, 1993) 327.
31 On the membership numbers of ARAC and other communist mass organizations in France, see "Renseignements avec donées statistiques préparés par Guyot pour la délégation française au CEIC: sur le front unique, le mouvement syndical, le 8e congrès du PCF, les écoles du parti, la presse du parti," RGASPI F 517 Op. 1 D. 1769.
32 See notice on the cover of *L'Humanité* of February 6, in which veterans were told to rally at 20:00 at the same Champs Elysées location the UNC had selected for their march. The PCF had been tracking public sentiment in relation to the Stavinsky affair and noted the "fascists" in France were successfully capitalizing on public anger and frustration at government corruption. The party decided to infiltrate "fascist" protest marches and deploy its agitation in order to redirect the passions of the masses to the communist united front. The first successful infiltration was reported at the political bureau meeting of the PCF on February 1, 1934: "… the communist youth joined the queue of the fascist march with their slogans. The fascists mixed with them and said: [w]ell, let us bring down the Government and after let us settle our affairs." Procès-verbal des séances du Bureau Politique du PCF February 1, 1934, RGASPI F. 517 Op. 1 D. 1626. The official report published after the February events for the Chambre des Députées confirmed the communists had

infiltrated the marches, their veteran's organization ARAC had marched together with both the UNC and Croix de Feu, had chanted pro soviet slogans and had provoked violence throughout. *Rapport général fait au nom de la Commission d'enquête chargée de rechercher les causes et les origines des évenements du 6 février 1934 et jours suivants.* Annexe au procès verbal. No. 3383. Contrary to later anti-fascist propaganda, The Political Bureau of the PCF admitted internally on March 1, 1934, that "on ne peut pas dire que le 6 les fascistes avaient l'intention de prendre le pouvoir." These data require a fresh look at the events of February 6, 1934, in Paris, with the PCF as a key agent provocateur in the marches, and not merely reacting to and surprised by them, as Vidal and Jackson suppose. *La Grande Illusion*, 78; *The Popular Front*, 28 respectively. See also, with a detailed fascist vs. anti-fascist interpretation of February 6, 1934, Brian Jenkins, "The Six Février 1934 and the 'Survival' of the French Republic" in *French History*, Vol. 20, No. 3 (2006) 333–51.

33 Cited in Gilbert Allardyce, "The Political Transition of Jacques Doriot," in *Journal of Contemporary History*, Vol. 1, No. 1 (1966) 61.

34 Vidal, "Le PCF et la Défense" 49–50. The quote this phrase is taken from appears at the top of an article attributed to A. Mortier and entitled "Tempête dans les camps de l'Armée Bourgeoisie" in *Cahiers de Bolshévisme* 11o Année, No. 18, September 15, 1934, 1085–90.

35 ... la action des réservistes et des soldats es por nous importante dans ce sens que brisant la discipline dans l'armée de la bourgeoisie. Mortier, "Tempête," 1088.

36 Informations du CC des JC au CEICJ sur la Lutte Contre la Militarisation de la Jeunesse, sur l'Unité d'Action avec les JS, September 1 through 30, 1935, RGASPI F. 533 Op. 10 D. 3327.

37 Cited by V. P. Smirnov in "Le Komintern et le Parti communiste français pendant la «drôle de guerre», 1939–1940" in *Revue des Études Slaves*, Vol. 65, No. 4 (1993) 681–4. Smirnov also discusses the Comintern debate on the topic, which concluded with instructions to the PCF to deploy the slogans "down with the imperialist war and for immediate peace," but without any mechanical copying of slogans taken from the prior imperialist war, such as "transformation of imperialist war into civil war."

38 L'Unité our la Victoire, Discours Prononcé par Jacques Duclos a l'Assemblée Commune des Partis Socialiste et Communiste le 2 Décembre 1935, Salle de la Mutualité à Paris (Paris: Imprimerie Française, 1936) 7.

39 Vidal "Le PCF et la Défense" 72.

40 B. Vasiliev's speech on the work of communists in the army. August 19, 1935, one day before the end of the congress. RGASPI F. 494 Op. 1 D. 434, text available online http://docs.historyrussia.org/ru/nodes/101402.

41 *L'Humanité*, February 6, 1935, p. 6.

42 "A la demande du ministre de la guerre, la Chambre disjoint les amendements prévoyant des réductions d'effectives militaires" in *Le Mayenne*, a local daily in Laval, December 28, 1935.
43 See L. Sampaix, "La Reduction du Temps de Service, est elle possible?" in *L'Humanité* August 15, 1936, in which Sampaix argued that the law increasing military service to two years had been the product of French fascists allied with Hitler and Mussolini.
44 Vidal, "Le PCF et la Défense," 54–5, 65.
45 In "Le(s) Communisme(s)," Latest online revision dated 2017.
46 Roberto Villa, 1917. *El Estado Catalán y El Soviet Español* (Madrid: Espasa, 2021). On the 100th anniversary of the 1917 events in Spain, Eduardo Gonzalez Calleja (ed.), *Anatomía de una Crisis* (Madrid: Alianza Editorial, 2017). The very structure of this earlier book serves to highlight the novelty of Roberto Villa's thesis. While Eduardo González Calleja's volume is divided into sections dealing with the political, military, and economic crisis, thus stressing their relative independence, Villa has shown the interconnectedness of all three strands, and the collaboration, however utilitarian and limited, of the leading actors in each domain to unsettle the political status quo. A solid review of Villa's book outside of the journals is Carlos Dardé, "España 1917; Tres Revoluciones o Solo Una?" in *Revista de los Libros*, July 14, 2021, online. Villa's response to Dardé led to a fruitful discussion between them.
47 Ángel Bahamonde Magro, "La Crisis Militar. La Reunión Corporativa de las Juntas de Defensa," in González Calleja, *Anatomía*, 80.
48 Villa, *1917*, 280.
49 On the meetings and agreements between Márquez and Cambó and Lerroux, see Villa, *1917*, 327–9.
50 Cited in Villa, Ibid.
51 Villa, *1917*, 542. See on this and other revolutionary publications in Spain in 1918, Paul Aubert, "La Propagande Étrangère en Espagne dans le Premier Tiers du XXe Siècle" in *Mélanges de la Casa de Velázquez* Année (1995) 31–3, 103–76, esp. 136. Limiting her research to the Servicio Histórico Militar, Ana Alonso has argued that seditious ideas were "totally absent" in the NCO Juntas, and that these were not Soviets. Ana I. Alonso Ibáñez, "Las Juntas de Defensa de las Clases de Tropa (1917-1918)" in *Cuadernos de Historia Contemporánea*, No. 21 (1999) 259–278.
52 "Sargentos y brigadas expulsados del ejército el pasado año ... Restituto Mogrovejo y Juan Antonio Montero." *La Época,* January 17, 1919.
53 See on this McMeekin, *The Russian Revolution. A New History* (New York: Basic Books, 2017) 128–9.
54 "Project de Directives our le Travail Anti au Maroc." In Procès-verbaux n° 26–8 des réunions du Présidium du CEIC et les matériaux annexes aux procès-verbaux (1er exemplaire). RGASPI F 495 Op. 2 D. 47. The Spanish press had been following

communist-inspired propaganda promoting sedition among the troops in Morocco since at least 1923, see "Propaganda Antimilitarista" in *El Sol*, August 23, 1923, 4.

55 On the Doriot-led Comité d'action des Jeunesses communistes de France et d'Espagne, see David Drake, "The PCF, the Surrealists, Clarté and the Rif War" in *French Cultural Studies*, Vol. 17, No. 2 (2006) 173–88; David H. Slavin, "The French Left and the Rif War, 1924–25: Racism and the Limits of Internationalism" in *Journal of Contemporary History*, Vol. 26 (1991) 5–32.

56 "Al Secretariado de La internacional Comunista. Moscú," a letter signed José Bullejos and written on official PCE letterhead. Correspondance du Secrétariat du CEIC en CC du Parti Comuniste d'Espagne. RGASPI F. 494 Op. 18 D. 464a.

57 "Informe sobre el Trabajo Anti," a thirteen-page handwritten report signed by "Julio" with a Russian translation, part of "Reports of Representatives of the ECCI in the Communist Party of Spain," RGASPI. F. 495. Op. 32.d. 223. We have identified Julio as Julio Suárez Rodríguez, thanks to the date of his arrest as provided in his report.

58 *Ahora* was a morning newspaper, and its articles were, for the most part, written the evening before. This note mentions the arrest took place "anoche," hence, the evening of March 7. See also *Libertad* of March 9, and details of his arrest and pending trial on the Archivo Histórico Nacional online: "Rollo nº 347/1934 del sumario 145/1934 instruido por el Juzgado de Instrucción nº 7 de Madrid (Tribunal de Urgencia) por reunión clandestina en el Café Platerías situado en la calle Mayor, nº 40."

59 Enrique Líster, *Memorias de un Luchador. Los Primeros Combates* (Madrid: G. del Toro, 1977) 63.

60 "Memorial Confidencial" August 14, 1934, part of "Letters of the Roman Secretariat of the ECCI to the Communist Party of Spain" RGASPI F. 495 Op. 32 D. 219.

61 Líster, *Memorias*, 62.

62 ¿Por qué Fui Lanzado del Ministerio de la Guerra? Diez Meses de Actuación Ministerial (Madrid: Espasa Calpe, 1934).

63 Ibid. 54–5, 146–7.

64 See, for example, "Hay que impedir a toda costa las maniobras militares de septiembre" in *Soldado Rojo, Órgano Nacional de la Federación de Soldados y Marinos Comunistas,* año 1, número 2, September 1934, repeatedly urging communist cell members to disable or destroy equipment needed for the exercises; "Abajo las maniobras militares de preparación de la guerra" in *Campamento Rojo*, Año 1, Número 3, July 1934, a pamphlet targeting the military installations in the Southwest area of Madrid known to this day as "Campamento." This issue mentions by name "fascist officers" in the base.

65 Ibid. 119, 84.

66 Ibid. 29–35. The officer in question, Lieutenant Colonel López Bravo, a battalion commander, was first thought to be sailing on the Segarra, a vessel which the ministry authorities failed to locate. Hours later he was located on the Miguel de Cervantes cruiser instead, whose captain was ordered to disembark the officer without delay. In his debate with Calvo Sotelo, Hidalgo affirmed that his investigation of the matter revealed López Bravo had only, in fact, told a group of friends that soldiers were not likely to shoot "their brethren," and had not promoted insubordination directly with the troops. The story of Lopez Bravo, as an example of fraternization frustrated by the government, made it to the pages of the French communist pamphlet *Le Choc de Deux Espagne*, written by Robert Blache (Paris: Défense Éditions, 1935) 12.

67 Espada describes his personal role as liaison for the communist cells on board in the arrangement of the meeting with López Bravo. "Informe del Camarada Espada a los Camaradas de la Dirección" in AHPCE Manuscritos 35, 1, 16–17.

68 See on this Roberto Villa, *1917*, 369. As the government monitored the preparation of armed insurrection by the socialist and anarchist unions, "no confiaba en la respuesta del Ejército, minado por unos junteros cada vez más soliviantados ... que además daban pábulo a las expectativas de los revolucionarios sobre el resquebrajamiento de la disciplina."

69 Transcript of the January 17, 1936, Meeting of the ECCI's Roman Lander Secretariat—Spanish Commission. RGASPI. F. 495. Op. 20.D. 269. See also on this J. A. Sánchez y G. Sauco, *La Revolución de 1934 en Asturias* (Madrid: editorial Nacional, 1974) 130–1, detailing, as does Codovilla in his January 1935 report, the presence of revolutionary cells at the aerodrome in Leon totaling at least twenty-eight individuals, and the insubordination of the base commander which forced senior officers to temporarily disable aircraft to avoid them being taken over by insurgents. As Sauco mentions, when the first aircraft appeared in the skies of Asturias, the insurgents fully expected them to be on their side.

70 Du Réau, *Daladier*, 327.

71 Sauco, *Revolución*, 130–1.

72 In an open letter addressed to the leadership of the socialist party, PCE leader José Díaz called for the suppression of the permanent army, "an instrument of capitalism" the "liquidation" of the officer corps, and the creation of a red worker and peasant army. Published on *Heraldo de Madrid*, March 6, 1936, 3–4. As of May 1936, socialist and communist militias were operating as one, and the joint May 1 parades of uniformed socialist and communist militias were widely reported in local and national newspapers. The troika-based structure of the militias was identical to that of the communist army cell network. See *MAOC. Órgano del Comité Nacional de las M.A.O.C.* Número 1, September 1934, 3.

73 In an interview with British newspaper *The Daily Telegraph*, Caballero asserted that the Azaña government was moving "lazily" in the implementation of the

Popular Front platform, and that what was needed was the republicanization of the army and the ministries. "Besteiro, Zulueta, Largo Caballero y José Díaz hacen declaraciones políticas" in *Heraldo de Madrid*, March 5, 1936, 2. More explicitly, the UGT's *Transporte*, in its May issue, celebrated the defeat of capitalism and feudalism, and called for both the punishment of the executioners who acted "illegally" in the repression of the insurrection and the republicanization of the army, the judiciary, and the state administration. "A las agrupaciones socialistas y organizaciones obreras pertenecientes a la Unión General de Trabajadores," article signed by Caballero for UGT and Juan Simeón Vidarte for the PSOE, in *Transporte*, Número 117, May 1936. In February 1936, *Soldado Rojo* was calling upon the "Popular Block" coalition to prioritize the democratization of the army, by which it meant, the elimination from its ranks of every reactionary and fascist officer. This required, according to *Soldado Rojo*, the united struggle of all antifascist soldiers, sailors, and corporals "before and after the triumph of the Popular Block." *Soldado Rojo*, Año 2, Número 13, undated but certainly either late January or early February 1936, 8.

74 For a detailed narrative of his arrest, charges against him and execution see the appendix to Rafael Salazar Alonso, *Bajo el Signo de la Revolución* (Astorga: Akrón, 2007) 45–66.
75 See Calvo Sotelo's speech in *ABC*, April 16, 1936.
76 Jessica Wardhaugh, *In Pursuit of the People. Political Culture in France 1934–1939* (Basingstoke: Palgrave, 2009) 200.
77 Both quotes cited in Du Réau, *Daladier, 19.1*.
78 Jackson, *Popular Front*, 57.
79 See on this Birnbaum, *Blum*, 68.
80 Leon Blum, *For all Mankind* (tr.) W. Pickles (New York: Viking Press, 1946) 174.
81 Manuilsky speech to the ECCI on the preparation of the XII Plenum of the ECCI, April 17, 1932, RGASPI F. 495 Op. 170, D. 5, L. 53–7. Available online http://docs.historyrussia.org/ru/nodes/101371.
82 The most influential work is Serge Berstein, *Le 6 Février 1934* (Paris: Gallimard/Julliard, 1975). Michel Dobry, "Février 1934 et la Découverte de l'Allergie de la Société Française à la 'Révolution Fasciste'" in *Revue Française de Sociologie*, Vol. 30 (1989) 511–33. More recently, for example, Brian Jenkins, "The Six Février 1934 and the 'Survival' of the French Republic" in *French History*, Vol. 23 (2006) 333–51; Chris Millington, "February 6, 1934. The Veterans' Riot" in *French Historical Studies*, Vol. 33, No. 4 (Fall 2010) 545–72; Emmanuel Blanchard, "Le 6 Février 1934, une Crise Policière?" in *Vingtiéme Siècle. Revue d'Histoire*, Vol. 128 (Oct.–Dec 2015) 15–28. See full bibliography in Millington and Blanchard.
83 Brian Jenkins and Chris Millington, *France and Fascism. February 1934 and the Dynamics of Political Crisis* (Routledge Studies in Fascism and the Far Right;

London: Routledge, 2015). See also Zeev Sternhell, *Ni Droite ni Gauche. L'idéologie Fasciste en France* (Paris: Éditions du Seuil, 1983).

84 But see Michel Winnock, "Revisiting French Fascism: La Rocque and the Croix-de-Feu" in *Vingtième Siècle. Revue d'Histoire*, Vol. 90, No. 2 (2006) 3–27. Jenkins and Millington's refusal to engage with definitions of fascism is central to their argument. See also Stanley G. Payne, *A History of Fascism, 1914–1945* (Abingdon on Thames: Taylor & Francis, 2003) 291–9.

85 Brian Jenkins, "Introduction. False Perspectives, False Conclusions—The Historiography of the 6 Février 1934" in Jenkins and Millington, *France and Fascism*, 10–11.

86 Thus, on authoritarianism, Jenkins attributes it repeatedly to the right-wing parties and leagues in France in the 1930s. Of twenty-three references to "authoritarian" or "authoritarianism" in his "The Six Février," all are in reference to the right-wing parties or the leagues, and not a single one to the PCF or left wing of the SFIO, who openly advocated the dictatorship of the proletariat and Soviet-style revolution (see my previous chapter). In Jenkins and Millington's 2015 *France and Fascism* volume, we find seventy references to "authoritarian" or "authoritarianism," of which a single one has a left-wing party as a referent (p. 2 in the introduction by Jenkins). Similarly, "radicalized" or "radicalization" appear six times in Jenkins's "The Six Février" and all are attributed to the right or to alleged fascist movements, never to the left. In their co-authored volume all seventeen instances of the words have the right or the leagues as a subject. Likewise, the term "extraparliamentary" is reserved, in "The Six Février," in six out of seven references for the leagues or for alleged fascists, with a single reference made in relation to the Popular Front as a movement. In their co-authored volume, of twenty-four references to "extraparliamentary" all but three are used in reference to the right or the leagues, and three of the Popular Front. In their qualification of just how the Popular Front was "extraparliamentary," however, the authors make their views transparent: the extra-parliamentary nature of the Popular Front involved grassroots institutions embedded in close-knit communities. That of the right, however, was chauvinistic, racist and nationalist (p. 16 in Jenkins's introduction). Lastly, in their discussions of an "insurrectional climate," both authors fail to mention the explicit and detailed insurrectional plans of the PCF and its front organizations, which included the publishing of the famous manual *L'Insurrection Armée* and were the object of careful French government surveillance (see on this my previous chapter). For Jenkins and Millington, communist armed insurrection existed only in the conspiracy theories of the right-wing leagues.

87 A key element in Jenkins and Millington's argument is the assertion that the conservative fear of the left in France in this period was "exaggerated," see, for example, Jenkins, "The Six Février," 343. Further, as we have already detailed, both

authors exclude both the PCF and the left wing of the SFIO from any references to authoritarianism, violence, and regime change. For Jenkins, the communists merely tried to exploit the scandal, and he believes Stavisky was not a good source for communist agitation. Jenkins, "Crisis and Conspiracy. The Prelude of the Six Février" in Jenkins and Millington, *France and Fascism*, 50. Logically, references to the significant communist involvement in the February 6 events are relegated to the footnotes and appendices, and not properly engaged with in their discussion. Thus, though the communist veteran's group "also joined" the marches to "protest" (Jenkins, p. 62), Instructions on *L'Humanité* for the communists to join the UNC marches are relegated to endnote 3 in Chapter 3, where Jenkins argues this instruction is given "somewhat confusingly." Further, the fact that "a large number of communists" were present is mentioned as part of a Shirer quote on endnote 53 of Chapter 3. Lastly, Millington quotes Shirer's account of the marchers moving towards the Madeleine at around 10 in the evening, a quote affirming the crowd "of leaguers and communists" was 10,000 strong, engaged in a fierce assault of the bridge and "almost carried it." Chris Millington, "The Veterans and the Paris Riot" in Jenkins and Millington, *France and Fascism*, 115.

88 Chris Millington, "Communist Veterans and Paramilitarism in 1920s France: The Association Républicaine des Anciens Combattants" in *Journal of War & Culture Studies*, Vol. 8, No. 4 (Nov. 2015) 300–314. Millington does mention the ARAC's involvement in the 6 Février in his chapter on the subject in the volume co-written with Jenkins, but this is mentioned in passing and not elaborated on. Chris Millington, "The Veterans and the Paris Riot" in Jenkins and Millington, *France and Fascism*, 101.

89 Procès Verbal des Séances du Bureau Politique du PCF du II Janvier 1934, Procès-verbal des séances du Bureau Politique du PCF, RGASPI F. 517 Op. 1 D. 1626, available online from PANDOR.

90 Procès Verbal des Séances du Bureau Politique du PCF du 18 janvier 1934, Ibid.

91 "essayer de jetter le trouble et de pénétrer sous cette forme, dans cette organisation fasciste d'anciens combattants que sont les Croix de Feu." Procès-verbal du Comité Central, 23 janvier 1934, RGASPI F. 517 Op. 1 D. 1609, available online.

92 "Au moment des manifestations sur les boulevards la semaine dernière, des J.C. se mettaient à la queue des manifestants fascistes avec nos mots d'ordre, les fascistes se sont mélangés avec à eux et leur on dit: Bien, mettons en bas le gouvernement et après on réglers nos affaires." Procès Verbal des Séances du Bureau Politique du PCF du Ier février 1934, Ibid.

93 *Rapport général fait au nom de la Commission d'enquête chargée de rechercher les causes et les origines des évenements du 6 février 1934 et jours suivants*. Annexe au procès verbal. No. 3383.

94 *Rapport général*, 461.

95 Ibid. 1019, 1020.
96 Ibid. 1119, 1128, 461, 546 etc.
97 Procès Verbal des Séances du Bureau Politique du PCF, February 15, 1934, Ibid.
98 Plumyène and Lasierra, cited in Payne, *Fascism*, 294.

Chapter 5

1 See on this E. H. Carr, *Twilight of the Comintern, 1930–1935* (New York: Pantheon Books, 1982), 7, 21–2 on the creation of the Revolutionare Gewerkschaftsopposition or RGO by the KPD in 1929, and the discussion in the context of the V Congress of Profintern, respectively; Kevin McDermott and Jeremy Agnew, *The Comintern. A History of International Communism from Lenin to Stalin* (Basingstoke: Macmillan, 1996) 33–6, 47 etc. See also Stéphane Courtois, "The Origins of the Trade Union Question in the Communist World" in *Journal of Communist Studies*, Vol. 64, No. 7–17 (1990) 7–16.

2 See, for example, a detailed account of the British experience in John McIlroy, "British Communists and the 1932 turn to Trade Unions" in *Labour History*, Vol. 56, No. 5 (2015) 541–65. The Spanish experience, as we shall see, also entailed a "both … and" approach.

3 Tim Rees, "Revolution or Republic? The Spanish Communist Party 1931–1936" in Manuel Álvarez Tardío and Fernando del Rey Reguillo (eds.) *The Spanish Second Republic Revisited* (Eastbourne: Sussex Academic Press, 2012) 156. Rees further implies that communist mass organizations in Spain were operating only in 1936, Rees, 163.

4 Antonio Elorza and Marta Bizcarrondo, *Queridos Camaradas. La Internacional Comunista y España 1919–1939* (Barcelona: Planeta, 1999) 178, 213–15.

5 Helen Graham, *Socialism and War. The Spanish Socialist Party in Power and Crisis 1936–1939* (Cambridge: Cambridge University Press, 1991) 79.

6 "The Party and the Trade Unions." The file is part of the West European Bureau material, RGASPI. F. 499. Op. 1.D. 2.

7 E. H. Carr, *The Russian Revolution from Lenin to Stalin (1917–1929)* (New York: Macmillan, 2004) 33.

8 RGASPI. F. 495. Op. 51.D.18. The commission was implementing the guidance on revolutionary opposition groups and other topics issued by the IV Congress of the Profintern, the Red International of Labor Unions.

9 "Rapports du Secrétariat Romain du CEIC portants sur l'Espagne," January 19, 1932. RGASPI F 495 Op. 32 D. 209.

10 *El Trabajo en las Células de Empresa* (Ediciones Joven Comunista; Barcelona: Myria). This is a twenty-nine-page booklet not bearing a publication date, though probably printed around 1932.

11 *La Internacional Comunista: ¡Proletarios de todos los países, uníos!*: Number 5—August 1932; Number 8-9—November 1932 etc.
12 On Pablo de la Fuente Martín's role in the rail workers union's OSR in the run-up to the October 1934 armed insurrection see Miguel Muñoz Rubio, "El Sindicato Nacional Ferroviario: cuatro decenios de lucha contra el franquismo en el exilio y en la clandestinidad" in *Transportes, Servicios y Comunicaciones* 42, March 2020. Muñoz Rubio affirms on the basis of data taken from another researcher that in October 1934 37.9 percent of the UGT in Madrid was controlled by communists. For de la Fuente's role in the SOE see Bericht aus Spanien, dated July 1935, in which his role and that of Rafael Ochoa are discussed, together with their infiltration of the metal workers' union. RGASPI F.495 Op.32 D.158.
13 Bericht aus Spanien, dated July 1935, RGASPI F.495 Op.32 D.158.
14 *Hacia la Unidad de la Lucha de Clase. Plataforma de Acción de los Partidos de la Unidad Sindical* (Madrid: Ediciones Unidad Sindical, 1932), with an introduction by Juan Astigarrabia, Secretary General of Comité Nacional de Unidad Sindical.
15 Rafael Cruz, "La Organización del PCE (1920–1934)" in *Estudios de Historia Social*, No. 31 (1984). Cruz mentions, in line with the two sources we cite, 221 delegates being present at the conference, but affirms these represented 175,000 "afiliados," mentioning *Frente Rojo* July 7, 1932, as his source. Cruz also argues that 150,000 is the correct figure based on a PCE-produced breakdown. Perhaps Cruz's accounting also has gaps, since his map showing OSR and red union members per province shows zero members in Cataluña, but the Comintern-held report of the conference mentions the participation of a Barcelona-based OSR representing 2,000 workers in that city. A June 1935 Comintern report mentions 1,500 OSR members in the city of Madrid, working in unison with the left-wing socialists against the right in those unions. "Sténogramme du Secrétariat Romain du CEIC sur la question espagnole" RGASPI F. 495 Op. 32 D. 174.
16 See on this Sandra Souto Kustrín, "Poder, Acción Colectiva y Violencia en la Provincia de Madrid 1934–1936" doctoral thesis at Universidad Complutense de Madrid, 2000, 103.
17 Fernando del Rey Reguillo, "Protesta Obrera y Sindicalismo en la Industria Tabaquera Española (1887–1939)" in *Hispania*, Vol. LX, No. 3, num. 206 (2000) 206.
18 RGASPI. F. 495. Op. 4.D. 441.
19 RGASPI F 494. Op. 32 D. 225. In our previous discussion we argued Albert is none other than Comintern agent Hugo Eberlein.
20 "Federation des ouvriers du tabac" is mentioned in first place by Barbusse. RGASPI F 543 Op. 1 D. 25, more details below.
21 For detailed numbers, see Marta Bizcarrondo, *Historia de la U.G.T., Vol. 3. Entre la Democracia y la Revolución* (Madrid: Siglo XXI, 2008) 17–24; Manuel Redero San

Román, "La U.G.T. en el Primer Bienio Republicano," in *Investigaciones Históricas: Época Moderna y Contemporánea*, No 10 (1990) 105–6.
22 Enrique Santiago, "Largo Caballero en el Ministerio de Trabajo" in *El Socialista*, April 16, 1931, two days after the proclamation of the II Spanish Republic.
23 See on this Bizcarrondo, *U.G.T.*, 19–21.
24 Manuel Redero San Román, "La Problemática de la Organización de la U.G.T. en la II República," in *Studia Historica. Historia Contemporánea*, Vol. 1 (February 2010) 67–88.
25 "Del Frente Único al Comité de Fábrica," Signed C.D. in *El Metalúrgico*, Año, Vol. VI, No. 57 enero (1932).
26 As reported on *Hoja Oficial del Lunes*, March 21, 1932.
27 J. Gonzalo Aceña, "Ante los Derechos Conquistados, la Obligación y el Sacrificio se Imponen," in *Transporte*, Suplemento al Número 74, 15 de febrero de 1932.
28 "Plan Orgánico" in *Fuerza*, Año 1 Número 1, April 1, 1932.
29 As reported in *El Sol*, June 19, 1932.
30 "Grupo Sindical Revolucionario de Artes Blancas" in *La Libertad*, July 14, 1932.
31 *Bajo el Signo de la Revolución* (Astorga: Akrón, 2007) 121–5. Salazar Alonso discusses in some detail the attempted general strike launched by the printers union in 1934 which targeted the monarchist daily ABC and other conservative newspapers.
32 Antonio Segura, "La Casual Pérdida de unos Textos Taquigráficos" in *Cartas y Carteros. Órgano del Sindicato Nacional de Carteros*, Año III, No. 52 (October 25, 1932).
33 Francisco Rebollo, "Actuaciones" in *Transporte*, Suplemento al No. 83, November 15, 1932.
34 "… hay que reconocer que en todas ellas prendió la agitación de los grupos oposicionistas … en una negativa labor de obstrucción y saboteo a todos los acuerdos llevados a discusión por las juntas directivas." "Unidad de Acción de los Grupos Sindicales Socialistas" in *El Socialista*, Año XLVIII, Número 7459 (January 1, 1933).
35 September 5, 1934, ECCI report entitled "The Situation in the Communist Party of Spain," RGASPI. F. 495. Op. 32.D. 144. L. 230–47. http://docs.historyrussia.org/ru/nodes/102017.
36 "La Lutte Economique et les Taches des Partis Communistes," May 27, 1929, Trade Union Commission of the ECCI, RGASPI. F. 495. Op. 51.D.18.
37 ECCI Letter to the Central Committee of the Communist Party in Spain on recruitment for the ILS. RGASPI. F. 495. Op. 32. D. 219 L 34–5. http://docs.historyrussia.org/ru/nodes/102016.
38 Bizcarrondo, *U.G.T.* 107.
39 RGASPI. F. 495. Op. 32.D. 144. L. 230–47. http://docs.historyrussia.org/ru/nodes/102017.

40 Secrétariat Romain. Question Espagnole, orateur: Codovilla. January 29, 1935. *RGASPI F. 495. Op. 32. D. 165.*
41 "Directives Interieures pour le Parti Communiste d'Espagne," March 2, 1935, RGASPI F. 495 Op. 32 D. 2.
42 For example, references to "grupos de oposición," "oposición revolucionaria," "oposición sindical" when in reference to the OSR groups etc.
43 See, for example, coverage in *El Siglo Futuro*, May 14, 1934.
44 ECCI Report "Situation in the Communist Party of Spain," September 5, 1934, RGASPI F. 495 Op. 32 D. 144 http://docs.historyrussia.org/ru/nodes/102017.
45 Codovilla's words repeated multiple times in his comprehensive report post October 1934 insurrection, delivered in Moscow in January 1935, RGASPI F 494 Op. 32 D. 165. The Communists insisted on adding "y campesinas" (and of peasants) to the socialist Alianzas Obreras (Alliances of workers). As a late comer into the Alianzas, communist strategy involved joining these to control and shape the content where possible "from the base," and to form them from scratch according to their vision of soviets where none existed. With the merger of CGTU with UGT (including its largest union, the agriculture workers union FNTT) a year later, this became a moot point.
46 Report mentioned above on the Spanish question, RGASPI F 495 Op. 32 D 165.
47 Report written by Luis G. de Linares, who found a red OSR membership booklet next to a dead miner, with the name page torn off. The booklet contained the program pushed by OSR groups everywhere, including two months of paid annual vacation, a seven-hour workday, the arming of the proletariat and the destruction of the capitalist regime. "Son estos dos últimos artículos, concluded de Linares, los que han intentado llevar a la práctica los revolucionarios asturianos."
48 Cited in Bizcarrondo, *U.G.T.*, 145.
49 Especially after losing the 1933 elections to the conservative—republican block. For example, in a speech to the printing unions in January 1934: "[f]rom the [communists] all that separates us is a question of name, since we both have our doctrinal roots in Marx's Capital and in the Communist Manifesto." Caballero also defended, in that speech, the violent seizure of power, which, he argued, even moderate socialists had accepted. As reported on *Ahora* January 2, 1934.
50 "Nota Sindical" in *La Región*, April 18, 1936.
51 Holger Weiss, *A Global Radical Waterfront: The International Propaganda Committee of Transport Workers and the International of Seamen and Harbour Workers, 1921–1937* (Studies in Global Social History 43; Leiden: Brill, 2021). The International Propaganda Committee was a network of revolutionary opposition groups in docker and sailor unions of several countries, which enabled the launch of a global communist union by the Profitern.

52 Alan Campbell and John McIlroy, "'The Trojan Horse': Communist Entrism in the British Labour Party, 1933–43" in *Labor History*, Vol. 59, No. 5 (2018) 513–54, and an ongoing research project at Middlesex University available online TROJAN_HORSE.pdf (mdx.ac.uk). See also Matthew Worley, "The Communist International, The Communist Party of Great Britain, and the 'Third Period', 1928–1932" in *European History Quarterly*, Vol. 30, No. 2, 190, in which Worley stresses the CPGB focused not on the set up of a communist union, but on the establishment on revolutionary opposition groups within the existing Labour Party unions.

53 The authors correctly trace the origins of this tactic to Lenin's own instruction to form communist nuclei in "every organization, union or association without exception" for the purpose of agitation and control. Although they focus on CPGB infiltration of the Labour Party, they show the communists did so "because of its umbilical connection with the trade unions" (3) and mention multiple instances of CPGB opposition activity within Labour unions (8, 10, etc.).

54 See Jonathan Haslam, *The Spectre of War. International Communism and the Origins of World War II* (Princeton: Princeton University Press, 2021) 11.

Chapter 6

1 *El Cielo Prometido. Una Mujer al Servicio de Stalin* (Barcelona: Planeta, 2016) 89.

2 Gounot has worked primarily with the Red Sports International material in Fond 537 of the RGASPI files. See, for example, "Sport ouvrier et communisme en France, 1920–1934: une rencontre limitée" in *STADION. Revue internationale d'Histoire du Sport*, Vol. 23 (1997) 84–112; "L'Internationale rouge sportive et le problème de l'établissement d'une 'culture physique communiste' (1921–1937)" in *Sport History Review*, Vol. 31, No. 2 (2000) 139–59; "Sports or Political Organization? Structures and Characteristics of the Red Sport International (1921–1937)" in *The Journal of Sport History*, Vol. 28, No. 1 (2001) 23–39; *Die Rote Sportinternationale, 1921–1937. Kommunistische Massenpolitik im europäischen Arbeitersport* (Münster: LIT Verlag, 2002); "El Proyecto de la Olimpiada Popular de Barcelona (1936): Entre Comunismo Internacional y Republicanismo Regional" in *Cultura, Ciencia y Deporte*, Vol. 1, No. 3 (2005) 115–23; "Social Democratic and Communist Influences on Workers' Sport across Europe (1893–1939)" in *Labour History*, Vol. 80, No. 1 (2015) 1–29.

3 In my view, the most valuable contribution of the article is his reference to and detailing of the communication between CCEP and Sportintern in the document entitled "Abschrift des Briefes des Comité Català pro Esport Popular, Barcelona vom 22. April 1936" in RGASPI F. 537 Op. 2 D. 67, a copy of which I have obtained

and is not available in the online repositories. In this document, the CCEP reports to Sportintern management on its achievements, especially the critical support from ERC and Estat Català, and concludes: "[i]t is now of the utmost importance for us that we maintain regular and quickly functioning contact with you ..."

4   L'Altra Olimpíada. Barcelona 1936 (2 Ed. June 2006; Barcelona: Llibres de L'Index, 2006). Volume sponsored by the Generalitat de Catalunya's Programa per al Memorial Democràtic.

5   James Stout, *The Popular Front and the Barcelona 1936 Popular Olympics* (Singapore: Palgrave, 2020) 60. Pujadas was involved in the editing of the volume and Stout is heavily dependent on the Santacana and Pujadas tome. Stout has also written a popular level account of the Barcelona Popular Olympiad published by The National Geographic in July 2021; "The Brutal Story of the 1936 Popular Olympics: A Boycott of Fascism and Hitler," available online.

6   For example, his reference to "German communist George Dimtriov[sic]," in reference to Georgy Dimitrov the Bulgarian communist who became Comintern General Secretary after his release from nazi imprisonment, Stout, 20; or his statement that the "Trofeo Thalemann [*sic*]" in Barcelona was "named after an executed German communist," in reference to Ernst Thalmann, executed in 1944, eight years after the Thaelmann Cup, Stout, 56. On that same page, Stout affirms it was 1937 when militias first took up the name Thalmann in Barcelona, but this happened already in late July 1936.

7   See Extrait de la Decision du Secretariat du CE de'l IC en date de 2 Octobre 1935, sur la Structure de L'Appareil du Secretariat du CE de L' IC., section 2, Section de Propagande et de Organisations de Masse. RGASPI. F. 495. Op. 20. D. 808 and Projet de Statut du Service de Propagande et de Organisations de Masse, dated June 6, 1936, same reference.

8   On Comintern mass organizations, see Witold S. Sworakowski, *The Comunist International and Its Front Organizations* (Stanford: Hoover Institution, 1965), dated but still useful and focusing primarily on publications from the Red International of Labor Unions, Communist Youth International, International Red Aid, International Peasants Council, Workers International Relief and the various Communist Women's organizations. See also E. H. Carr, "Fronts and Movements" in *Twilight of the Comintern, 1930–1935* (New York: Pantheon, 1982) 385–400; Brigitte Studer, *The Transnational World of the Cominternians* (Basingstoke: Palgrave, 2015); Stephen Koch, *Double Lives* (New York: Enigma, 2004), for the best treatment of the network of front organizations managed by the "Münzenberg trust."

9   Bericht des Genossen Inkpin über die Tätigkeit des Bundes des Freunds der Sowjetunion, dated July 5, 1935. RGASPI F. 494 Op. 20. D. 898.

10 RGASPI Fond 495. Op. 4.D., 254.

11 As acknowledged, for example, by PCE leader José Bullejos in *La Comintern en España* (Mexico: Impresiones Modernas, 1972) 157–8. See also Elorza y Bizcarrondo, *Queridos Camaradas*, 230; see also Chapter 1.
12 See, for example, August 7, 1935, letter from "Rafael" of the provincial SRI committee in Jaén to the Executive National Committee: "… en esta provincia existe una gran simpatía por nuestra organización. De ello se encarga, en gran parte, el Secretario General, que es socialista, pues en todo [sic] los actos habla por el SRI"; August 8, 1935 letter from SRI in Ecija to the Executive National Committee on the members of the new local committee: "Presidente: Socialista, Secretario General: Comunista, Secretario Administrativo: Sin partido"; September 26, 1935, National Committee of SRI "A todos los comités regionales y provinciales," detailing the members of the new national committee, which for Cataluña was to be "un miembro afiliado a la Esquerra" and for Vasconia "un miembro nacionalista o socialista." AHPCE Microfilms XIV -171.
13 See for references and discussion of this Chapter 2.
14 See on the Sportintern Gounot, "Sports or Political Organization?" Anna Khorosheva, "The Activities of the Red Sport International 1933-1937" in *Rossijdksiskaya Istoriya*, Vol. 5 (2018) 105–15; Barbara Keys, "Soviet Sport and Transnational Mass Culture in the 1930's" in *Journal of Contemporary History*, Vol. 38, No. 3 (Jul. 2003) 413–34.
15 Proposition du Comité Exécutif de l'International de Sports. November 11, 1921, RGASPI. F. 495. Op. 18.D. 34.
16 Resolution of the Political Secretariat of the ECCI on the Sport Movement in Finland and Latvia. RGASPI. F. 495. Op. 20.D. 869. Similarly, the "decision on the sport question," January 21, 1934: "… the bourgeois sport organizations in all countries have been placed under the military authorities and have become converted into an integral part of military training of the toiling masses … the Red Sport organizations have placed themselves at the head of the struggle … in the field of sport." The document includes country-by-country instructions, including a paragraph addressing the Spanish section. RGASPI. F. 495. Op. 20.D. 869.
17 GARF F. R7576 Op. 2 D. 2 cited in Khorosheva, "The Activities" 106. In a similar vein, a 1924 Sportintern document explained that the aim of the organization was "to better prepare sportsmen for civil war," cited in Gounot, "L'Internationale Rouge Sportive et le Problème de l'Establishment d'une Culture Physique Prolétarienne (1921–1937)," in *Sport History Review*, Vol. 31 (2000) 145.
18 See on this Gounot, "Sport or Political Organisation? Structures and Characteristics of the Red Sports International, 1921–1937" in *Journal of Sports History*, Spring 2001, 26.
19 F. 495. Op. 12.D. 146.

20 Gounot, "El Proyecto" 117-18; Francisco de Luis Martín, *Historia del Deporte Obrero en España* (Salamanca: Ediciones Universidad de Salamanca, 2019) 234-47.
21 de Luis Martín, *Deporte Obrero*, 240, citing a 1933 PCE report. Gounot, citing Sportintern estimations, gives a figure of 9,500, 5,000 of which were Madrid-based. Gounot contrasts this figure with the relatively low numbers of communist party members in Spain. "El Proyecto de la Olimpiada," 117.
22 See on this Stanley Payne, *The Spanish Civil War, the Soviet Union and Communism* (New Haven: Yale University Press, 2004) 36.
23 "Aus den Berichten und Diskussionen auf den Internationalen Sportberatung vom 9-August 11, 1937." This material is held within the Gottwald secretariat section, RGASPI. F. 495. Op. 13.D. 72, not consulted by Gounot in his work.
24 RGASPI. F. 495. Op. 18.D. 1051.
25 Gounot, "El Proyecto de Olimpiada," 133.
26 "Pour mieux developper le travail parmi les sportifs progressistes et unir toutes les forces contre la Olympiade Hitlérienne, on crée le Comité International 'Fair-Play—Pour la défense de l'Idee Olympique.' L'Internationale des Sports appliquait la, por la premiere fois, une nouvelle méthode de travail … Le comité a agi comme association indépendante." Information sur le Travail de l'Internationale des Sports en 1936. The report mentions both the Committee and congress, as well as the Barcelona Olympiad, among Sportintern successes in 1936. RGASPI F. 495 Op. 20 D. 871.
27 *L'Altra Olimpíada*, 94-5. The authors naively list the participants, coming from "a variety of social sectors" as evidence of independence and non-partisanship. Following the two Catalan authors see Stout, *Popular Front*, 36, though he grants, forced by the evidence presented by Gounot, that "it seems to have shared space with the Red Sports International."
28 RGASPI. F. 495. Op. 12.D. 146. For example, instruction that the Fair Play Committee should create an organ in the United States or be expanded in England.
29 Olimpiada Popular de Barcelona, "Press Service," June 8, 1936, 4. On Miravitlles' roles in International Red Aid, Friends of the Soviet Union and Thälmann Committee in Catalonia see Ramón Batalla i Galimany, "Jaume Miravitlless I Navarra, Revolucionari I Home de Govern. Els Anys Joves 1906-1939," Doctoral thesis at Universitat Autónoma de Barcelona, 2010, 380; Neus Moran Gimeno, "El CADCI, Guerra i Memoria Espoliada," Doctoral Thesis at Universitat de Barcelona, 2018, 136.
30 Note from W. J. Bolton to Sir Walter Citrine, with headline reading "Barcelona Olympiad," making reference to the International Fair Play Conference held in Paris in June 1936. Bolton writes: "… suspicion was thrown on this organization by Schevenels … the Fair Play Committee is mentioned as one of those … in which

the Executive should not participate." Warwick University Archive of the Trades Unions Congress.
31 See, for example, the coverage on *Mundo Deportivo* of Barcelona from March 23 to April 12, 1936. Interestingly, in the brief announcement of March 23, Mundo Deportivo uses CCEP and "Comité pro Thälmann" interchangeably.
32 See my Chapter 2 discussion of the launch of the Comité Anti-Fascista in Spain during the Comintern-funded and Münzenberg Trust-managed visit to Madrid by Henri Barbusse and Ellen Wilkinson.
33 De Luis Martín, *Historia del Deporte*, 187.
34 Cited above, RGASPI F. 495 Op. 13 D. 72.
35 Gounot, "El Proyecto," note 54, p. 199.
36 "Contra l'anada dels espanyols a l'olimpíada negra," *La Humanitat*, April 23, 1936.
37 Protokoll (A) No. 47 der Sitzung des Sekretariats der ECCI am May 29, 1936. RGASPI. F. 495. Op. 18.D. 1092. The discussion covered several topics related to Comintern operations in Spain.
38 "Informe del Comité Català pro Esport Popular," containing also, according to the archival labeling, the norms of the committee. According to the archival labeling, the name of the publisher is Joventuts Socialistes Unificats de Catalunya, Comité Executiu. The location of the document in the archive classification scheme was: Político-Social Madrid, Joventuts Socialistes Unificats de Catalunya, Comité Executiu. That is, the document was found as part of a larger collection of files belonging to the JSU in the Catalonia region. Since 2014 the file is located at Arxiu Nacional de Catalunya, FONS ANC1-886. The Catalan archive retains the classification scheme placing the document under the JSUC files.
39 Bericht über die Internationale Sportberatung vom 9-August 11, 1937. Found in the Gottwald Secretariat section of the Comintern archives. RGASPI F. 495. Op. 13.D. 72.
40 Santacana and Pujadas, *L'Altra Olimpiada*, 196. Also ignoring Comintern management of the Commissariat is Xavier Pujadas i Martí and Aleix Augé Bailac, "La Institucionalización Deportiva en Plena Guerra Civil. La Creación del Instituto de Educación Física y Deportes en Cataluña en 1937" in *Athlos*, Vol. III (2012) 123–43.
41 Ibid. 64.
42 Letter written in English to Walter Citrine in the UK on June 12, 1936. WUATUC.
43 Eulogy by Segis Álvarez on *Mundo Obrero*, September 11, 1936.
44 Cited in Gregorio Luri's monograph on the Mercader family, *El Cielo*, 90.
45 Catalan Communist Party leader Hilario Arlandis speaking in Moscow during the meeting of the Spanish Commission: "gracias a la iniciativa de nuestra dirección en Cataluña se efectuó en el local del CADCI …" September 5, 1935, RGASPI F. 494 Op. 32 D. 117.

46 On CADCI and Aznar see Moran Gimeno, "El CADCI" 27–32.
47 Lettre au Comité Central du Parti Comuniste d'Espagne, September 16, 1934, section entitled "Le mouvement de liberation national." The Comintern was instructing the Spanish section that, in order to conquer the masses in Catalonia, it must put forth a united front against "Spanish colonialism," as well as the idea that only soviet power could liberate the Catalan people from national oppression. This concept was well understood by the leadership of Estat Català, who had travelled to Moscow with Spanish communist leader Bullejos in 1925 in order to request weapons and support for an armed insurrection against the Spanish Government. RGASPI f. 495 Op. 4 D. 310.
48 Russian language list of Spanish Komsomol students at the International Lenin School, with Andres Martín listed as number 21 of 28. RGASPI F. 531 Op. 2 D. 122. Among the requirements for admission into the school in 1935–6 were "serious experience in mass work … participation in civil war or armed insurrection." "Conditions de Admission a la Ecole Leniniste Internationale 1935–1936" RGASPI F. 531 Op. 1 D. 43. The curriculum included doctrinal as well as military training in guerrilla warfare, see my discussion in Chapter 1.
49 An interesting, if brief, biography of Andres Martín, "Hero of Saragossa" in *Legkaya Atletika*, Vol. 9 (September 1966) 30.
50 See de Luis Martín, *Historia del Deporte*, 186.
51 On JSU membership numbers post the merger, before and after the outbreak of war, see Burnett Bolloten, *The Spanish Civil War* (Chapel Hill, NC: UNC Press, 1991) 130. This is also the number given by PCE leader José "Pepe" Diaz to his French counterparts in Paris on May 25, 1936. See Sténographies des Séances du Comité Central du PCF; "Deuxième Séance, Fonds de la Section Française de l'Internationale Communiste," PANDOR.
52 The June 27 issue of *Juventud* dedicated the entire front page to the Barcelona event, including an article by Andrés in which he declared the Spanish Olympic Committee a cadaver, and a number of stories and instructions for the event. On July 17, *Mundo Deportivo* announced that *Juventud* had moved its publishing operations to Barcelona in order to create a special issue of the daily based on the Oympiad.
53 *La Voz*, October 15, 1936. Surprisingly, José Palma Leon, of Sevilla, is listed as executed in postwar repression by the Franco regime. See https://todoslosnombres.org/content/personas/jose-palma-leon.
54 For example, Parramon and Verdera, the CCEP executive members mentioned above, see "Lo que fue la Olimpiada Popular de Barcelona" in Frente Rojo, December 10, 1937, 2; Antonio Noguera, a student who went to the Olympiad and moved from the track to the war front, in *Mundo Obrero* June 5, 1938, 8; José Sanchez, who writes to Largo Caballero in April 1937 to apply for a commissar

job and mentions he had traveled from Oviedo to the Popular Olympiad on July 16, and ended up in the Thälmann group of fighters in late July, in RGASPI F. 545 Op. 1 D. 17.

55 150 Mallorcans who had come to Barcelona to participate in the Olympiad formed a full company, including both men and women. *Las Noticias*, August 8, 1936, 2.
56 Thus, in *Las Noticias* July 24, 1936.
57 AHPCE, JSU Informes, Caja 151 3/6.
58 April 21, 1936, Comité Central PCE, responsable de las MAOC a todos los comités del partido. AHPCE Microfilms XIV 183.
59 Présidium du Comité Exécutif de l'I.C., Séance du 22 Mai 1936. Jesús Hernández reporting to Dimitrov, Moskvin and others. RGASPI F. 495 Op. 2 D. 245. Hernández gave up-to-date numbers on the socialist and communist youth post the merger of those organizations, as well as on the unified militia, its weapons and tactics, with follow-up questions on the latter by Moskvin.
60 Information sur le Travail de L'Internationale des Sports in 1936, dated March 25, 1937, RGASPI F. 495 Op. 20 D. 871.
61 Federation des Jeunesses Communistes aux Regions. In PANDOR. Fonds français de l'Internationale Communiste, Internationale Communiste de la Jeunesse, Documents des unions de jeunesses communistes de différents pays Directives, lettres, appels, tracts et autres matériaux du CC des JC.
62 *Le Jour*, July 25, 1936.
63 RGASPI. F. 495. Op. 12.D. 152. On the frictions between Sportintern and the Soviet High Council for Physical Culture, see Susan Grant, *Physical Culture and Sport in Soviet Society* (New York: Routledge, 2013) 34; Keys, "Soviet Sport and Transnational Mass Culture in the 1930s" *Sport and Politics*, 413–34. Keys argues that the Supreme Council was primarily focused on raising the level of Soviet sport and lacked the Sportintern and Communist Youth's International focus on advancing Soviet revolutionary goals globally.
64 As late as July 16, the Comintern was communicating to the Central Committee of the Spanish Communist Party that "Soviet athletes will take part in the Olympic Games in Barcelona. Please let us have detailed information about the events of the Barcelona Olympic Games." Cyphered communication as monitored by the British MASK program, in TNA HW17/14, July 16, 1936.
65 Minutes of the meeting of the secretariat of the ECCI and related materials, April 28, 1938, Instructor to Dimitrov. RGASPI F. 494 Op. 10 D. 1085.
66 Propositions de la commission instituée par le Secretariat sur la question de la réorganisation de la Section de Propagande et d'organisations de masse. The mass organisations section was being closed and the management of the various areas was distributed to various leaders. RGASPI. F. 495. Op. 20.D. 808.
67 On Moskvin see the summary in the volume written by Osip Pyatnitsky's son, Vladimir, *Osyp Pyatnitskyi i Komintern* (Minsk: Charbest, 2004) 335–6.

68 TNA HW 17/26 February 6, 1936, "Medina" to "Monaco."
69 For the secret unpublished clauses of the VII Congress on mandatory military work by the sections see RGASPI, F. 494, Op. 1, D.437, l. 2. http://docs.historyrussia.org/ru/nodes/101403. The document was given to the sections with a cover letter signed by "Walter," who would later move to Spain and operate as "General Walter" in the Civil War.
70 RGASPI. F. 495. Op. 13.D. 72.
71 See full report and potos on *L'Humanité* July 6, 1936.

Conclusion

1 New York University Jordan Center, "Why Was the Second World War Inevitable?", a conversation with Professor Jonathan Haslam on his recent book, *The Spectre of War. International Communism and the Origins of World War II*. Available online.
2 James McPherson, "Revisioninst Historians," Letter from the President, September 1, 2003, available on the AHA's website.
3 "Ampliación del Consejo de Ministros de Hoy," As reported by *El Mundo Futuro*, September 13, 1935.

Epilogue

1 The Russian translation of the report is also available, but, as it is often the case in the Comintern archival system, it is filed in a haphazard manner. Thus, the Russian text of the report and discussion is stuck in the middle of the material related to the Czech question which was discussed first on the same day. Transcript of the meeting of the Presidium of the ECCI, May 22nd, 1935. RGASPI F. 495 Op. 2 D. 245.
2 Elorza and Bizcarrondo are highly selective in their discussion of the material, failing to mention Dimitov's assessment of the readiness of Spain for Soviet power, discussion of the progress in communist army work in Spain, armed militias, etc. See *Queridos Camaradas* (Barcelona: Planeta, 1999) 283–5. Thus also Tim Rees, "Revolution or Republic? The Spanish Communist Party 1931–1936" in Manuel Álvarez Tardío and Fernando del Rey Reguillo (eds.) *The Spanish Second Republic Revisited. From Democratic Hopes to Civil War (1931–1936)* (Eastbourne: Sussex Academic Press, 2013). In a slight modification of the majority view, Rees argues that the PCE was marginal in terms of real power and influence, and that its growth, especially starting in late 1934 was due to unplanned developments in Spain outside of its control. Consistently with that view, Rees ignores the relative success of the communists within the socialist union UGT starting in 1932 and

relegates the activities of Comintern front organizations in Spain to 1936. Contrary to well-known processes we have detailed in this book, Rees believes that the Bolshevization of the socialist union and youth organization "reduced the appeal of the much smaller [PCE]" thus ignoring the intentional and progressive efforts of the Comintern and its Spanish section to infiltrate and win over both organizations. In line with that interpretation, Rees also adopts the majority view on the Comintern's VII Congress as an about turn with anti-fascism displacing Bolshevik revolution. Rees's reference to the May 22, 1936, ECCI Presidium documents is given in the context of his assessment that the militias were not well-armed and that the Comintern was urging restraint because it stood in "support of the regime." As we shall see, such a view is at odds with a careful reading of both documents and the June 1936 directives. Less valuable still is Fernando Hernández Sánchez, "El Partido Comunista de España en la Segunda República" in *Bulletin d'Histoire Contemporaine de l'Espagne* [online], 51|2017. Hernández engages in a selective Reading of TNA material and mentions the May 22, 1936, article, dismissing completely the far more detailed report which he assumes is merely a French copy: "hay también una copia en francés." His overall conclusion is that in early 1936 the party had completed a turn away from insurrectional tactics to "un espacio de centralidad".

3 I will not reproduce here the discussion on Soviet foreign policy in the 1930s we included in the introduction. Suffice it to say that, as Kotkin and others have shown, and the documentary evidence I have discussed confirms, there was, in fact, no genuine pursuit of a collective security policy by Stalin after the VII Comintern Congress or even in the spring of 1936. Duplicity, with an unchanging commitment to insurrectional and revolutionary tactics through the Comintern, while at the same time the foreign commissariat pursued diplomatic and commercial deals, including with nazi Germany, was the norm.

4 Thus Caballero as reported by *El Sol* on April 7, 1936: "Es indudable … que hay que ir rápidamente a la unificación del proletariado." In the same rally, JSU leader Santiago Carrillo had also addressed the single proletarian party that, in his view, was about to be created.

5 Directives for the Communist Party of Spain, March 3, 1936, RGASPI F. 495 Op. The directives insisted on the continued relevance of agitation and on the enforcement of the five requirements for unity with the socialists communicated at the VII Comintern Congreess. These included commitment to Soviet power and the proletarian revolution.

6 Roman Lands Secretariat, report from Codovilla on January 29, 1935. RGASPI F. 494 Op. 32 D. 165. Interestingly, in his June 1936 report to the Roman Secretariat, Pepe Díaz again identified Alianzas Obreras y Campesinas with soviets. In conversations with Caballero, Díaz had suggested to the socialist that Alianzas and

soviets were one and the same. He added "we must destroy the machinery of the state. The name matters little." Sécretariat Romain, Commission Espagnole, Pepe Diaz in dialogue with Manuilsky and others. RGASPI F. 495 Op. 20 D. 269.

7   The article from *Avance* reprinted on the cover of the local socialist youth organ in Zaragoza. "Fortalecimiento y desarrollo de las Alianzas Obreras" in *Vanguardia*, February 29, 1936. It is interesting to note that the article compares the period of revolutionary transition from the "democratic bourgeois" revolution in Spain to the 8-month period between the February and October revolutions in Russia.

8   On the breakdown of the rule of law in the countryside during the Popular Front Government, especially May and June 1936, see Edward Malefakis, *Agrarian Reform and Peasant Revolution in Spain. Origins of the Civil War* (New Haven: Yale University Press, 1970) 369–73.

9   Dimitrov's response could have been framed as a question. His follow-up comment is fully transparent, however.

10 "Si c'etait partout, on pourrait faire la république soviétique, parce que des choses semblables ne peuvent pas renforcer la république démocratique." The Russian translation has "Soviet power" here.

11 Decisión sobre La Cuestión Española, June 7, 1936, RGASPI F. 495 Op. 18 D. 1092.

12 Ibid.

13 The word used here for coup is perevorot. See my discussion of these terms in chapter 1. Speech of G. Dimitrov at the meeting of the ECCI, July 23, 1936, RGASPI F. 495 Op. 18 D. 1101, available on the online repository of the Russian Historical Society http://docs.historyrussia.org/ru/nodes/102023.

14 On the politization of justice, and the mass arrests of conservatives during the Popular Front Government see Stanley Payne, *The Collapse of the Spanish Republic* (New Haven: Yale University Press, 2006) 225, 263.

15 See for example Bilbao's *El Nervión* of April 18, reporting the arrests of members of Falange, as well as a right-wing judge, a number of youths who "had nothing to do with Falange," the expropriation of a factory, etc.; "Se intensifican las detenciones de personas de significación derechista en toda España," detailing the arrests of priests, pharmacists, civil servants etc., on *ABC* April 21, 1936. In addition to the violation of fundamental civil rights, these widespread arrests led to the withdrawal of parties on the right of the political spectrum from the polling to elect delegates to the Presidential election. See *El Sol* April 22, 1936.

16 See *Ahora*, May 5, 1936: "El Partico Comunista ... declara que es una patraña el rumor del envenenamiento de niños. Ruega a sus afiliados no tomen actitudes levantiscas ni obedezcan órdenes que puedan perturbar la paz pública."

17 In addition to the burning of churches, convents and homes, the leader of the opposition mentioned various acts of aggression against ladies accused in the poisoned candy hoax. His speech was covered on *ABC* May 17, 1936. For

the foreign press coverage of the burning of churches during the Popular Front Government, see for example "A Trail of Arson through Spain," on *The Illustrated London News* of March 17, 1936.

18 On JSU membership numbers post the merger, before and after the outbreak of war, see Burnett Bolloten, *The Spanish Civil War* (Chapel Hill, NC: UNC Press, 1991) 130. The number given by PCE leader José "Pepe" Diaz to his French counterparts in Paris in April 1936 was 150,000. See Sténographies des Séances du Comité Central du PCF, Deuxième Séance, Fonds de la Section Française de l'Internationale Communiste, PANDOR.

19 In the words of the August 1934 report of the Spanish Commission to the ECCI, worker and peasant militias were to be organized in coordination with the socialists "encubriéndolas con el pretesto [sic] de que temenos que defendernos del fascismo … debemos procurar no decir desde el primer momento que organizamos las milicias para la toma del poder." RGASPI F. 495. Op. 4.D. 441.

20 The extra judicial arrests of citizens by "elementos extraños a la autoridad" was witnessed to in the press. Occasionally, the local civil governor would forbid such arrests and free those detained. See "Prosiguen las detenciones en toda España de personas significadas en el campo derechista" in *Siglo Futuro*, April 23, 1936.

21 A few days before Hernández gave his report in Moscow, the socialist leader had given his perspective on the militias at a rally in Madrid. Caballero described them as "ejército contra el enemigo común con una organización militar … ¿con que objeto? Defensiva cuando el enemigo nos ataque. Ofensiva para apoderarnos del Poder." "Un Importante Discurso de Largo Caballero" in *Heraldo de Madrid*, April 31, 1936.

22 Haslam's full reflection refers not to the Comintern and its Spanish section only, but to the political left as a whole: "[w]hen the left finally got to power ….in 1931 they thought, 'now the revolution will happen' ….and they victimized those on the right. There were assassinations, there were land seizures, they attacked monasteries and convents … priests had to wear civilian clothes to avoid being attacked … This is before Franco tries and succeeds in taking power in 1936, so there was a revolution going on in Spain before this counter-revolution." New York University Jordan Center, "Why was the Second World War Inevitable?", a conversation with Professor Jonathan Haslam on his recent book, *The Spectre of War. International Communism and the Origins of World War II*. Minute 45.50. Available online.

Index

Abramov-Mirov, Alexander 18, 27, 172–3 n.11
Abramson, Paulina 80, 203 n.78
Alba, Santiago 43
"Albert." *See* Eberlein, Hugo
Alberti, Rafael 45, 76, 123
Alfred. *See* Lehén, Tuure
Alianzas Obreras 28, 107, 130, 161, 180 n.75, 219 n.45
Alonso, Bruno 42, 186 n.20
Alsace-Lorraine 33, 92–3, 95, 145
Amsterdam-Pleyel movement 35
Amutio, J. Martinez 48
anti-fascism 32, 47, 49, 100, 134, 140, 143
Anti-Fascist Front 20, 30–3, 37, 60, 99
Antuña, Graciano 41–2, 186 n.16
Araquistain, Luis 31, 34, 36, 180 n.79
armed insurrections
    Bolshevik tactics 10, 89–92
    ECCI approval 28, 30
    forms of 27
    October 1934 in Spain 26, 28, 39, 41, 53, 57, 73–8, 88, 107, 110, 129–30, 145–6, 177 n.50
    against Popular Front government 16
    preparation 24–30
army work
    Bolshevik task of 91
    in France 87–101, 154–5
    post-October 1934 110
    in Spain 88, 101–9
Arquer, Jordi 144–5
Association Républicaine des Anciens Combattants (ARAC) 95, 114, 116
Asturias
    Communist party officials 161–2
    October 1934 insurrection 41, 88, 106
Azaña, Manuel
    with Caballero 50
    on a European trip 50–1
    left-wing electoral coalition 36
    political orientation 52–3
Aznar, Pere 145–6

Barbusse, Henri
    anti-fascism 32–3
    and Concentración Popular 49–50, 124
    F.T.E. endorsement 124
    visit to Moscow 51
    visit to Spain 49
    and World Committee 33
Barcelona
    EEA's move to 65–73, 155
    Popular Olympics 12–13, 80, 133, 141, 147–8, 150
Barón, Lucía 55, 75, 193 n.76
Bertrand. *See* Wertheim, Johannes
Berzin, Yan Karlovich 25
Blum, Léon 10, 91, 111, 156
Bolshevik faction
    in the civil war 90
    debate with the Mensheviks 120
    in October 1934 insurrection 10
    PCF and Comintern 90–2, 97–8
    and the PSOE 8
"Bono." *See* Quaglierini, Ettore
Bourthomieux, Charles 42
Brest-Litovsk Treaty 89–90
Bullejos, José 18, 20–2, 173 n.13, 174 n.24
    PCE leadership 88, 104
    and Spain 22
Bush, George W. 153

Caballero, Largo 10, 169–70 n.38, 212–13 n.73
    and the left-wing coalition 50
    and U.G.T. 36, 125, 130
Calvo Sotelo, José 111, 163–4, 179 n.64
Carl Hoym Verlag (publishing house) 70–1
Carrillo, Santiago 165, 204 n.80, 228 n.4
Chamberlain, Neville 4
Cical, Libert 66–7
Claudin, Fernando 12, 171 n.1
Codevilla, Carlo 27, 173 n.11

Codovilla, Victorio 10, 58, 188 n.35
  and Asturian orphans 46
  and Communist army work 107–9
  and ECCI 9, 11
  January 1935 report 107, 130–1, 161
  and 1934 insurrection 46, 129, 188 n.35, 193 n.79
  and the PCE leadership 28
  and PSOE 48
  and Red Aid 48
  in September 1936 24
Comintern funds. *See* funding/finance
Communist army work 87–9, 98–110, 212 n.72
Communist Youth International (KIM) 142, 164, 201 n.54, 204 n.80
Concentración Popular 6, 49–50, 52, 124
Confederación Nacional del Trabajo (CNT) 8, 19, 24, 26, 57, 123–4, 144

Daladier, Édouard
  national defense 99–100
  Popular Front government 111
del Vayo, Julio Álvarez 27, 34, 48–9, 178 n.54, 178 n.55, 187 n.25, 189 n.46
  and Ercoli 10, 49
  solidarity movement 49
Democracia (newspaper) 36, 75, 177 n.50, 183 n.98
Diaz, José 21, 67, 162, 165, 168 n.21, 178 n.54, 190 n.51, 191 n.61, 194 n.88, 213 n.73, 225 n.51, 228–9 n.6, 230 n.18
  in Moscow 109
  on Mundo Obrero 58
  path of October 60
  permanent army, suppression of 212 n.72
Dimitrov, Georgi
  conditions for joining the Third International 57
  iconography 84
  at the VII Comintern Congress 57
  vote for 75
Doriot, Jacques 96, 103
Duclos, Jacques 98, 138, 151

Eberlein, Hugo 182 n.90, 208 n.29
  affair 33, 95, 158
  and Barbusse campaigns 50, 55
  and Popular Front campaign, slogans 33–5, 53
Edeya 70–1
Ediciones Europa América (EEA) 66–7, 70–1, 74, 81–2
El Socialista 9, 128, 169 n.37, 170 n.38, 173 n.16, 176 n.42, 185 n.15, 201 n.55, 218 n.22, 218 n.34
"Ercoli." *See* Togliatti, Palmiro
Espada, Manuel 29, 212 n.67
Executive Committee of the Communist International (ECCI) 42, 83, 135
  budget 18
  Manuilsky and 22, 30
  O.S.R. operations, success of 129–30
  and PCE 28
  political commission of 26, 43, 47
  preparatory commission 23
  Presidium of 159
  Trade Union Commission 121, 128
  and Zaisser 27–8

February 1917 revolution 89, 101
Federación Cultural Deportiva Obrera (FCDO) 133, 137–8
  primary aim of 157
  against "reactionary" leadership 140–1
  Sportintern and 146
  vision and action 139–40
Federación Tabaquera Española (F.T.E.) 124
"Fiesta del Libro" 204 n.81
France
  Communist army work in 87, 100, 154
  Communist mass organizations in 96
  "the Eberlein Affair" 33
  fascism/fascistization 115, 208 n.32
  internal intelligence service 95
  national security of 29
  fraternization, Communist concept of 88, 94, 97, 112, 212 n.66
French Communist Party (PCF) 88–90
  on Alsace 95
  Comintern and 91

Political Bureau on February 15 116
role of 114
"Stavisky affair" 96
front organizations 9, 21, 96, 134–7, 144–5, 149, 228 n.2
funding/finance
Comintern and the PCF 91
dependence 17
Moscow 61, 64
OMS responsibility 18
Red Aid 48, 155
for Spanish 18

"Gilbert." *See* Trepper, Leopold
Gil, Evaristo 32
Giménez Siles, Rafael
Cenit, focus of 71–2
Comintern's publishing organization and 69
Gonzalo Aceña, José 126
Gottwald, Klement 65, 134–5
Great War 3, 39, 95

Hernández, Jesús 142, 157, 159–65, 228 n.2
Hidalgo, Diego 107–10
Humbert-Droz, Jules 18, 31

Ibarruri, Dolores 12, 32, 34, 46, 54, 57, 78–9, 188 n.39, 189 n.41, 201 n.56, 203 n.75
Iglesias, Pablo 102, 186 n.15
Internacional Comunista 75, 81, 122
International Committee for the Computerization of the Comintern Archive (INCOMKA) 11
International Lenin School (ILS) 25–8, 59, 129, 146
International Red Aid (MOPR in its Russian acronym) 9, 20–1, 32, 44, 47–8, 54–5, 59, 75–6, 122, 131, 135, 175 n.27, 177 n.49, 184 n.4, 192 n.72, 192 n.74
leadership 59, 136, 155
primary task of 47
"serpent's embrace" 21
World Committee and 45
International Relations Department of the Comintern (OMS) 27, 172–3 n.11

Jiménez de Asúa, Luis 32, 34, 176 n.39, 182 n.92
Juntas de Defensa 102–4
Juventudes Socialistas Unificadas (JSU) 36, 142–3, 145–7, 151, 156–8, 164–5, 175 n.30, 179 n.63, 224 n.38, 225 n.51, 228 n.4, 230 n.18

Katz, Otto 42, 70
Kent, Victoria 34, 50
"Klavego." *See* Quaglierini, Ettore
Kreps, Mikhail 65, 75, 78–9, 201 n.53

Lehén, Tuure 27, 105, 178 n.56
Lenin, Vladimir 2–6, 98–9
Lerroux, Alejandro 40–1, 44, 154
L'Humanité 88, 93, 99, 115–17, 207 n.21
Lina. *See* Abramson, Paulina
Lister, Enrique 28, 106, 178 n.61
Listowel, Lord 42–3, 49
Llopis, Rodolfo 72, 200 n.48
López Bravo, Miguel 109–10, 212 n.66
López Ochoa, Eduardo 41, 110

Manuilsky, Dmitry 21–2, 30, 56–8
on ECCI 22, 30
inadequate slogans 22
NSDAP 112
O.S.R. operations 121–2
self-criticism 23
"work in the army" 92
"Maria." *See* Modotti, Tina
Marín, Ricardo 70, 72, 80
Marley, Lord 32, 43, 187 n.24
Márquez, Benito 102
Martín, Andrés 133, 144, 146
Martin-Hajdu, "Jordi", (Gyorgy Martin Hajdu) 143–4
Marty, André 94, 97–8, 195 n.9, 196 n.17
mass organizations. *See* front organizations
McPherson, James 153
"Medina." *See* Codovilla, Victorio
Menendez, Álvaro 135, 143, 146, 150–1
Merás, Dolores 44, 136
militias
communist/MAOC 106, 139, 147, 160, 164–5
socialist 139, 165

Mínev, Stoyán Miniéevich (known in Spain as Moreno) 17, 20, 22, 26, 48, 174 n.26
Miravitlles, Jaume 138, 144–5
Mission Militaire Française (MMF) 89–90
Modotti, Tina 19
Mundo Obrero 57–8, 68, 70–1, 138, 198 n.30, 201 n.49
Münzenberg, Willi (Willi)
  and comintern publishing 70, 82, 122
  and "Franz" 70–2, 78, 199 n.41, 200 n.46
  in Madrid 12, 82–3
  trust 33, 39, 45, 135, 221 n.8
  World Committee 42, 45, 51

Navarro, Francisco del Barrio 19
Nelken, Margarita 48–9, 60, 75–6
network effect 61, 66, 80, 120, 123, 157
  bourgeois distribution 72, 84, 155
  Comintern publishing 13, 21, 64, 70, 81
  party-controlled organizations 121
Nielsen, Daniel. *See* Eberlein, Hugo

O.S.R. groups 119–25, 157, 217 n.12, 217 n.15, 219 n.42, 219 n.47
  in Spain 122
  and U.G.T. 126–32, 156
"Otto." *See* Trepper, Leopold

"Pablo." *See* Quaglierini, Ettore
Pasionaria. *See* Ibarruri, Dolores
PCF. *See* French Communist Party (PCF)
Popular Front/Volksfront
  in February 1936 24
  French 35–6, 111, 151, 174 n.23, 183 n.96
  Spanish 11, 15–16, 20, 22–5, 31, 33–40, 48, 61, 140
  victory 24, 56–7, 75–6, 139, 146
Popular Olympics, Barcelona 12–13, 80, 133–4, 140–2, 147–50, 220 n.2, 223 n.29, 225 n.54
Pravda 11, 60, 167 n.12, 172 n.8, 182 n.90
prisoners
  and children 40–8
  political utilization of 47
  population 186 n.18

Propaganda and Mass Organizations Department (Gottwald) 65, 149
Pyatnitsky, Osip 17–18, 23, 149, 177 n.48

Quaglierini, Ettore 13, 66, 70, 77, 195 n.11, 197 n.23
  Bertrand's support for 74
  and Mikhail Kreps "Bruno" 75
  and Cical's behavior 67, 69
  "Nuestro Pueblo" 77

"Raul." *See* Codevilla, Carlo
Rebollo, Francisco 127
Redizdat (Comintern publishing)
  organizational chart 83
  Spain operations 64–6, 70, 78–80
revolutionary opposition groups. *See* O.S.R. groups
Roces, Wenceslao 77–8, 80–2

Salazar Alonso, Rafael 56, 110, 127, 193 n.79, 218 n.31
II International 8, 10, 32, 120
Second World War 51, 113, 132, 190 n.56
VII Comintern Congress
  army work instructions in 28, 37, 87–9, 91–2, 96–110, 154–5, 164, 206 n.12, 227 n.2
  interpretations of the 21, 40, 43, 93, 114, 133, 149, 153
  socialists attending 28, 130, 154
Simeón-Vidarte, Juan 36, 41, 185 n.10
Sindicato Nacional Ferroviario 19, 122
socialist party
  French 90
  leadership 155, 212 n.72
Socorro Obrero Español (S.O.E.) 122–3
Socorro Rojo Internacional (SRI). *See* International Red Aid (MOPR in its Russian acronym)
Soldado Rojo 28–9, 105, 110–11, 213 n.73
Soviet foreign policy 1–3, 5–6, 153, 228 n.3
Soviet Union
  Friends of the 9, 20, 135, 139, 157
  popularization of 65, 71
Spanish Communist Party (PCE) 8, 70, 88
  leadership and the Comintern 22, 88, 106, 163

Spanish II Republic 6, 8, 13, 18–19, 29, 63, 71, 125, 158, 195 n.5, 203 n.66
  in April 1931 53
  historiography of 61, 160
Spanish Socialist Workers Party (PSOE) 8, 19, 25, 28, 31, 41–2, 48, 50, 53–4, 57, 70, 102, 136, 173 n.16, 175 n.27, 183 n.95, 213 n.73
Sportintern 133–41, 143–51, 156–8
Stalin, Joseph 1–6, 15–16, 24, 30, 33, 37, 59, 71–2, 78, 84, 124, 166 n.2, 171 n.1, 181–2 n.88, 199 n.42, 228 n.3
  personal archive 2
  and the Soviet leadership 2
  Soviet Union, encirclement of 3
Stasova, Elena 12, 19, 39, 43–7, 54–5
Stavisky affair 96, 113–15
Stepanov. *See* Mínev, Stoyán Miniéevich (known in Spain as Moreno)
Suárez Rodríguez, Julio 105–6
Sverchevsky, Karol 24–5, 176 n.46, 227 n.69

Togliatti, Palmiro 10, 15, 45, 67, 171 n.2, 180 n.74
  ECCI Presidium 36
  and Popular Front 157
  and Popular Olympiad 142
Trepper, Leopold 51–4, 190 n.56, 190 n.58, 192 n.72

Unión General de Trabajadores (U.G.T.)
  for the Anti-Fascist Front 20
  leadership 42, 125, 128–30, 156
  O.S.R. activities in 124–31
Union Nationale des Combattants (U.N.C.) 96, 113, 115–16
Uribe, Vicente 21, 80, 82, 106

Vasiliev, Boris 98–9, 209 n.40
Vassart, Albert 92–7, 99
VEGAAR publishing house 65, 72, 80
Vicéns, Juan 72, 200 n.47
Voiriot, General Léon 91

"Walter." *See* Sverchevsky, Karol
Wertheim, Johannes 69–70, 74, 77, 79–83
Wilkinson, Ellen 13, 32, 42–3, 136, 181 n.84–5, 187 n.25
Wollenberg, Erich 177 n.48
"Women against War and Fascism" 136
World Committee against War and Fascism 33, 42–3, 45, 47, 52, 64, 69

Zaisser, Wilhem 177–8 n.52, 178 n.59
  and ECCI 27–8

www.ingramcontent.com/pod-product-compliance
Lightning Source LLC
Chambersburg PA
CBHW071825300426
44116CB00009B/1438